1961

HROTSVITHA:

The Theatricality of Her Plays

PLATE I

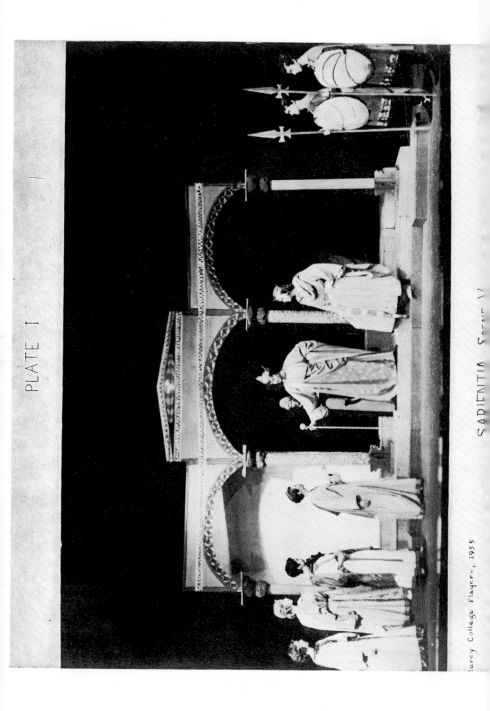

SAPIENTIA Scene VI

Mercy College Players, 1955

HROTSVITHA:

The Theatricality of Her Plays

by

**Sister Mary Marguerite Butler,
R. S. M.**

PHILOSOPHICAL LIBRARY   **NEW YORK**

Printed in the United States of America

To
Pastor Felix Hardt
of Bad Gandersheim
who now in Heaven
will learn
from Hrotsvitha herself
the whole story
of her life and her time

FOREWORD

The "strong voice of Gandersheim" has been stilled too
long. Now, Sister Mary Marguerite Butler, R.S.M., has released that voice once more by helping us to understand not
only the tenth-century religious, Hrotsvitha, but also the literary, social, and political environment which influenced her
life and her works.

Sister Mary Marguerite has assiduously researched and sur-
veyed all available data about Hrotsvitha and about the
Gandersheim monastery where this nun-dramatist spent her
adult years. She has applied to these data her own knowledge
and intuitions as a religious in order to interpret the acts of
Hrotsvitha, and thus, to reach a fuller understanding of her
character and religious status. Sister concludes, for example,
that Hrotsvitha must have been a canoness rather than a
cloistered nun; and, of course, she corrects the otherwise
reputable reference works which confuse the playwright,
Hrotsvitha, with an abbess of Gandersheim of the same name.

Theatre historians used to tell us that drama lay dormant
from the seventh century A.D. until the mystery plays took on
dramatic form in the twelfth and thirteenth centuries. They
have shrugged off too easily a religious who, during the latter
half of the tenth century, wrote six plays extolling the Christian virtue of chastity. They hastily dismissed these plays as
curious, disconnected phenomena having neither roots nor
influence. It was obvious to these scholars that if these plays
had been performed, it would have inexorably confused the
accepted account of theatre history, *ergo*, they were not performed. Recently, Benjamin Hunningher and others have

cast doubt upon this theory of a long period of hibernation of theatre, and have demonstrated the existence of theatre during the five centuries of accepted vacuum. Sister Mary Marguerite presses the inquiry about this vacuum further and defines her position by identifying certain dramatic and theatrical vestiges clearly apparent in the plays of Hrotsvitha, and by suggesting the possible influence which the nun-dramatist may have exerted on subsequent drama.

In her effort to exhaust all available sources of information about Hrotsvitha, Sister investigated the historical and architectural records of Gandersheim. She visited the site of the Gandersheim monastery, examined codices in Munich and Cologne, and searched for additional data at the Vatican Library and elsewhere. This foreign study was made possible by a fellowship grant from the Horace H. Rackham School for Graduate Studies, University of Michigan.

Sister Mary Marguerite supported her thesis by producing two of the plays in order to examine their practical stage-worthiness. We are proud that she presented these plays in the Lydia Mendelssohn Theatre of the University of Michigan under the sponsorship of the Department of Speech. She informed these productions with her own devout belief in their message, with her fine aesthetic judgment in the settings and costumes reconstructed from tenth-century sources, and with her unerring taste in the mixture of piety and theatricality which she continually demonstrates in her theatre productions at Mercy College in Detroit.

There have been a number of valuable studies of Hrotsvitha's plays from a literary standpoint—more in German than in English—but Sister Mary Marguerite has made the first study of any length which has investigated the plays from a theatrical point of view. In consequence, she has revealed many surprising aspects of the plays, including the practicality of their performance both in our day and in Hrotsvitha's day. In contradiction to the traditional opinion of literary scholars, namely, that the plays were not written for performance,

Sister's study, as well as her experimental production, goes a long way to indicate the likelihood that the plays were written for production and were performed under the direction of their author.

WILLIAM P. HALSTEAD
Professor of Speech
University of Michigan

TABLE OF CONTENTS

LIST OF ILLUSTRATIONS

PREFACE

This study is one of the first attempts to present the dramatic works of Hrotsvitha of Gandersheim from the viewpoint of theatre rather than from that of literary history. The genesis of the problem is related here because its subsequent development demonstrates its controversial character as a research problem and provides the basis for its legitimacy.

As early as August, 1953, I decided to make the dramatic works of Hrotsvitha the subject of my doctoral dissertation. After a few months of study and discussion, I was prepared to state the problem as follows:

Among theatre and literary scholars through the years there have been two schools of thought regarding the purpose this Benedictine nun had in mind when she wrote her plays. One school maintains that the dramas were written merely as pious exercises to glorify laudable Christian virtue as a counter to the pagan works popular at the time. Opposed to this theory are those who contend that the plays were written for production. Life within a medieval monastery, the spirit of the time, and the mind of the Church—all seem indicative of the practicality of the performance of such virtuous lessons. This is my thesis.

Supplemental to the theoretical research are plans to produce several of the plays in authentic medieval settings before critical audiences.

Confirming this statement of purpose was a second one made on October 17, 1953, to accompany an application for a scholarship to study medieval art and architecture abroad and to do research of original sources in the monasteries and libraries of Germany, England, Italy, and France:

At present I am preparing an acting text of three of the plays of Hrotsvitha for presentation for critical audience reaction: the first to be given in one of the rooms of the Cloisters in New York City; the second at the Art Institute of Detroit; and the third one on the campus of the University of Michigan. It is hoped that the performance of the plays in settings conceived as nearly like the original as possible will furnish a basis for further study of the proposed problem.

By November, 1954, after further analysis, the problem began to assume a different pattern. By that time I had decided that my study should confine itself to "The Dramatic Possibilities Found in Hrotsvitha's Plays as Demonstrated in their Performance." This seemed to negate the original statement in which I proposed to prove that the plays of Hrotsvitha were acted in her monastery in her own time. It seemed now that such a problem could yield only a speculative conclusion. Therefore, I supported my more recent proposition with the preparation of an acting text of the plays which would prove more conclusively their dramatic value.

I was convinced that these acting texts would be a definite contribution to medieval drama since existing translations do not lend themselves easily to production, nor do they give us the spirit of Hrotsvitha found in the original Latin text or in the French translation of Magnin.

After preparing an acting text for "Dulcitius" and "Sapientia," I arranged to stage the plays at the Lydia Mendelssohn Theatre on the University of Michigan campus in January, 1955. This experience resulted in a further rephrasing of the problem, in which the emphasis was shifted from the dramatic possibilities to the theatrical possibilities of the plays. I deduced that this change was justified by the semantics of the term "theatrical" as opposed to the term "dramatic." I refer here to the fact that "dramatic" pertains primarily to the literary form whereas "theatrical" pertains to the total science of dramatic representation. At this point the title became "Hrotsvitha: A Study of the Theatrical Possibilities of her Plays" or "The Theatricality of Hrotsvitha." This brief recapitulation of the steps which resulted in the final statement of the problem does not begin to represent the scope of exploration in reading, discussions, formal interviews, and travel.

The inclusion of the chapters pertinent to the origin and welfare of monasticism in general, and to Gandersheim in particular, in its historical, social, and structural aspects, was deemed indispensable to the study. The prime requisites of theatricality are not only inherent in the essence of the dramatic form and subject matter, but they are also dependent upon a suitable acting locale and a receptive audience.

Using the force of the principle of analogy, emphasis was placed upon the impact of three existing dramatic influences on Hrotsvitha's plays. The principle was further applied to a comprehensive analysis of the experimental aspect of the study.

This doctoral project would have been considerably curtailed, and possibly not realized at all, had it not been for a Carl Braun Fellowship awarded to me by the University of Michigan on the recommendation of the Faculty of the Speech Department. This grant made possible several months of European study. I am most grateful to the University for this opportunity to explore primary sources and for the privilege of completing this study under the direction of its Faculty.

In particular, I acknowledge the interest and generosity of the late resident pastor of the Katholische Kirchengemeinde at Bad Gandersheim, the Reverend Felix Hardt, who made accessible to me several important documents from the Archiv der Stadt Bad Gandersheim relative to Hrotsvitha and her time. Even after I had returned to the United States, Pastor Hardt's interest and solicitude followed me. His sudden death deprived the cause of Hrotsvitha of an ardent advocate and scholar.

I also wish to express my appreciation for an interview with the distinguished historian and canon of the Hildesheim Cathedral, Dr. Konrad Algermissen, into whose care has been entrusted the priceless illuminated manuscripts from the Bernward School of the Ottonian Renaissance; for the opportunity of working with the *Cologne Codex* in the Municipal Archives of Cologne and with the *Emmeram-Munich Codex* in the Bavarian State Library in Munich; for permission of Dr. Kenneth J. Conant of Chevy Chase, Maryland, to use the most complete floorplan of Cluny now available through the Medieval Academy of America; for conferences with Dr. Guy Ferarri, O.S.B., of the staff of the *Princeton Index* in Rome who suggested pertinent sources of information on Hrotsvitha as a canoness; and for the invaluable assistance of Dr. Giannina Spellanzon at the Vatican Library, of Sister Mary Judith Hiller, S.S.N.D., of Kloster Brede, Brakel, Germany, and of Peter Gallasch, Bad Gandersheim, district editor of the *Braunschweiger Zeitung*.

In conclusion, I wish to express gratitude to Professor Henry W. Nordmeyer, Chairman of the Department of Germanic Languages and Literatures, for his painstaking editing of the text; to Professor Frank O. Copley of the Department of Classical Studies; to Professors Lamont Okey and Hugh Z. Norton of the Speech Department; and to the Chairman of my committee, Professor William P. Halstead, whose direction and encouragement were invaluable. To my community, the Sisters of Mercy, who gave me the opportunity for study and research, I am sincerely grateful.

Sister Mary Marguerite Butler, R.S.M.

Feast of St. Roswitha of Alsatia
September 16, 1958

Chapter I

INTRODUCTION: THE PROBLEM

Among theatre and literary scholars of the last century and a half, there are two schools of thought regarding the purpose which motivated Hrotsvitha, the nun of Gandersheim (*ca.* 932-1002) when she wrote her dramas. The one school is of the opinion that she wrote the plays for performance in her monastery during her own lifetime; the other maintains that she wrote them only to be read as pious exercises or dramatic colloquies glorifying laudable Christian virtues, as opposed to the licentious matter found in the pagan works popular at the time.

In an article appearing in *Speculum* in 1945, "Were Hrotsvitha's Dramas Performed During Her Lifetime?",[1] Edwin Zeydel calls attention to the importance of this argument. He points out that an answer in the affirmative would necessitate a rewriting of the history of European drama between the tenth and twelfth centuries, because historians have ignored Hrotsvitha's dramas in relation to other existing contemporary or subsequent dramatic activity. Zeydel then presents the conflicting views of the most representative authorities of these schools of thought and shows how they "have followed each other in almost regular succession for over a century, without either being able to efface the other."[2] Until there is positive evidence to support either view, this question will continue to be a controversial one. Thus far, research has failed to reveal any record of the production of the Hrotsvithan plays during her lifetime.

It is regrettable that a review of these critical opinions presents but one point of view—that of the literary historian. Conrad Fiedler in his book, *On Judging Works of Visual Art*,[3] speaks of the learned connoisseur, the collector, and the scholar who often concern themselves with those characteristics of works of art which have no relationship to artistic form and purpose. This kind of preoccupation, according to Fiedler, can result in scientific research without an understanding of the work of art.

It would seem that this observation applies to those Hrotsvithan scholars whose research, for the most part, has been concerned with conventional purpose and literary form rather than with an artistic comprehension of her plays within their dramatic framework. These scholars have not taken into consideration that the playwright, as an artist, works in a medium with which he is familiar. He knows its capacities and its limitations. If he is a truly creative artist, his play will come to life on whatever kind of stage a group of actors give it form.

Any attempt to analyze Hrotsvitha's plays within a dramatic framework must be done in the light of certain historical facts. She lived in an age of which it is erroneously said there are no established data to prove the existence of a living theatre.[4] Drama was said to be an alien literary form. Theatre arts, because of their misuse of man's capacities in his Christian way of life, were said to have been completely and finally suppressed by the Church through the conciliar banns issued at the Trullan Synod, held in Constantinople in 692 A.D.[5] Documented data prove the contrary.

St. Isidore of Seville (530-636), in his *Etymologia*,[6] reveals the status quo of public entertainment during the seventh century. Some scholars[7] make a point of the fact that Isidore's description of theatre, in general, is expressed in the present tense, but when he comes to the physical stage and its Greek origin, he reverts to the past tense. And when he warns the Christians to avoid the obscene and licentious activities engaged in by public entertainers, referring to the latter as

2

mimi, histriones, et ioculatores, he again uses the present tense. "All this," Nicoll says, "goes to prove that acting of a kind was being continued [at this time] with performers who had carried over from classic days the old tradition of mimic impersonation with its 'imitation' of life and its secular tendencies."[8] The argument for a living theatre, based merely on the tenses of the verbs in the *Etymologia,* might not satisfy the scientific historian, but when reinforced by the following excerpts from the Church Councils, it gains force.

Nicoll,[9] in calling attention to the wording of the various banns of the Trullan Council, emphasizes the kinds and universal patronage of public entertainment at this time. Canon fifty-one as quoted from Mansi "condemns the mimes and their theatres, hunting spectacles involving wild beasts, and dancing on the stage. And for those who disobey this canon, . . . clerics will be deposed, and laymen excommunicated."[10] Canon sixty-two condemns the "pagan festivals of the Kalends . . . dancing . . . the wearing of women's clothing by men, and the wearing of men's clothing by women . . . as well as the wearing of the comic, satyric, and tragic masks,"[11] —all were forbidden. And again there is the decree of deposition of the clergy and excommunication of the laity who disobey this canon. Canon sixty-six upbraids those who, on the holidays, rather than attend the "sacred mysteries of the Church service praising Christ with psalms, hymns, spiritual exercises, desert the Church for public shows;"[12] and in Canon seventy-one there can be no doubt in the minds of those who read the laws as to what is intended, the theatre itself is mentioned. There is a final warning of excommunication for those who do not conform.[13]

From this time on, church legislation, as recorded, is the strongest evidence for the case of a continual living secular theatre. A careful examination of the pronouncements made by subsequent Councils and Synods, which convened periodically during the next three centuries, reveals continued warnings and prohibitions against all public entertainment and association with the entertainers. The following pronouncements clearly indicate that a secular theatre to which the public had easy access, continued to exist without interruption in the West and that this same secular theatre, because of its licentiousness and obscenity, was of grave concern to the Church hierarchy.

The Synodus Francica, called by Pope Zachary sometime before 742, mentions again the earlier condemned pagan festivals.[14] Amusements preceding great church festivals come under heavy censure in the Council of Clovesho in 747;[15] and the Synod of Nicaea held in 787 attacks the licentious living of the actors.[16] St. John Damascene, writing in the eighth century, mentions the public shows—their continued popularity, their licentiousness and obscenity—in contrast with the spectacle of the Mass. Nicoll observes that "from St. John's words it is easy to see that he might have considered the making of religious plays as a rival attraction."[17]

The letters of Alcuin, written at this time from the court of Charlemagne, bear frequent testimony to the unbecoming conduct of the clergy in their association with the *histriones*. Corresponding with the Abbot Higbald of Lindesfarne, he said, "Better for the poor to eat at your table than actors and luxury-lovers."[18] Later, in a letter to Abbot Adalhard of Corvey, Alcuin expresses his concern for one of his colleagues, the poet-monk Angelbert, when he writes:

I fear lest Homer [Angelbert] be angry at me for forbidding certain plays and devilish fantasies, all of which sacred scripture prohibits. St. Augustine says, 'A man who introduces actors, mimes, and dancers into his home does not know what great disorder of soul follows this defilement.'[19]

Councils held throughout the ninth and tenth centuries consistently warned priests and clerics as well as laymen to avoid public spectacles. There were the Councils of Mayence[20] and Châlons,[21] both held in 813; the Council of Aix-la-Chapelle,[22] 816; the fourth council of Paris,[23] 829; and one

4

at the beginning of the tenth century from the Archbishop of Sens,[24] 909-916, exhorting both clerics and laymen to stay away from public shows; and to shun the company of "actors and mountebanks . . . and endeavor to avoid the danger of scandal." The church authorities continued these warnings against the *histriones,* the *mimi,* and the *ioculatores* throughout the century.

Liudprand of Cremona, as representative of Berengar II to the court of Constantinople in 949-950, in describing the robes worn by one of the rulers, ridiculed them, likening them to garments or costumes of the actors or mimes—*histrionum mimorumve more.*[25] And somewhat later, as ambassador to the same court in 968-969, he wrote to the Emperor Otto I that the Church of Santa Sophia had been turned into a theatre where he had been received on the occasion of the presentation of the play *Elijah.*[26] These two records are important; they indicate a casual mention of the mime and the enactment of a kind of religious play in the East contemporary with the appearance of the *Concordia Regularis* in the West.[27]

Thus we have documented evidence that the Church, through her bishops, was unable to obliterate a kind of mimetic drama which stemmed from the deep-rooted ethnic activities of ancient Greece and Rome, and flourished throughout the centuries from Byzantium to Spain as a well-developed secular drama. So "surprisingly" developed was this drama that Hunningher, in his essay on *The Origin of the Theater,*[28] says of the play of Adam le Bossu, *Jeu de la feuillée,* which appeared in 1250, it was "so well-constructed, indeed, that it clearly betrays his reliance upon existing traditions."

Hunningher, in pointing out the weaknesses in the theory of the ecclesiastical origin of modern dramatic art, which, he says, "has been canonized in numberless handbooks and textbooks," juxtaposes two alleged facts which he critically analyzes:

5

Without a theatrical vacuum in the middle ages, there could have been no growth of an autonomous religious theatre; and without the secularization of religious theatre, there could have been no liturgical origin for dramatic art.[29]

He then proceeds to explain that a complete theatrical vacuum from the seventh through the tenth centuries would imply "the existence of an iron curtain between Eastern and Western Europe . . . and a temporary withering of human insights . . . tendencies . . . and capacities."[30] There is evidence to prove a continual, if erratic, communication between the East and West during these years;[31] nor was there a withering of instincts, tendencies, and capacities during this age.[32] Therefore, Hunningher says, "we must allow the theatre historian to ascribe the idea of a theatrical vacuum to a 'pure' scholarship lacking in both human and artistic insight."[33]

There is every evidence that there was an independent dramatic stream, flowing parallel with the secular drama, which did not come under the Church banns placed on the latter. This dramatic element is found in the ceremonials of worship which began in the early days of Christianity. One of the first records is from the fourth century. It recounts an already well-developed ritual in dialogue performed by congregations in Palestine at the site of Christ's birth, passion, and death during the Christmas and Easter seasons.[34]

These ceremonials, through the centuries, gradually entered the liturgy of the West, but it was not until the banns were placed on secular theatre that they acquired distinction in theatre history. Karl Young, in his study of medieval church drama, says that even though many of these ceremonials in themselves are

highly theatrical and can easily be transformed into dramatic pieces . . . the effectual beginnings of religious drama are found not in the elaboration of the elements present in the traditional forms of worship, but in the deliberate, unsanc-

6

tioned, literary additions to the authorized liturgical text,
. . . conveniently called tropes.[35]

Young shows how the germ of the liturgical drama lies in
the tropes—interpolations, hundreds of which appear in the
liturgy of the Mass from the seventh to the tenth centuries.
These tropes may be found in the records of the Court
School of Charlemagne; in the records of such famous monastic centers as Metz, St. Gall in Switzerland, Jumièges in
France, Montecassino in Italy, and in the well-known tenth-
century *Concordia Regularis* of Ethelwold at Winchester, in
which we find specific directions for the correct conduct of
the *Quem quaeritis* of Easter, which trope, many contend,
marks the beginning of medieval church drama.

Concerning this work of Karl Young, Hunningher says, it
is

an indispensable collection of extant liturgical texts . . . an
extensive study which covers the entire field, and nothing
seems to have escaped his searching eye—except the need on
the part of readers and critics for a clear annotation of
dates.[36]

He finds it difficult to accept so late a date as the tenth century for the origin of this new dramatic form, the trope.[37]
To prove his thesis, he cites "a richly illuminated troparium
with miniatures," produced sometime before the tenth century at the abbey of St. Martial in Limoges, and now in the
Bibliothèque Nationale in Paris.[38] The miniatures, he says,
"are of great importance to us, for they portray various
mimes in their performances."[39]

Hunningher questions the appearance of mimes in these
tropes. "What business," he asks, "have these enemies of the
Church in a collection of monastic songs?"[40] The only conclusion we can draw, he says, is that the artist—the miniaturist, who enjoyed much greater freedom than the scribe
—depicted vividly and realistically what he had seen—mimes

7

singing, dancing, "accompanying themselves on musical instruments" while they enacted the tropes.

Upon the premise that the Church followed its customary practice of "sanctifying those worldly elements from which its congregations would not be parted,"[41] Hunningher explains his entire thesis. He uses this argument to show how the Church, recognizing the need for aesthetic performance, added the impersonation of the mime to the symbolism of liturgical drama in the trope. "This best explains," he says, "how drama sprang from the tropes—or rather how the tropes developed into drama."[42] However, this did not affect the old secular craft of the mime against which the conciliar banns continued to be issued. Thus, it was that the Church, in self-defense, created its own attractions, and it is not difficult to understand how easily the liturgical plays of the next three centuries evolved from the interpolations between the traditional scenes of the Christmas and Easter plays.

History relates that such a development of the trope was taking place in Germany as well as in England and France. Paul von Winterfeld suggests that Hrotsvitha might have known the sequences of Notker Balbulus and might even have written some of her own tropes.[43] Or, if she were influenced by the tropes, she might have taken her precedent from the monastery of Corvey, a fruitful source of codices and troparia. Through Agius, a Corvey monk and son of the founder of Gandersheim, there may be traced a close connection between Corvey and Gandersheim, which fact is significant for this study.

Agius was a brother of the first three abbesses of Gandersheim and was influential in the establishment and direction of the monastery from its very beginning. Corvey had become an important monastic center in the West after its foundation from Corbie in France in 822. Numbered among the monks who made the foundation at Corvey under Adalhard as abbot, was Adelricus, a famous miniaturist; and under Abbot Warinus, who soon succeeded Adalhard, is listed Hrodgarius, an equally famous scribe. It is to these two—the minia-

8

turist and the scribe—that Jones and Morey[44] have attributed certain Vatican Terence manuscripts. Where these manuscripts were executed by these two monks—Corvey in Germany or Corbie in France—is not a question which concerns this study; what is significant is that such important scribes and miniaturists were at work on classical codices and liturgical troparia in the monastery so closely associated with Gandersheim. This documented fact would indicate that Hrotsvitha had access to the literary and art relics of the scriptoria of both monasteries.

In spite of all the existing evidence, little stress has been placed on these three dramatic traditions which existed during the so-called "dark" centuries—the *liturgical* drama, which had its beginnings as early as the fourth century, came to full flower in the tenth, and continued to exist in its simplest form without any notable change until the sixteenth century; the *mimetic* drama which survived the disintegration of the Roman Empire and existed as a secular theatre in spite of the Church restrictions placed upon it;[45] and the literary tradition of *classical* antiquity which was preserved in the works of Seneca in the ninth and tenth centuries, though he was not popularly read before the fourteenth,[46] and in the Terence manuscripts which have been traced chronologically from the fifth through the twelfth centuries.[47]

A critical examination of Hrotsvitha's works in the light of these three existing dramatic traditions will reveal that she was a playwright intuitively capable of creating plots within a dramatic form. Her plays will show a marked influence of all three traditions. She herself says that she did not hesitate to imitate Terence "in that self-same form and composition,"[48] but the imitation ceased to exist with the form; for even though she reached back into antiquity for her sources, she is an artist with a creative mind. Her plays, written in Latin, are imbued with her Benedictine way of life and overflow with the lyricism of the liturgy. A theatre practitioner will be inclined to disagree with Mantzius, who finds her "one of those quiet poetic minds who eagerly studied behind monastic walls imitating favorite classic writers without making any reverberations beyond their limited circles,"[49] and would rather accept Magnin, who, writing in the mid-nineteenth century, says of her, "One senses an author who wrote not for chanting from choir galleries but for production in the great halls of the Chapter House."[50]

Karl Young, in discussing the influence of Terence upon Hrotsvitha, believes that she probably did not know that his plays were acted upon a stage, and concludes, "Certainly her freedom with the *Unities* of time and place would have made impossible a performance after the manner of the master."[51]

This study will attempt to show that Hrotsvitha's plays, when brought to life upon a stage, do not violate the one and "only dramatic Unity enjoined by Aristotle . . . the Unity of Action"[52] and that, in addition to the classic tradition and liturgical influence found in her writing, there are evident many and varied realistic theatrical tricks of the mime whenever her plots are taken from the script and put into action. To test this thesis, it was decided that the historical approach supplemented by an experimental problem would provide the most satisfactory resolution.

Survey of Performances

There are records of some private and semi-private performances of individual plays of Hrotsvitha, both in this country and abroad. In January, 1914, there was a production of "Paphnutius" by the Pioneer Players at the Savoy Theatre in London.[53] This production was done under the direction of the late Edith Craig with Ellen Terry playing a leading role. Christopher St. John, who had translated the play from the Latin for this English production, served in an advisory capacity for the stage presentation. Considerable

10

interest in the performance resulted in the publication, in 1923, of the first complete English edition of all six plays as translated by St. John. This was followed closely by another English translation, that of H. J. W. Tillyard.[54]

In December, 1934, The Snarks, a non-professional group of players, staged "Abraham" in the parish auditorium of the Church of St. Ignatius Loyola in New York City.[55] The St. John translation was used for this performance.

On May 3, 1952, students of the Classical Department of Bryn Mawr College, Pennsylvania, staged a Latin performance of "Gallicanus" in the cloisters of the campus library.[56]

The year 1952 marked the eleven-hundredth anniversary of the foundation of the monastery at Gandersheim. In anticipation of this observance, a group of professional players was brought up from southern Germany in August of 1950 to Gandersheim to enact the play "Abraham."[57] It was performed in view of the tenth-century church and the buildings which have through the years replaced the original monastery where Hrotsvitha lived and wrote.

In January of 1955, in preparation for this study, two of the plays, "Sapientia" and "Dulcitius," were prepared for performance in the Lydia Mendelssohn Theatre on the University of Michigan campus.[58] This production provided a working experiment to determine what theatrical qualities the plays possessed when presented as theatre pieces. The fact that there was no available record of performance for either of these plays influenced the selection.

An important factor in the application of experimental techniques to the historical data was the availability of critical reviews of the London and New York performances and of the performance in Gandersheim. In writing about the London performance, the *Times* reviewer says:

The name Hroswitha, the tenth century Benedictine nun of Gandersheim, is well known to students of dramatic literature. Her plays were the sole link between the drama of Imperial Rome and the drama of the Medieval Church.

11

They were Terentian in style, . . . we believe Miss 'Christopher St. John' to be the first person who has translated one and got it on the stage. The Pioneer Players acted it last night . . . and a very interesting hour it was.

The play chosen was *Paphnutius* . . . the story of the conversion of Thais by that ardent hermit of the Egyptian desert. A true picture of life in the Egyptian desert would probably be intolerable to the modern senses, but the sacks heaped in the corners of the Savoy's 'apron stage,' the coarse habits of the holy man's disciples, the wicker baskets they were knitting, and their simplicity of mind gave all one wanted for an impression. After a brief and very quaint lecture to these backward pupils in quadrivium, Paphnutius told them how his soul was burdened with the guilt of Thais and the eternal destruction of all men who sinned with her, and how he was resolved to venture into Alexandria to save her soul. To Alexandria he goes, looking very young and very handsome in the worldly garments donned over his habit; making his way to the house of Thais . . . he begins by making love to her. A very gallant . . . and experienced manner he had of doing it. But very soon the lover and the lover's garb were thrown aside, and the holy man was revealed in his dingy habit, with words of denunciation on his lips. The conversion of Thais . . . must have seemed surprisingly sudden to anyone who failed to understand that in the mind of Hroswitha and her contemporary hearers, the change would have been divinely prepared before ever Paphnutius set out from the desert. . . . Thais puts on the penitent's garb and disappears from the world. . . . Years pass . . . there is the vision of celestial bliss and Paphnutius' visit to the repentant sinner and her death in his arms. There are no half measures about Hroswitha. She pits the world against monastic virtues with no half-tones or saving clauses. But to a modern hearer the living merit of her play (which whatever may be the Latin, is not the least Terentian in significance) is the clearness and beauty with which she brings out the love of Paphnutius for his convert, the profound tenderness that underlies his appallingly severe treatment of the sick soul and sinning body. The last scene is loftily ecstatic. There is no doubt that Hroswitha is a good dramatist.[59]

12

John Mason Brown, writing in *The New York Post* following the Snarks' production in 1934, says:

On Friday last the Snarks offered their audiences an interesting escape into the drama's past by presenting, with all due reverence . . . Hroswitha's 'Abraham,' a script which was written a thousand years ago by the nun who added playwriting to her other acts of piety and who referred to herself as the 'strong voice of Gandersheim.'
If her voice no longer seems a strong one; if what was unquestionably daring in her own time has now taken on the quaint beauty belonging to all primitives; and if instead of being shocked by her boldness, one smiles—or wants to smile—at her naïveté she shows in writing her more worldly scenes, the reason is of course that a thousand years have robbed her of her strength, but they have not robbed her of her charm, her intensity, her simplicity or her desperate earnestness.[60]

In speaking of her object in writing her plays, Brown quotes from Hrotsvitha's prefaces, then says of her, "She was embarrassed by what she had to do to achieve her noble ends, but she anticipated the Channing Pollocks of today in the justification she found for herself."[61]
Writing in the *Braunschweiger Zeitung*, Peter Gallasch says of the Calderon Players performance:

The 'Schützenhaus' was almost packed up to the last seat when the curtain rose upon the performance of Hrotsvitha's play, 'Decline and Repentance of Mary, Niece of Abraham the Ermit,' done by the 'Calderon-Institute' of Munich. The performance proved that you can perform Hrotsvitha's plays now-a-days and that the public will enjoy them. The Nun-dramatist and poetess possessed a fine sense of 'milieu' which she brought to the stage with accurateness. Therefore her secular scenes are as well done as the religious passages. Those who thought that the Calderon would prove more 'up-to-date' (as Calderon lived nearer our time than Hrotsvitha did) felt that they had gone the wrong way long.[62]

13

There is a consistency in these reviews. Here are the records of three productions widely separated in time, place, and performance, yet all three leave very nearly the same impression, namely, that they are the works of a playwright who created intuitively for an audience. Hrotsvitha "pits the world against virtue" and the latter is triumphant in a manner not "intolerable to the modern sense," but entirely acceptable to the "now-a-days audience" because of the "clearness and beauty" with which she develops her themes, because of her "charm, intensity, simplicity, and desperate earnestness."[63]

Survey of Historical Data

The assumption that Hrotsvitha and her works fell into practically complete oblivion after her death (*ca.* 1002), until the discovery of the *Emmeram-Munich Codex* in 1493 by Conrad Celtes, has been, according to Zeydel, "repeated so often that it is now axiomatic."[64] He points out that the fairly recent discovery of certain manuscripts and the identification of other fragments, discovered in the nineteenth century as Hrotsvitha's writings, have increased the number of primary sources to such a degree that there is serious speculation about "Hrotsvitha's position as a possible factor during these five hundred years [1000-1500] of important literary development."[65]

The primary sources available and those to which the writer had access include the following manuscripts: the *Emmeram-Munich Codex*[66] which contains all the extant works of Hrotsvitha except the "Primordia Coenobii Gandeshemensis." These extant works are the six plays[67]—"Gallicanus," "Dulcitius," "Calimachus," "Abraham," "Pafnutius," and "Sapienta," with a preface and the argument for each play; the poems—"Maria," "Ascensio," "Gongolfus," "Pelagius," "Theophilus," "Basilius," "Dionysius," and "Agnes," with a general preface; and the "Gesta Ottonis" which has an ex-

14

planatory preface. This codex was found in the monastery of St. Emmeram at Regensburg in 1493 by Conrad Celtes, a fifteenth-century humanist, who edited and published the manuscript in 1501. It is now located in the Bavarian State Library in Munich.

The *Cologne Codex*,[68] a copy of the first four plays as they appear in the *Emmeram-Munich Codex,* was discovered by Goswin Frenken in 1922 and is now in the Municipal Archives of Cologne. There are varied opinions about this manuscript. Some maintain it was copied from the earlier codex during the twelfth century; others support the view that it represents not a copy of the *Emmeram Codex* but a better, purer text, possibly one of several manuscripts sent out from Gandersheim, during Hrotsvitha's lifetime, to prominent patrons of the monastery after the completion of these four plays.[69]

The *Munich Codex, Gallicanus,*[70] is also in the Bavarian State Library. It is believed to have been copied from the *Emmeram Codex* and dates from the twelfth century as a part of the Austrian Passional in Alderspach, Bavaria. Discovered by O. Holder-Egger in 1888, it was identified by Paul von Winterfeld in 1902.

In addition to these manuscripts, there are the *Klagenfurth Fragments*.[71] They comprise sheets containing a part of the legend "Maria" and a part of the play "Sapientia." These fragments were allegedly copied in the eleventh century from the *Emmeram Codex*. They are known to have been in the Dominican Library in Vienna before 1513 and are now in Klagenfurth.[72]

Although these primary sources are limited in number, they are significant because of the internal evidence which they provide. The secondary sources, much more numerous and highly controversial in nature, have appeared over the last five centuries in erratic manifestations of interest in Hrotsvitha.

Much of the available historical data about Gandersheim is based on the work of two eighteenth-century clerics,

Johann Georg Leuckfeld and Johann Christoph Harenberg, who had access to the monastery archives. Leuckfeld published *Antiquitates Gandersheimenses* [sic] in 1709;[73] and Harenberg, *Historia Ecclesiae Gandershemensis Cathedralis ac Collegiatae Diplomatica*[74] in 1734. These works are not wholly reliable because critical analyses have shown that they contain many errors and much pure fabrication. However, they are of some value because they contain copies of some very early manuscripts which have since been lost; chief among these is the above-mentioned "Primordia Coenobii Gandeshemensis," the only Hrotsvithan work not contained in the *Emmeram Codex*. The writer had access to the Leuckfeld and Harenberg works through the Archiv der Stadt Bad Gandersheim.

Other secondary sources also made available to the writer through the Gandersheim Archives were the *Syntagma ecclesiae Gandesianae* (1550)[75] based on *De scriptoribus ecclesiasticis* of J. Tritheim;[76] "Hrotsvitha und ihre Zeit" by Franz Löher (1858);[77] and "Canonissin des Stifts Gandersheim, die älteste deutsche Dichterin" by R. Steinhoff (1882).[78]

The *Théâtre de Hrotsvitha,* Charles Magnin (1845),[79] and *Le Moyen Age,* Philarète Chasles (1876),[80] were two important French works used in this study.

In 1867, Joseph Aschbach of the Imperial Academy of Sciences in Vienna published his *Roswitha und Conrad Celtes.*[81] He sought to prove that Hrotsvitha never existed; that her works were a mass of colossal forgeries, the work of Celtes. However, at an assembly of the German Historical Society in Munich in 1869, eminent scholars unanimously declared the *Emmeram Codex*, the only then-known manuscript, to be a genuine eleventh-century document and not a falsification of the fifteenth century, as Aschbach claimed. This declaration of the German Historical Society settled the controversy for several years.

In 1902, Paul von Winterfeld edited *Hrotsvithae Opera;*[82] in 1906, the Teubner edition of *Hrotsvithae Opera* by Karl

16

Strecker[83] was published. In 1909, Karl Steinacker published a monograph, "Stift Gandersheim," in the *Jahrbuch des Geschichtsvereins für das Herzogtum Braunschweig,*[84] which was concerned with the changing structure of the Gandersheim monastery since its very beginning. This was the first attempted architectural study. A year later, 1910, Steinacker expanded this monograph and published, in complete book form, *Die Bau- und Kunstdenkmäler des Kreises Gandersheim* (with 21 plates and 272 illustrations).[85]

Though this work is not considered valuable as an historical source, it has some merit as an architectural-monument study and places Gandersheim in the realm of the accepted conventual monastic plans—those of Cluny and St. Gall which are the generally accepted models of medieval monasteries. This work, not widely circulated, was made available through the archives at Bad Gandersheim.

"Die Anfänge der sächsischen Frauenklöster," a doctoral dissertation by Johanna Heineken, published in 1909 at Göttingen,[86] though not a complete study, does furnish valuable information about Saxon women's cloisters during Hrotsvitha's time. However, more recent critical examinations of the Gandersheim documents reveal the limitations of this work so that the extent to which it is used in this study is only in the consideration of the canoness branch of the foundation.

In 1923, as was previously mentioned, two English translations of the plays appeared. The first, a work of Christopher St. John, was published in London;[87] the second, *The Plays of Roswitha* by H. J. W. Tillyard, was also published in London the same year.[88]

In 1945, the Aschbach controversy was reopened by Zoltán Haraszti with the publication of an article in which the authenticity of Hrotsvitha's works was again challenged.[89] Zeydel in his discussion of the "Authenticity of Hrotsvitha's Works,"[90] calls attention to the fact that no attempt has been made to examine the manuscript paleographically with all the modern scientific tools at hand. He feels that such an

17

examination would settle the controversy conclusively. In a second note (of the same year) he points out that no humanist (Conrad Celtes) could have fabricated the good Old Saxon name, "Hrotsvitha," and rendered it correctly into Latin.[91]

The examination of the above-mentioned sources has been supplemented by recent documentation, most of which has been in progress since the last war. Among the works of Hans Goetting, state archivist of the Gandersheim area, the following have a particular bearing on the history of Gandersheim: "Zur Kritik der älteren Gründungskunde des Reichsstifts Gandersheim" (1950),[92] "Die Anfänge des Reichsstifts Gandersheim" (1950),[93] and "Das Fuldaer Missionskloster Brunshausen und seine Lage" (1953-1954).[94]

Konrad Algermissen, canon, eminent scholar, and historian of the Diocese of Hildesheim, attests to the thoroughness of Goetting's documentation and findings.[95] Algermissen's articles have appeared in the 1952 and 1954[96] issues of *Unsere Diözese,* an official publication of the Diocese of Hildesheim, the jurisdictional See of Gandersheim.

In the preparation of a text for this study the writer used the *Emmeram-Munich Codex,* the *Cologne Codex,* the French edition of Charles Magnin, the Teubner edition of Karl Strecker, and the English edition of Christopher St. John. Original tenth-century illuminated manuscripts furnished tableaux structures and rich colorful patterns for creating stage space and costume design. Access to these manuscripts was through the Hildesheim archives.

The historical research is particularly important to this study because it reveals the fact that the political and social impact of the time created the climate for the flowering of Hrotsvitha's genius. Life in a medieval monastery, the spirit of the time, and the mind of the Church[97]—all indicate the practicality of such virtuous lessons which her plays provided as an antidote to the continued popularity of the pagan writers.

The fact that there is no external historical evidence to prove that the plays were ever acted or intended for performance at Gandersheim in the tenth century supports the theories and assumptions of those who maintain that the plays were never intended for performance. Likewise, there is no positive statement nor external evidence to prove that the plays were not performed at Gandersheim. Thus, with a complete awareness of the claims for and against Hrotsvitha's plays as acting dramas, the purpose of this study is to analyze the plays for their stageworthiness. To do this effectively, it is necessary to examine the culture in which this tenth-century nun lived and to ascertain the possibility of probable performance.

The significance of such a study in the field of drama and theatre should be contributive since there has been no evidence, heretofore, of a critical theatre approach to the plays. Because of their time and place in theatre history, the plays of Hrotsvitha deserve a thorough investigation.

Chapter II

THE ORIGIN OF GANDERSHEIM

At the beginning of the middle ages, there were in Germany three cultural currents—the classical heritage of antiquity, Christian humanism, and the creative urge inherent in the Germanic peoples. The blending of the Christian spirit with the Germanic life forever distinguishes the antiquity of Europe from western culture as we know it today.[1]

The Christian influence gradually permeated the culture of the West and provided a climate for the medieval synthesis of "German, Roman, and Christian elements," which was supported by the Christian theologians and poets of the Patristic Age. It was they who kept alive the "Hellenistic and classical traditions" together with the "Church and Scriptures," and who were responsible for the ultimate rise of medieval art, architecture, and literature in Europe. These "aspects of waning and rising social orders were powerful stimuli in a period of transition."[2]

Medieval Life and Monasticism

It was during this period of transition that monasticism, which had originated in the East as a simple life forsaking all human associations and cultural achievements, developed in the West into a way of life in which cultural activities received due consideration, but were ordered to the supreme end of Christian life. Thus, monasticism became a leading political and cultural force throughout Western Europe.

Under the Rule of St. Benedict this way of life flourished throughout Germany. The monks not only exerted a powerful influence in learning and research, but also in the arts and crafts. In order to meet significantly the demands of an actual day-to-day existence, they taught the people the "dignity of manual labor."[3]

When the great age of Charlemagne seemed to have spent itself through "war, famine, and death, the Benedictine monasteries kept the flame of culture alive. . . . The Carolingian Abbey was a self-sustaining organization, a miniature city where churches, schools, granaries, hospitals, intellectual culture, agrarian economy,"[4] and the cultivation of the arts and sciences culminated in a kind of security which is best described by the old German proverb: "'There is good living under the crozier' (*Unter'm Krummstab ist gut leben*)."[5]

Although the monastic community, which represents a society of peace and security, was in direct contrast to the tribal societies which, as bands of warriors, were ultimately to become the founders of the German state, there is an obvious parallelism in their structure and function.[6] On the one hand, there was the tribal chieftain and his followers whose sworn fealty was to the death; on the other, the abbot and his subjects who vowed loyal obedience to a death which meant eternal life. Among the tribes there was the code of honor and fidelity, and the worship of the hero; in the monastic way of life there was the code of sacrifice and penance, and the devotion to the saint and the martyr. For the tribe there was the oral tradition of heroic deeds in epic poetry; in the monasteries there was the literary tradition of the Sacred Scriptures and the lives of the saints.[7]

This similarity within the structural framework of pagan and Christian cultures accounts for the ease with which men could renounce a pagan cult with its mysteries and accept the practices and beliefs of Christianity. This they could do

21

without losing vital contact with their old social tradition, which was sublimated and transformed, but not destroyed or lost. Thus, family and regional loyalties came to centre in the hereditary monastery and in the hereditary saints of the clan or kingdom, and the abbot became the spiritual chieftain.[8]

The fact that the abbot was very often a kinsman of the founder accounts for the appeal monasticism made to the ruling element of society, and why so many men and women of royal blood entered the cloister:

Men like SS. Illtud, Cadoc, and David in Wales; Colomba and Finian in Ireland; Adhelm and Bede in England; Willibrord, Winnibald, and Boniface in Germany—all descendants of nobility, espoused monasticism and took a leading part in the conversion of their kinsfolk.[9]

It was through papal grants that monasteries and convents were established by the heads of royal families providing the right of abbatial succession to their sons and daughters. Thus, with the resources of royal estates at their command, they were able to contribute greatly to the growth of Christian culture by the transmission of monastic tradition.

The development of western culture was marked by "political experiment, economic expansion, and intellectual discovery."[10] By the middle of the tenth century, Europe steadily and aggressively had gained a position of respect and power. There were no spectacular military triumphs, no organized political revolutions, but an inevitable constant changing spawned by a deep migratory unrest. The battle of the River Lech, a victory for Otto I in 955, is seldom mentioned among those world events which mark turning points in the history of civilization. Nevertheless, "it ensured the territorial stability of the European nations and was perhaps no less important than Marathon in the formation of Greece."[11] This defeat of the Magyars in August of 955 and the subsequent victory over the Wends at Mecklenburg in October of that same year influenced the history of this period to such an extent that the Germanic people "may be called the great organizers among the European nations, taking upon their shoulders the world-historic responsibility of shaping the Christian Middle Ages." [12]

In 962, after responding to the appeal of Pope John XII, Otto the Great restored law and order in Italy, and in turn, received from the Sovereign Pontiff the imperial crown, which marked the beginning of the Holy Roman Empire of the German nation, and thus re-established the continuity of the ancient as well as the Carolingian tradition.[13] Thus, the Carolingian ideal of a universal Christian empire under the leadership of emperor and pope survived the century of decline, and contact with the Carolingian tradition was restored by the ascendancy of the Saxon dynasty.[14]

However, the intervening years were marked by far-reaching social and political changes—changes relatively important to this study because they set the stage for Hrotsvitha and her work at Gandersheim.

In an attempt to explain how the cultural formation of the ideal goal of the Christian and German middle ages was derived from a philosophical and religious ideology and how it was sanctioned by society, Reinhardt, through a parallelism, reveals

a unity of opposites reconciled in a God-centered civilization . . . the ideals of knighthood and cloister, cruelty and tenderness, sensuality and spiritual ecstasy, rational analysis and child-like faith, the claims of an authoritarian State and Church and respect for the dignity of the individual and social group, exploitation of the peasant and tender consideration for the poor and downtrodden, for widows and orphans and the sick and suffering, for lepers and outcasts: the cleavage between the ideal demand and the imperfect reality is overcome by a generally accepted and approved standard of moral values.[15]

23

Within this picture of a seemingly unified German state, the Saxon emperors were gradually establishing their supremacy in outlying districts. History testifies to strife between classes and groups, between emperors and popes; there were battles and crusades, peaceful colonization and violent conquests; zealous missionary labors and bloody persecutions as well as cruel inquisitions.[16] However, the strong tribal patriotism of the Saxons is exemplified in the kind of leadership which emerged. Here were not only conquerors, but architects of the Christian Middle Ages. It was Otto the Great who freed the papacy from distressing entanglements and brought a renewed harmony between German civilization and the Christian and classical traditions. Other German leaders, too, through the Saxon dynasty were able to transcend the confines of tribal interests to the extent of establishing a definite relationship between their civilization and the civilizations of the past.[17]

The first rulers of the Saxon dynasty were descendants of the founders of Gandersheim. Their heritage can also be retraced to the court of Charlemagne. Their family titles are found among the leaders of both Church and State—abbots and abbesses in monasteries, dukes and queens in affairs of state.

This affiliation between temporal and spiritual leaders brings into focus the monastic home of Hrotsvitha and emphasizes the importance of her two historical works, "Gesta Ottonis" and "Primordia Coenobii Gandershemensis." The former is a record of the heroic deeds of Otto I, and the latter is an account of the foundation of the Gandersheim monastery, from its beginnings to the death of the Abbess Christine, the last of the founder's daughters. These works are valuable as a mirror of the period.[18]

Hrotsvitha wrote the "Gesta" at the insistence of Otto's son and of the Abbess Gerberga II. This was a tremendous task because there were few written sources available to her.[19] She had to rely on the testimony of those closely associated with Otto to obtain the facts concerning his military exploits and the establishment of the empire.[20]

Through her writing of the "Primordia," Hrotsvitha shows that the working relationship between court and monastery is significant, and that the history of Gandersheim reflects the political, social, and religious life in the changing period which bridged the Carolingian and Saxonian dynasties. The study will now proceed to trace the historical facts relating to Gandersheim and its development, which facts contribute to an understanding of the tenth-century culture which produced a Hrotsvitha.

Foundation and Political Development

With the establishment of the Benedictine monastery on the river Gande in 852, the name Gandersheim occurs at intervals in critical literary history. Continued interest in the monastery and in its relative importance to literary and theatre history has been periodically aroused by controversies concerning the foundation documents and the genuineness of the literary works attributed to Hrotsvitha. The year 1952 marked not only the eleven-hundredth anniversary of the royal foundation, but also drew attention to recent documentation of the foundation records by state archivists.

During the tenth century the monasteries, besides being centers of culture, pivots of political activity, and places of private religious observance, were "gradually becoming centers of public intercession and prayer, performing a necessary service for the well-being of founders, benefactors, and society in general."[21] Gandersheim, an imperial foundation, with the daughters of the royal family in ruling positions, was just such a center—one ideally conditioned to foster the talents of its members during the years of a cultural renaissance. In order to understand clearly how such an establishment functioned, a consideration of those religious, social, and political institutions which influenced its growth and development is of primary importance.

Algermissen, a canon at the Cathedral in the Diocese of Hildesheim, under which ecclesiastical jurisdiction the monastery of Gandersheim is geographically located, recently published the results of a critical study of the early Hildesheim sources. His study, which contains valuable information concerning Bishop Altfrid and Count Liudolf, the co-founders of Gandersheim, also draws attention to the work of Goetting. In the examination and documentation of papers of the archives of monastic foundations in the Braunschweig area, Goetting has established definite and conclusive facts concerning the foundation of Gandersheim as well as additional facts concerning its subsequent development.[22]

Earlier there had been partial investigations of several of these documents which Goetting has now evaluated and categorized in their relation to one another. His critical examination furnishes reliable source material on the origin of Gandersheim. By sifting the genuine from the false he emphasizes the fact that even the latter are valuable in this instance, because they contain copies of earlier lost manuscripts. From a maze of material, constituting all available sources, he proves that there exists up to his time no complete scholarly history of the imperial Gandersheim foundation.[23]

In his 1952 article, "Bischof Altfrid," Algermissen introduces other information related to the Gandersheim foundation gleaned from various critical sources. As for the "Vita Hathumodae," the life of the first abbess of Gandersheim written by Agius, her brother, who was a monk at the nearby monastery of Corvey, Algermissen points out that this work was not intended as an historical document because there are neither historical dates nor the names of Agius' parents, the founders of Gandersheim, nor is there any mention of the other members of his own family who were closely associated with the foundation.[24] Though Agius seemed to have written primarily to show the virtuous life of his sister, Hathumod, the abbess of the monastery, medieval scholars consider his work one of the biographical monuments of the Middle Ages.[25]

In addition to this work of Agius, Algermissen also mentions as source materials, the *Hildesheim Chronicles,* particularly the "Memoirs of Thankmar," the seventh bishop of Hildesheim. Concerning these, Goetting, in his critical analysis, has this to say, ". . . they are true and accurate translations and are valuable to us as such."[26]

As for the genuineness of the Gandersheim foundation documents, there has been some doubt in the minds of scholars. Goetting, after careful critical investigation and documentation, has confirmed these suspicions, and he has been able to place these particular documents definitely in the twelfth century. However, he considers them important and revealing because he finds that their twelfth-century author actually compiled them from several genuine ninth-century documents which have since been lost. The lost documents were prepared by Duke Liudolf himself, the royal founder of the Stift Gandersheim, and are important and significant for this study because they are the sources which Hrotsvitha used in writing her history of the foundation.[27]

About this history written by Hrotsvitha and entitled "Primordia Coenobii Gandeshemensis," Goetting says that prior to the eighteenth century all opinions held about the foundation were based on this work. And he further states that

even though Hrotsvitha has used reliable sources, her work contains a serious gap in at least one very decisive passage in the history of the foundation [of the *Stift*] and, in general, is written from the standpoint of her own time with distinctly noticeable coloring. Heretofore only the opposition, namely, the Hildesheim sources on the history of the imperial foundation of Gandersheim, has been decried as being subjective, . . . [Be this as it may,] there can, however, be no doubt that the facts, as given in Thankmar's "Memoirs" and the later *Chronicon Hildeshemense,* . . . can be exploited to the full.[28]

Regarding the many previous attempts to write a reliable history of the foundation at Gandersheim, Goetting in effect says that

anyone interested in the literature concerning this eleven-hundred-year-old imperial foundation, Gandersheim, the oldest cultural center in the Braunschweig area, must still, whether he likes it or not, go back to the works of two eighteenth-century historians, J. G. Leuckfeld and J. Chr. Harenberg.[29]

Johann Georg Leuckfeld, a temporary secretary to the abbess of Gandersheim with access to the monastery archives, was able to publish in 1709, his *Antiquitates Gandersheimenses* [*sic*].[30] Goetting points out that this work is entirely uncritical and contains many errors but, despite this fact, he shows wherein it is still very valuable because it contains the original publication of the oldest documents and narrative sources of the Gandersheim history. Among these documents are Hrotsvitha's "Primordia Coenobii Gandeshemensis," which Goetting says was copied from a manuscript that has since disappeared.[31]

Johann Christoph Harenberg's *Historia Ecclesiae Gandershemensis Cathedralis ac Collegiatae Diplomatica* appeared in Hanover twenty-five years after Leuckfeld's work (1734).[32] Harenberg was at that time rector of the foundation school; in this position he had access to the archives. His publication contained the entire documentary fund of the foundation up to the fourteenth century and beyond, and serves as a tremendous source of historical information on the entire area. But it has been proved that much of the work was the product of Harenberg's imagination. He was forced to admit this and to publish a retraction in 1735. This retraction consisted in handing over to the authorities a copy of his work in which he had indicated on the margins the location of all the liberties he had taken with his texts.[33] However, Harenberg's retraction did not reach the general public before his work had entered modern literature, where it was subsequently used as genuine source material.[34]

In 1909, Karl Steinacker, an official connected with the study of monumental art and architecture in the Gandersheim district, dared to work over the material at hand and published a short summary entitled "Stift Gandersheim."[35] This work was not entirely successful because, according to Goetting, it lacks critical analysis of the older sources.[36]

It is to the advantage of this study, therefore, that more recent critical investigations concerning the foundation of the Gandersheim monastery, namely, those of Goetting and Algermissen, have been pursued. These studies have resulted in the establishment of certain facts which were previously misrepresented or unconfirmed.

In reviewing the history of any religious institution of the middle ages, it is important, from a religious as well as a political point of view, to keep in the foreground the relationship between the Church and State. Therefore, in a consideration of the Gandersheim area, it is well to note that in his efforts to colonize and Christianize Saxony and to bring Germany into the Franconian Empire, Charlemagne made strong political allies by awarding vast land grants to numerous loyal Saxon leaders. There was intermarriage among the wealthy Saxon and Franconian families. Their genealogies list many religious as well as worldly titles. In the first decade of the ninth century, even before Charlemagne's death, the Christianizing of Saxony was well under way. This tremendous task had been undertaken by the great monastic foundations which, under royal patronage, established numerous missionary foundations. Important among the early monasteries having this royal protection was the great Bonifatius Cloister of Fulda which, with its many strong branch convents, served as a church center until the Saxon bishoprics were established.[37]

The name Gandersheim, which Goetting has established as appearing in documents as early as 802, was first known as the missionary foundation from Fulda called Brunshausen.

This concept of the origin of Gandersheim as a mission-cloister is only a few years old.[38] Little is known today about Brunshausen, originally a Benedictine monastery for monks, situated on the upper Gande about one and one-half kilometers north of the present location of the town of Bad Gandersheim. However, Goetting mentions that in the early history of Gandersheim there are several formerly ignored accounts which refer to Brunshausen. From these it can be inferred that there already existed a monastery settlement—one not identical with the Gandersheim foundation—which was transformed into a women's cloister by Liudolf in 852. These references may be found in the *Annals of Quedlinburg,* in Hrotsvitha's history, the "Primordia," in the "Memoirs of Thankmar," and vaguely in the "Vita Hathumodae" of Agius.[39]

The chartularies of Fulda, during the reign of Abbot Baugulf (780-802), and his successor Ratgar (802-817), show a relationship between Fulda and the monastery in the Gandersheim area.[40] Brunshausen, a name which can be traced to one of the early Saxon families, is derived from *Brun* or *Bruno.* It was a Bonifatius cloister, that is, one stemming from the first monastic foundation made in Germany by St. Boniface. It was erected by the grandfather and father of the later Duke of Saxony, Liudolf,[41] and, as the private property of the Liudolfians, subsequently became Gandersheim. The name *Bruno* occurs significantly in each generation of this wealthy Saxon family. Brunshausen was able to contribute greatly to the imperial foundation of Fulda, and the royal protection which it received in return made it an important link in the missionary foundations of the Church. The papers of Ludwig the German reveal that in the fourth decade of the ninth century a member of this family ruled as lay-abbot. This is confirmed by Algermissen who says that Duke Liudolf himself, in the year 840, acted as lay-abbot of Brunshausen.[42]

When the diocese of Hildesheim was established (*ca.* 804), its boundaries extended far south of Brunshausen, encompassing the area which included Gandersheim. The ecclesiastical center then shifted from Fulda to Corvey, a monastery newly established within the boundaries of the Hildesheim diocese. This new monastery was for young Saxon monks who had been educated and made their religious profession at Corbie in France, hence, the new Corbie or Corvey. It was governed by the reverend abbot, Adalhard,[43] a relative of Charlemagne, and a grandson of Charles Martel. Corvey then became, by and large, the recipient of the economic support formerly given to Fulda. This fact may have brought an end to the Fulda missionary work as well as account for the establishment, about the middle of the ninth century, of many private family cloisters by large, rich and powerful, aristocratic landowners. Among these families was the *Liudolfinger,* of which Duke Liudolf was a member; among the monasteries was Gandersheim, whose establishment, Goetting says, appeared in documents between 802 and 817. This Fulda missionary-foundation known as Brunshausen, subsequently as Gandersheim, appears listed among the possessions of the Liudolf family as early as the fourth decade of the ninth century.[44]

The prestige of the family may be determined by the fact that Liudolf and his wife Oda, who was also a descendant of a powerful Saxon family with a long line of ancestors stemming from Charlemagne's court as well as from imperial monastic abbeys, made a pilgrimage to Rome. The purpose of this journey, besides being a pilgrimage, was to place the newly planned monastery under papal protection; to obtain permission to install the minor daughter of the family, Hathumod, as abbess; and to obtain relics for the monastery church. The last-mentioned reason had a very special significance at this time for the newly Christianized Saxons, since it was customary to place newly erected churches under the patronage of Christian martys and, whenever possible, have their relics enshrined in the church.[45]

The pontifical papers of Sergius II establish that this trip to Rome by Liudolf and Oda occurred sometime during his reign as pontiff (844-847).[46] It obviously would take some time for the preparation of the monastery. Algermissen quotes from Hrotsvitha, "We know of a certainty, from other sources, that Brunshausen was the place where, in 852, the canoness convent was founded by Liudolf until a more suitable place could be determined."[47] This date also marks Hathumod's recall from the monastery school at Herford to be installed as abbess of the newly founded Gandersheim monastery.

Hathumod, who was born in 840, was the second eldest daughter of Liudolf. She had been placed in the nearby canoness convent of Herford, a Fulda mission, where her maternal grandmother and aunt had been successive abbesses. It is assumed that she had been sent there to prepare her for her future role as abbess of Gandersheim.[48]

Liudolf and Oda had six sons and six daughters. According to age they were as follows: Bruno, Otto, Ekbert, Enda, Hathumod, Gerberga, Christine, Liudgard, Thankmar, and two unindentified sons and a daughter who died at an early age. In order to retain the family's temporal power, Liudolf's two sons, Bruno and Otto, remained in the world. Ekbert and Thankmar entered the monastery at Corvey, insuring the family's prestige in Church affairs. Ekbert became the monk Agius, the biographer of Hathumod; Bruno, the eldest and heir, was killed in battle with the Normans in 880. He was succeeded by Otto the Illustrious, the second eldest, whose son, Henry I, was the founder of the German Empire and father of Otto the Great. Thus, Liudolf was rewarded for his foresight in arranging for his posterity.

Algermissen asserts that the founding of the Gandersheim monastery must also be regarded in the light of the politics of this celebrated family. It was to be a private convent for the daughters of the Liudolf family who were to hold ruling positions insofar as it was possible.[49] Enda, the eldest daughter, was married. After the death of her husband she joined her sisters in the monastery. Hathumod, the first abbess, died in 874 and was succeeded by her sister, Gerberga I, who ruled as abbess until her death in 896.

This record reveals how carefully Liudolf had protected his family holdings and power in both Church and State. Through his marriage to Oda he had greatly increased his power and wealth. Oda, as an Egbertine, shared in rich estates in Westphalia; her brother, Warin, was abbot of Corvey from 826 to 856. Another close relative, Altfrid, the monk at Corvey who became fourth bishop at Hildesheim, exerted a powerful influence for the family while he lived. He not only assisted with the foundation of the Gandersheim monastery, but he also served in the diplomatic service of Ludwig the German.[50] After his death in 874, there was evidence of strained relations between Gandersheim and the bishopric seat of Hildesheim. This apparently was due to the fact that there was no immediate member of the Liudolf family able to succeed Altfrid as bishop at Hildesheim.

This threat to Gandersheim's hope for an independent imperial status was anticipated by Hathumod before her death. Agius recounts in the "Vita" a conversation wherein she expressed her worry concerning the affairs of her foundation, because it had not yet received the royal protection. Agius calms her fears by saying that this protection can be easily secured, since the bishop is *fidelis et familiaris* and with the help of friends and relatives at the court the royal patronage certainly can be obtained. Hathumod doubts that she will live to see this day.[51]

Algermissen, quoting from Agius, states that this conversation took place in the spring or early summer of 874; Bishop Altfrid died in August of that same year. Liudolf of Corvey, a cousin of Agius and Hathumod, was named as successor to Altfrid. However, Liudolf died before his installation and Agius mentions as Liudolf's successor, ". . . a Bishop Markward, who stood at the deathbed of Hathumod, November 29, 874, in that frightful year in which a third of the German and Gallic population died of famine and pestilence."[52]

33

The royal protection was acquired only after the Liudolfians had formed a family relationship with the Carolingian
royal house through the marriage of Liudgard, the last-
named daughter, with Ludwig the Younger. In 877, a large
document containing four diplomas, two of which are still
preserved in the original, gave to Gandersheim, not only
immunity and royal protection, but also a guarantee that the
daughters of the Liudolfian family would govern the community as abbesses. With this document there were large
real estate gifts in Thuringia, and in addition, the right to
collect customs for the river traffic in regions between the
Rhine and the Elbe rivers. These revenues were made out
to Oda, as the mother-in-law of Ludwig. She became the recipient with the stipulation that the gifts, together with the
revenues collected therefrom, would fall to the possession of
Gandersheim at her death. Thus, the royal marriage, in addition to pressure from the brothers, Bruno and Otto in
Frankfurt, brought about the Royal Protection Charter.[53]

Goetting, through careful analysis of this document entitled, *Diploma of Ludwig the Younger,* has determined that
it was not drawn up by the Royal Chancellery as had been
stated by earlier investigation; he claims that the form shows
that it must have been dictated by a learned member of the
Church, one familiar with the proper phraseology for such
documents, saying in substance:

On the basis of certain similarities with the older Gandersheim foundation document, I believe the dictation might
have been by Agius. He was the most important clerical
member of the founder's family and could well have participated in formulating the Royal Diploma of Gandersheim
which appears to have the same basic form that had been
used in the drawing up of the foundation documents for
Corvey.[54]

Since in the Diploma, there is no reference to the Bishop of
Hildesheim, the Liudolf family contended that the foundation would continue to be controlled by its heirs. Gerberga,

who succeeded Hathumod, was abbess when the Royal Protection Charter was finally obtained.[55]

Relative to the change in location from Brunshausen to Gandersheim, the "Primordia" states:

There already existed a small church on top of a mountain across the banks of the Gande, and from this they named the celebrated spot Gandersheim. There, worthily paying homage to the Lord until a place better suited could be found, they united many maidens in community life, and they destined their own daughter, Hathumod, to become like unto these in mode of living.[56]

Other available sources also indicate that, four years later, the monastery was transferred one and one-half kilometers south to the eventual location. There have been various reasons given for this change which, according to Hrotsvitha, was intended from the very beginning, "Dum locus investigari posset magis aptus." Her explanation in the "Primordia" gave rise to a legendary feature of "divine intervention." She recounts that on All Saints Day, light rays appeared to Liudolf in this very place (Gandersheim), thus designating the new site by a sign from Heaven. In other words, as Goetting says, it was a supernatural appearance as is often indicated in many of the documents of these early foundations. However, there are also practical reasons advanced for the move. The high road and the elevation of the ground on which Brunshausen was situated permitted no room for expansion. Certainly, the new location was more easily accessible, and, another very important factor, it would place the monastery at a vantage point, that is, at the intersection of two very important crossroads.[57] Of this location Algermissen says in substance:

The new location one and one-half kilometers to the south provided a better protection by means of a large forest and swamp. At the same time there were more proper accesses of travel and transportation since two large main roads crossed each other at that point. One, the west-east road from the Rhine to the Elbe, was formerly an army road of the Franconian troops, and the north-south road was a connection between Göttingen, Northeim, Lamspringe, and Hildesheim.[58]

Goetting affirms that, thereafter, the older Brunshausen served primarily to support the new monastery at Gandersheim, and since it had lost its original significance as a mission cloister, it continued to exist only in the shadow of Gandersheim. Algermissen adds that after the more favorable location at Gandersheim had been found, the construction of a large convent and church was begun at the new site. At the time of the moving of the convent from Brunshausen to Gandersheim (881), there is evidence that some members of the community remained at the Brunshausen site.[59] Both houses, the new and the old, flourished since both represented in their membership the most highly respected families of the countryside. Algermissen uses the term *Kanonissenkonvent* in reference to this move, thus supporting the fact that there must have been a distinction of status among the members of the community.[60] Such a distinction would have some significance for this study.

Goetting indicates that, through the efforts of Agius and with the permission of Pope Sergius II, two other Saxon canoness convents had their beginnings the same year as Gandersheim, one at Essen on the Ruhr, and the other at Lamspringe, just northeast of Gandersheim. Recent research has brought to light the relationship of these monasteries. They were foundations promoted by Altfrid, and made by wealthy Saxon families at relatively the same time. It was mentioned earlier that Hathumod had been placed in a monastery school at Herford, one which apparently served as a model for the three canoness convents which Altfrid later fostered. Thus it appears there is a definite pattern for these private-family foundations with vast powerful holdings retained in the name of the Church.[61]

Through the Hildesheim sources, particularly the "Memoirs of Thankmar," Altfrid's influence in establishing these foundations is revealed. According to these documents his name is mentioned with reference not only to the foundation of the Gandersheim monastery, but also to its later transfer and its dedication. The original convent at Brunshausen was under Altfrid's direction, and four years later he is said to have examined the new location, to have named the foundation, and with the Duke's approval, to have begun its construction.[62]

Wersebe has proved that the original Gandersheim church is a typical "Altfrid" construction with architectonic bases that correspond exactly to the original plans of the cloister church at Corvey.[63] In the year 851, when Altfrid became Bishop of Hildesheim, he began the construction of his new Cathedral with the first square crypt in which were housed altars in honor of the protomartyrs, St. Stephen and St. John the Baptist.[64] It is significant that these same saints are honored with altars at Corvey, at Gandersheim, and at Hildesheim because it indicates clearly the close relationship between Gandersheim and Hildesheim at the time of the foundation.

It is recorded that Duke Liudolf continually made large gifts of land and buildings to the foundation. Agius participated by being counselor to his sister, Hathumod, and guided the spiritual welfare of the newly founded monastery. About the year 860, Agius was instrumental in having Liudolf legalize the donation of the land and buildings which belonged to the Gandersheim foundation. These original documents which first listed Liudolf's possessions—both land and holdings—indicate that certain definite areas belonged to him and others to his wife, and that later they were to be placed in the hands of his daughter, Hathumod.[65] These holdings included three parts of the "Flenithigau," the area of a relatively closed region along the upper Gande river. This is sometimes referred to now as the old Gandersheim area. There are the names of various settlements such as Liudolfhausen, immediately to the west of the present Gandersheim, and North Liudolfhausen, south of Dankelsheim, neither of which survives, and finally, Brunshausen —names which show that the Liudolf family controlled this entire area.[66]

After the passing of the immediate Liudolfian family, the bishops of Hildesheim seem to have gained control of the monastery at Gandersheim. Goetting infers from this fact that it is not mere coincidence that Hrotsvitha's "Primordia" ends at this point.[67] From this date, historically speaking, the activities of the monastery are available only through the Hildesheim sources. They refer merely to the functions which require the bishop's presence or assistance; the monastery's position seems to be the same as that of other branch monasteries under the bishop's rule. However, relations between the monastery and the bishopric of Hildesheim must have strained to the breaking point to bring about a move made by Otto I, in January of 948. He, through Hathumar, the reigning abbot of Fulda, effected a new protective privilege from Pope Agapet II, in Rome, placing the Gandersheim monastery directly under the Holy See. [68] Here Goetting has quoted Harenberg's source which also confirms Stengel's proof of the genuineness of the *Agapet Privilege*. This document conforms strictly with a series of papal privileges which were concerned with the monasteries of Fulda, Hersfeld, Essen, and Quedlinburg. In the case of Gandersheim, the text of the *Agapet Privilege* was lost when there was an attempt to falsify the original foundation documents in the twelfth century.[69]

This protective privilege, which placed the monastery directly under papal jurisdiction, is said to be the strongest anti-bishopric protective order issued in this period. The Pope placed Gandersheim under his immediate care by expressly emphasizing that it is *nostrum monasterium,* whose establishment is referred to *Otto, comes de Saxonia,* and that no other clerical powers should have any jurisdiction whatsoever over the foundation. The Pope further stated that any bishop who dealt contrary to this privilege would fall under his interdict. The abbess was to be chosen from her own Chapter (that is the monastic community), but installed by the King.[70] This event marks the initial step towards the final dissolution, centuries later, of a genuine religious community life which eventually turned to Protestantism and, finally, to total deactivation.

The Hildesheim sources reveal the physical progress of the monastery's growth. They show that the abbess Hrotsvitha (916-927), who succeeded Christine, completed the western spire and the gallery of the monastery church. Windelgard (927-955), the next abbess, was instrumental in having another church constructed in honor of the Blessed Virgin. The record also shows that the latter building was consecrated in 939 by Bishop Diethard (928-954). Windelgard died about 955.[71] She was succeeded by Gerberga II, the daughter of Henry the Fowler and niece of Otto I. She, like the other abbesses before her, despite the *Agapet Privilege*, was installed by the Bishop of Hildesheim.[72] During the Christmas synod of 967, Gandersheim received an extensive privilege from Pope John XIII, on demand and in the presence of Otto I and his son, the future Otto II. This new privilege did not expressly refer to the bishops; it merely served to emphasize the independence of the foundation.[73]

Under the rule of Gerberga II, Gandersheim enjoyed the period of its greatest achievement. It was during this time that the young Hrotsvitha entered the monastery; Algermissen says it was probably in 957, when she was about twenty-seven years of age:

In 973, the old canoness cloister and church burned to the ground, and the very capable abbess, Gerberga, had a new church and monastery constructed. While this construction was going on, Hrotsvitha worked on her poetry, and about the year 985, Sophia, the daughter of the already deceased Otto II, entered the monastery of Gandersheim as canoness.[74]

39

With Sophia's entrance the strained relations which apparently had prompted the request for the *Agapet Privilege* developed into what became the famous "Hildesheim quarrel." During the bishopric of Osdag (985-989), there was an attempt by the canonesses of Gandersheim to separate completely from Hildesheim and join the archdiocese of Mainz. The high point of this attempt was reached at the time of Sophia's reception of the veil. She refused to accept the veil from the hands of Osdag, the Bishop of Hildesheim, and she asked the Archbishop and Chancellor, Willigis of Mainz, to perform the ceremony.[75] Bishop Osdag protested in the presence of both her mother, the Empress Theophano, and her brother, Otto III, but the bishop had to concede to a compromise; together with the Archbishop Willigis, he performed the ceremony upon Sophia, and the remaining novices who were to have received the veil at the same time had a private ceremony on another day with only the Bishop of Hildesheim officiating.

In the year 1000, when the newly constructed church was to be consecrated, Sophia, who was in charge of arrangements because the elderly abbess, Gerberga, was ailing, once again ignored the Bishop of Hildesheim and invited the Archbishop of Mainz to officiate at the ceremony. Gerberga, in spite of her illness, insisted that the Bishop of Hildesheim, Bernward (993-1022), be invited for the consecration ceremony. However, when Bernward arrived on September 14 for the ceremony of the elevation of the cross, he was denied admittance by Sophia. He appealed to the Empress and to the Pope, but no immediate reconciliation seems to have been effected. Gerberga died in 1001 and was succeeded by Sophia. After making several attempts, Bishop Bernward finally consecrated the Church on January 5, 1007.[76]

There are no details of this internal struggle mentioned in the account by Algermissen; he merely refers to it indirectly when he says:

Hrosvitha, [the dramatist], was no longer living at this particular time. However, she did experience the earlier days of this unrest at Gandersheim. What position she had taken in the quarrel is not known to us. Because of her friendship with Gerberga and her advanced age, let us assume that she did not belong to the group of rebellious nuns who under the leadership of proud Sophia [prevented Bishop Bernward from entering the Church] as is known from the seventeenth chapter of Thankmar's 'Vita Bernwardi.' [77]

The Hildesheim-Gandersheim difference continued and was responsible for the earlier-mentioned attempt to falsify some of the foundation documents at the beginning of the twelfth century, so that Altfrid's name might be omitted entirely, leaving only the founder's family name and that of the Pope. Algermissen notes that Hrotsvitha does this same thing when she makes her presentation of the foundation of Gandersheim, omitting the name of Altfrid.[78]

The Abbess Matilda (1195-1222) had earlier started a suit in Rome against Bishop Hartbert (1199-1212) on the basis of the earlier privileges of Popes Agapet II and John XIII. The trial and process were won by Matilda. On May 8, 1208, the Gandersheim convent monastery achieved its goal in obtaining complete separation from the Bishopric of Hildesheim through Pope Innocent III (1198-1216). The convent was free to turn to any bishopric, whenever necessary, and the bishops of Hildesheim no longer had any relationship with Gandersheim.[79] In the year 1589, the abbess of Gandersheim, Margareta von Chlum, and her successor, Anna Erika von Waldeck, together with the entire community, turned to Protestantism. Until the year 1802, the convent was represented at all national events as an imperial worldly free "Reichsstifts." In 1810, King Jerome of Westphalia deactivated it. Algermissen concludes, "this was the end of Liudolf's and Altfrid's at one time venerable foundation."[80]

This comparatively detailed account of the historical and political development of Gandersheim, with particular emphasis on the tenth century, shows the status of the monastery government in relation to the Church and State. The fact that Otto the Great obtained papal privileges to keep Gandersheim under direct imperial protection, and this coincidental with Hrotsvitha's lifetime at the monastery, is of considerable consequence because it emphasizes this close interlocking of activity and communication between monastery and court.

In the preface of the "Gesta Ottonis," Hrotsvitha addresses herself confidently to Gerberga, at whose request she had written the poem, calling her "Illustrious Abbess, esteemed no less for her integrity than for her descent from a royal race." And addressing herself devotedly to the son of the Emperor, she says:

Bright scion of the august and revered Otto, . . . spurn not the poor composition of a poor nun! Thou thyself, . . . has lately ordered it to be presented to thy keen gaze. . . . If I were not urged by thy dread command, under no circumstance, should I have such self-assurance as to presume to offer to thy scrutiny this little book with its lack of polish.

To the Emperor himself she courageously pleads:

Otto, mighty sovereign of this empire of the Caesars, . . . do not reject the small offering of this poem, but may this proffered tribute of praises, which the least of the flock of Gandersheim accords thee, be pleasing. This kind solicitude of thy forebears has assembled it, and the constant desire of rendering service owes it thee.[81]

From these respectfully humble salutations to her Abbess and Emperor, there may be inferred a certain familiarity of address that reveals a friendly relationship between sovereign and subject—a relationship which indicated an established social intercourse between monastery and court. Löher, writing of Hrotsvitha and her time, says:

Hrotsvitha was in close contact with Archibishop Wilhelm of Mainz who was an important man in the later period of Otto the Great. She was well known to many other famous scholars. . . . The young king Otto [Otto II] was always the first who wished to read her new poems . . . and it was at his insistence, strongly supported by Gerberga and the Archbishop Wilhelm, that Hrotsvitha began to write the historic poem about her great contemporary, Otto, and his deeds.[82]

Such an intimate relationship between monastery and court, as implied here, would lend support to the opinions of Magnin, Chasles, Löher, and others. Gandersheim, as one of the most noted cultural centers in northern Saxony, was, according to Magnin, a gathering place for

the intellectual aristocracy and the clergy. In place of the circus and amphitheatre which had brought together huge crowds for the same purpose in the same enclosure . . . one sees the rise of churches, . . . which on solemn festal days, could hold, without confusion, the faithful of all stations in life, the barons and the clerics, . . . the townspeople and the serfs, and present thus, in spite of the vast class distinctions, that which drama needs more than anything, a great audience completely united in sympathetic bond by a common emotion, . . . in the enclosure of the monasteries, these privileged sanctuaries which opened their portals to all ranks [stations in life], and on certain days invited seculars to their feasts. In the shelter of these sanctuaries of learning, of piety, and of the fine arts, the drama of the middle ages could develop more openly, more poetically, and unhampered by inflexibility of the ritual. . . . In fact, we know, without any doubt, that it is in a famous Saxon abbey that the dramas of Hrotsvitha were produced, probably in the presence of the diocesan bishop and his clergy, before some noble ladies of the ducal house of Saxony and a few high dignitaries of the imperial court, without counting the audience in the background—the gaping crowd of peasants from nearby, and (who knows?) farther back on the steps of the great stairway, a few serfs, or craftsmen of the rich and powerful abbey.[83]

Thus, Magnin has presented a picture of the medieval monastery as the community center of the middle ages—a meeting place which did not preclude drama. Also through Löher's eyes we see such a segment of medieval life:

The Emperor, his knight and scholars, the nuns and noble women of the neighborhood, . . . the servants and common people in the background—all in front of a stage which must be considered simply arranged.[84]

In reply to those who doubt the possibility of Hrotsvitha presenting those scenes which are of a questionable nature, especially in monasteries, Löher replies, "Well, if a nun could write them, then her sister-nuns were hardly horrified to watch them.[85]

This is the medieval life—it was prepared to accept drama.

Chapter III

THE MONASTERY OF GANDERSHEIM

The Structural Aspects

A study of the physical aspects of the monastery serves as an important link in the history of Gandersheim as well as a guide for the consideration of the plays as theatre pieces.

There is little left today of the alleged original monastery and church (see Plate II). There was little more even in 1845 when Magnin expressed concern lest what remained at that time of the physical structure of the monastery and church might be lost forever:

This magnificent church, as well as the buildings and their dependencies is still standing. It would be very desirable, while there is still time, if prints could be made of all the details of construction and of arrangement of the interior and exterior of this venerable abbey to which are attached so many and such precious remembrances.[1]

This was subsequently done, for there are sketches, prints, and detailed accounts of the monastery's establishment and expansion in *Die Bau- und Kunstdenkmäler des Kreises Gandersheim,* an elaboration of an earlier published monograph by Steinacker.[2] Though the work, published in 1910, relies for its historical details on Harenberg and Leuckfeld (see Fig. 1), both of whom Goetting[3] has shown to be unreliable as historians, this does not preclude its value as the most

45

complete architectural study available. Interest in the monastery buildings is important in this study primarily for the purpose of determining a focal point from which the theatrical possibilities of the plays of Hrotsvitha might be considered.

The most reliable historical description of the original church and foundation is Hrotsvitha's "Primordia." It indicates that at the very beginning a massive construction had taken place:

Then at length [881], when all preparation for the celebration of the festival [All Saints] had been duly made, Wicbert, blessed bishop of the Lord, dedicated this magnificent church to the glory of God for endless praise throughout the ages to all saints whose feast was then worthily commemorated.[4]

The *Hildesheim Chronicles* record that in 973, fire destroyed the original monastery and cathedral. They were rebuilt immediately. Despite the fact that these records mention occurrences pertinent to the growth and development of Gandersheim only when the local bishop participated in the monastic activities, they reveal such points of interest as the solemn thoroughness and permanent construction of the buildings which "Bishop Wicbert consecrated and dedicated on All Saints Day, the [anniversary] day of the year of the local appearance of the lights." Later in the same *Chronicles* we learn that, "only in 926, under Bishop Sichart, was the construction of the 'turris occidentalis' completed; . . ."[5] This would indicate that when Hrotsvitha entered the monastery (*ca.* 955), Gandersheim was already a well-seasoned structure. Steinacker records the interment of Henry, Duke of Bavaria, in the church in 995, and the controversy surrounding the reconsecration of the new buildings. In Bodo's *Syntagma* there is an account of a second fire. He says, "The Abbess Adelheid II (1063-1094) had the foundation reconstructed after the second fire."[6]

Steinacker, in his historical identification of the present

PLATE II

Steinacker, XV

GANDERSHEIM, 1910

PLATE III

Steinacker, 270

CLOISTER GARDEN SHOWING THE EAST AND NORTH SIDES
OF FIG. 3. a_1-c WITH MARKINGS ON WALLS INDICATING

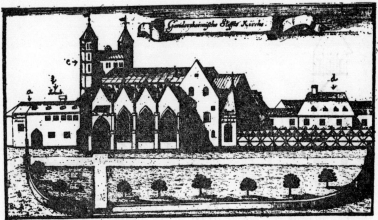

Leuckfeld

Leuckfeld

FIG. 1.— CHURCH AND ABBEY AT GANDERSHEIM, 1709

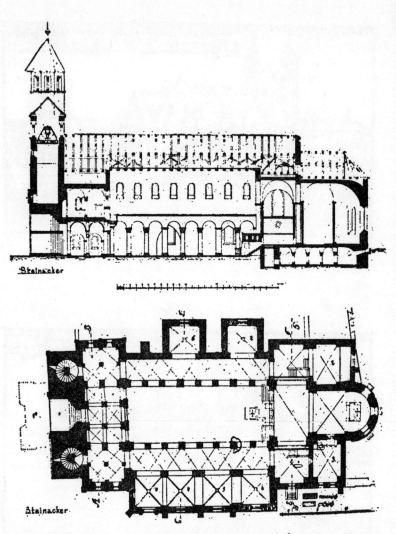

FIG. 2.—LONGITUDINAL SECTION AND FLOOR PLAN OF CHURCH AT GANDERSHEIM, SHOWING HISTORICAL DEVELOPMENTS

structure (1910), indicates that the main nave of the church doubtless belongs to the tenth century (see Fig. 2).[7] His basis for this statement is the similarity which the church at Gandersheim bears to the cathedral at Quedlinburg consecrated in 1129. He further points out that there was a very close relationship between these two abbeys during the eleventh and twelfth centuries. This relationship, he says, would indicate that Quedlinburg shows a dependence architecturally upon Gandersheim and the latter, in turn, upon Hildesheim. He also mentions the close similarity of the Gandersheim church to the cathedral at Goslar which was completed as early as 1055, and concludes this statement by saying:

Since it is well documented that a new consecration took place between 1063 and 1094 [dates coinciding with Bodo] we may, on the basis of the architectural forms, very well connect this act with the nave of the cathedral, which accordingly was built in the last quarter of the eleventh century.[8]

Churches in the middle ages traditionally faced the West. They were, as at Cluny, usually situated on the north side of the monastic buildings, but occasionally the church was located on the south side. In the case of the Gandersheim construction, the church and some of the buildings were constructed on the south side to serve as a protecting wall along the road which was, at that time, a military highway.[9]

In his description of the abbey which is accompanied by a floor plan (see Fig. 3) Steinacker says:

The name *Abtei* [abbey] designates all the former living quarters and outbuildings of the convent, all of which belong today [1910] to the ducal domain and are grouped around the existing church, i.e., especially the remnants of the oldest convent buildings which formerly enclosed the cloister, the deanery, and the abbey buildings in a narrower sense.[10]

Steinacker relates an interesting account, found in the "Vita Bernwardi" of the *Hildesheim Chronicles* of 1001, point-

47

ing out the similarity of the original structure of the abbey to a *castellum* (or bishop's residence). According to the Bernward report, the abbess had "the towers and defense works around the church manned with men at arms, soldiers who thus protected the *castellum* against the peacefully approaching bishop." [11] This description refers to the incident when Bishop Bernward was denied admittance by Sophia to the consecration ceremonies which had been planned in the year 1000.

This statement, in which Steinacker speaks of the monastery of Gandersheim as similar to a bishop's residence, raises the question that there might have been some characteristics in the monastic planning of Gandersheim which would differentiate it from the conventional monastery of the ninth and tenth centuries, but research shows that the monasteries of the West, from the ninth century on, were consistently alike in architectural planning. Cluny (see Fig. 4) is representative of most medieval abbeys. Although the floor plan of Gandersheim presented by Steinacker dates from approximately the fourteenth century, comparison with Cluny, which is much larger and more elaborate in structure, shows a striking similarity in general outline and in detail.

Steinacker attempts to follow the outline of the monastery from its beginnings until the nineteenth century. Though his floor plan covers more structure than the scope of this study, that part of the structure which is actually known to have been in existence in the fourteenth century is significant because there are in it some remnants which can be identified with the very earliest tenth-century structure.

At the entrances there were facilities for the lay people who used the church. Such facilities (see Figs. 1 and 3) included a guest house, school, ladies' dormitory, rectory, and other buildings—easily accessible from the outside. The *Kronenhaus* (see Figs. 1,a and 3,h) located west of the church towers, was at the disposition of notable guests and is mentioned as early as 1351.[12] Between the *Kronenhaus* and the *Südturm,* that is the southern spire of the church (see Fig.1,c)

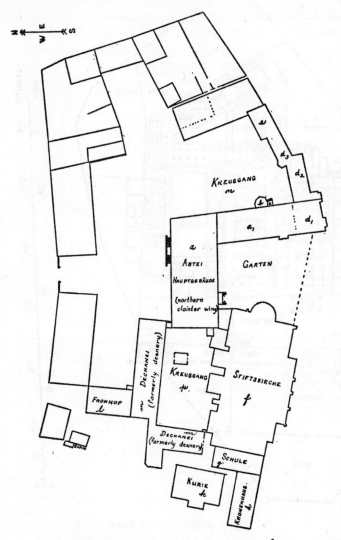

N ← W ← S

KREUSGANG
m

e

d₃

d₂

a₁

t g

d₁

a

ABTEI

GARTEN

HAUPTGEBÄUDE

(northern
cloister wing)

DECHANEI
(formerly deanery)

KREUSGANG
w

STIFTSKIRCHE
f

FRONHOF
l

DECHANEI
(formerly deanery)

SCHULE
g

KURIE
k

KRONENHAUS
h

FIG. 3.— FLOOR PLAN OF GANDERSHEIM (AFTER STEINACKER, 104)

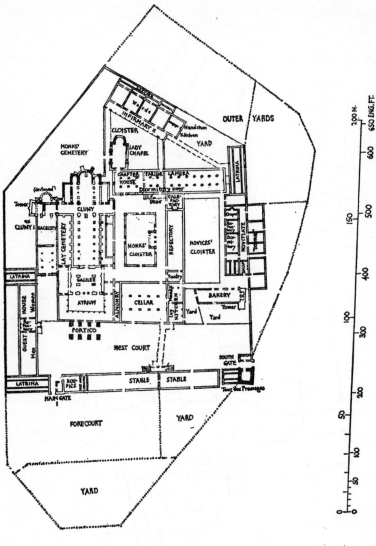

Fig. 4.—FLOOR PLAN OF CLUNY

OUTER YARDS

CLOISTER
INFIRMARY II
Wards

CLOISTER

MONKS'
CEMETERY

LADY
CHAPEL

Mandatum
Kitchen
YARD

LATRINA

CHAPTER
HOUSE
PARLOR
CAMERA

(archiepisc)

Tower
CLUNY

Dormitory over

CALE
FAC
TORY

Stair

of
CLUNY I

SACRISTY

LAY CEMETERY

Library

Chapel

NOVITIATE

Tower

MONKS'
CLOISTER

REFECTORY

NOVICES'
CLOISTER

SHOP

LATRINA

GALILEE

Pantry

ATRIUM

ALMONRY

CELLAR

Lay
Brothers'
KITCHEN

Yard

BAKERY

Tower

Yard

GUEST HOUSE
Women

Men

PORTICO

WEST COURT

SOUTH
GATE

LATRINA

HOS-
PICE

STABLE

STABLE

Tour des Fromages

MAIN GATE

FORECOURT

YARD

YARD

200 M.
650 ENG. FT.

600

150

500

400

100

300

50

200

50

100

50

0
0

was the *Stiftsschule,* the convent school of externs (see Figs. 1,b and 3,g). The *Fronhof,* probably a corruption of *Frauenhof,* according to Steinacker,[13] was the ladies' dormitory (see Fig. 3,1). This same structure is mentioned almost a century later as the *Schlafhaus.* The *Kurie,* house for the clergy (see Fig. 3,k), was located north of the *Kronenhaus* and *Schule.* The *Dechanei* housed the rooms for the administration of the institution and occupied the space between the *Fronhof* and the street (see Fig. 3,m). These buildings were equivalent to the extern quarters provided at Cluny.

The abbey buildings which made up the enclosure for the religious of the monastery were constructed on the opposite side of the church with the various apartments opening on a court or garden. This court was the cloister. In order to consolidate the gallery and provide shelter in inclement weather, the outer side of the arcade was divided into a series of small arches supported by single or double *colonnettes,* sometimes alternating both. These *colonnettes* rested on a low wall forming an enclosure which was broken at intervals to provide entrance into the court or garden from the various apartments which opened on the arcade or cloister walk.[14]

The monastery quarters consisted of three wings (see Fig. 3,a-e), with wing a, extending eastward joining a_1, then extending south becoming d_1, finally extending eastward again as d_2, d_3, and e, thus forming the protecting wall along the highway. This corresponds to the Leuckfeld sketch (see Fig. 1,d-k).

These parts of the enclosure probably point to a very early date. For example, in the wing marked deanery (see Fig. 3,m) in the uppermost floor in the southern wall close to the corners, there were two small round-headed Romanesque windows. In the western gable of the deanery, there was also an early Gothic window with a column in the middle, its capital decorated with involuted leaves.[15] These details indicate renovations of the building on the same location or foundation. The deanery, together with the *Kreuzgang* or

49

cloisters (see Fig. 3,p) on the north side of the church and the cemetery, all mentioned according to Steinacker in recent (eighteenth century) inventories, were torn down during the first half of the nineteenth century.[16]

St. Michael's Chapel (see Figs. 1,g and 3,d₂) is in the third wing and is the oldest part of the abbey. It is mentioned in Steinacker's reference to a document from 1393 as the *curia habitationis venerabilis domine Abbatisse* or residence of the venerable lady abbess.[17] Its Romanesque windows are easily detected in the Leuckfeld sketch, which also shows a passage to the abbey-courtyard on which the chapel opens (see Fig. 1,g and h).

The Steinacker plan clearly shows that the very early buildings opened on cloister courts and gardens, the one for externs and guests and the other (see Plate III) for the religious members of the community. Though Steinacker does not indicate all of the apartments of the community which might have opened on the cloister, we assume that Gandersheim followed the tradition of the time, that is, having the chapter room, the refectory, kitchen, pantry, etc. on the lower floors and the sleeping quarters or dormitories on the upper floors.

Thus, the architectural pattern of the monastery and the location of the conventual apartments therein could easily have provided appropriate settings for Hrotsvitha's plays. The arched colonnades forming the cloister walk adjacent to the garden could well have served as locales. The repetition of the architectural pattern of these arcades would have permitted their use as emperor's throne room, battle ground, torture chamber, wayside inn, prison cell—all side by side— offering to the performer natural acting areas. To support the possibility of such stage arrangement, the illuminations of two of the Terence manuscripts are offered as reference. That Hrotsvitha had ready access to these codices is historically sound.

The Corvey manuscript brought to Hrotsvitha the illuminations which, according to Nicoll, "are unquestionably based on some lost original made at a time when the comedies were still being presented on the Roman stage," thus justifying her use of the adjacent locales as legitimate theatre practice.[18]

The Leyden manuscript, believed to have originated in a northern scriptorium (*ca.* 1000), shows "the first stage of the dissolution of the antique iconography," for its miniatures are definitely marked by the Romanesque style:

The masks are gone, figures are omitted even when their labels are retained, the portals are developed mediaevally into complexes of roofs and towers, the literary reticence of the old cycle begins to give way to dramatic illustration with gestures and postures that are no longer classic. The chlamys replaces the antique pallium; old men acquire a staff; the Greco-Roman rule that one hand only should gesture is broken in favor of the mediaeval preference for two; the crossing of arms is introduced; and the profile is sometimes substituted for the traditional Hellenistic three-quarter view of the face.[19]

This brief reference to theatrical portals is not only a carry-over from antiquity but even seems to foreshadow the mansion stage of a century later. So in Hrotsvitha's possible use of the cloister arcade we find a meeting of the old and the new.

As an alternate setting for possible production of the plays within the cloister, the accepted location would be the chapter hall or the common room. This room was used as a gathering place for the community members for certain religious functions as well as for recreational purposes.

Larger monasteries, such as Cluny, show, in addition to the chapter house, a calefactory, or heated living room, and an auditorium within the cloister proper. Most monastic planning provided for the calefactory, and we may assume that there were such living accommodations at Gandersheim (see Fig. 3), both within the wing, marked former deanery, and the abbey proper.

Chasles supports the contention that the plays were acted in the church because of the character of the Romanesque nave.[20] However, this study is more in accord with Magnin's statement [21] than with Chasles', because of the realistic nature of the plays. It must be remembered that during Hrotsvitha's literary period, the trope came to full flower under the aegis of the Church. To suggest the willingness of the Church to sponsor secular drama contemporaneously with the liturgical trope is to imply an unthinkable alliance.

Magnin says, though he says it is strange to say, but as true as it is singular, that the Gandersheim monastery structurally and culturally was to the tenth century what the royal house of St. Cyr was to the seventeenth century, "a required subject for study by all serious historians of the theatre." [22]

The Canoness Cloister

It is significant that among recent critical studies of the *Foundation Documents* of Gandersheim the terms *Kanonissenkonvent, Kanonissenkloster*, and *Kanonissenstift* occur frequently.

The term, canoness, as applied to religious orders of women, appears for the first time toward the close of the eighth century.[23] It was used to distinguish those who led an essentially religious life in common, but who were bound by less stringent rules than the regular monastic orders of women, just as the order of canons for religious clerics differed from the stricter monastic orders of monks.[24]

There are only a few works which deal with women's cloisters in early Saxony: "Die Anfänge der sächsischen Frauenklöster" by Johanna Heineken, which treats in a general way of early Saxon nunneries; [25] the nineteenth-century work, "Canonissin des Stifts Gandersheim die älteste deutsche Dichterin," by Steinhoff; and the more recent works of Goetting and Algermissen, which are concerned with the foundation and character of the canoness cloisters of northern Saxony in the ninth and tenth centuries.

The Steinhoff work focuses attention on Gandersheim, in

particular, and in view of more recent critical studies, it has considerable merit. Heineken's dissertation reviews the rise of the various kinds of women's cloister foundations, the establishment of the various cloister quarters, and the cloister as an ecclesiastical foundation under church government. Goetting says that Heineken's work had only limited success because of the absence of a critical analysis of the original documents, which were available to her only in eighteenth-century print.[26] Despite his lack of confidence in Heineken's scholarship, Goetting supports her use of the word canoness, for he himself uses the term when he speaks of Herford as being "closely connected with Corvey, . . . and serving as an example for the many Saxon canoness foundations." [27]

In his "Kritik," Goetting refers to the "petition made by the canonesses of Gandersheim to Pope Paschalis in an original *littera clausa.* . . ." He also mentions "Brunshausen . . . the forerunner of the actualized convent of canonesses in 852." And he links Gandersheim with other canoness convents.[28]

In Algermissen's historical writings of the Diocese of Hildesheim, it is expressly stated that Gandersheim as well as Lamspringe and Essen were canoness convents. All three were established by Agius with Bishop Altfrid as co-founder. The latter laid the cornerstone of the three monasteries and that of the Cathedral of Hildesheim the same year (852).[29]

Algermissen, quoting from the Hildesheim sources, reports that only at the time of consecration and dedication in 881

did the changing of the canonesses from Brunshausen to Gandersheim take place. The convent at that time had twenty-four nuns. . . . It soon grew in size and importance and eventually became the richest in the bishopric of Hildesheim. . . .[30]

Not only do Goetting and Algermissen establish the fact that Gandersheim is rightly referred to as a canoness convent, but they also show evidence that there was at Gandersheim some distinction among its members regarding separate enclosures, rules of social intercourse, and way of life, especially occupation, education, and dress.

Concerning the matter of separate enclosures, Goetting says:

Before, not very much was known about Brunshausen situated on the upper Gande about one and one-half kilometers north of the city of Bad Gandersheim, other than that there had been founded there the later imperial monastery of Gandersheim in the year 852. There had been made there provisionary shelter for canonesses of the cloister before the building at Gandersheim was started in the year 856 [and until it was finished in 881], . . . and in regard to the fact that at a later time the existence of a nunnery in Brunshausen, dependent on the monastery of Gandersheim, could be proved, it was explained that, with the transfer of the cloister to Gandersheim, either a small convent remained at Brunshausen, or that at that time, a new convent was founded there according to the rule of St. Benedict.[31]

Goetting further mentions that

a remark by Agius of Corvey, in the poetical history of his sister Hathumod, which he deliberately kept free of definite data, may here be used, namely, that at Brunshausen the canonesses had at first to be sheltered *extra in villula* [apart in a little country house].[32]

Again, quoting from the Thankmar "Memoirs," he substantiates his statement supporting the distinction of enclosure for members of this community, as existing ". . . after the abbess and the canonesses [but no one else] were moved from Brunshausen to Gandersheim."[33]

This clearly indicates that between the years 852 and 881, i.e., during the construction of the Gandersheim convent, there existed in Brunshausen two distinct religious groups—the canonesses who lived, wholly or partly, *extra in villula* and later moved to Gandersheim, and the group who eventually remained at Brunshausen to become *eine neue Stiftung nach der Benediktinerregel*.[34] The distinction between these two groups is best understood in the words of Gasquet:

Both, indeed, set before themselves as an aim the realization of the Gospel counsels; both, too, have much in common as to principles, traditions, and usages. But while the former [canonesses] are societies, instituted at various periods in the Church, taking up the religious life as a means towards carrying out that special end, the latter [Benedictines Regular] is a systematized form of a life according to the Gospel counsels, existing, for its own sake, as a full expression of the Church's true and perfect life.[35]

Externally, this distinction is most strongly marked in the rules controlling secular intercourse. The fact that the canonesses took only the two vows of chastity and obedience, sets them apart from the Benedictines Regular who took a third vow, namely, poverty. The life of the canonesses, therefore, was essentially freer than that of the members of an actual nunnery [36] who separated themselves "from actual contact with the world and all that might interfere with their renunciation of it." [37]

According to Algermissen, the young canonesses who entered the monastery were the daughters of noble families in the neighborhood. They lived in a common convent, occupying their time with the recitation of the Divine Office, the care of the Church vestments, and the education of the young, particularly, the daughters of the nobility. As canonesses, they were permitted to receive guests and to keep servants. They were also permitted to leave the religious community if they so desired.[38]

Steinhoff, one of the first to refer to Hrotsvitha as canoness, in his description of the canoness school at Gandersheim, says that Latin was used exclusively in the classroom. Religion and the seven liberal arts were taught. The reading of the *Vulgate,* the *Fathers of the Church,* and the writings of the

Roman authors—all were compulsory. This frequently led to versifying in imitation of these early authors.[39] Nor were the sciences neglected since Hrotsvitha mentions her interest in them and her reluctance to participate in scientific discussions lest she might be considered "too uneducated" by the experts in this field. The faculties of these canoness schools were dedicated and devoted teachers who spent their entire lives transmitting to their pupils, not only a compendium of knowledge, but their own love of learning.

Goetting remarks that Hathumod, the oldest daughter of Liudolf, was placed in the famous foundation at Herford for education.[40] Thus, he shows that the canoness convents were renowned as educational institutions which were patronized by nobility. This statement, together with Gasquet's distinction between the monastic and religious orders, would logically lead to the conclusion that the Benedictines Regular were more of a contemplative character while the canonesses were an active group.

From Hrotsvitha we learn that the canonesses wore a less pretentious garb than the women of the world. In the "Primordia," she says, speaking of Gerberga, who, though betrothed to an influential man named Bernhard,

had secretly consecrated herself to Christ by means of the sacred veil, . . . yet, because of her desire to avoid civil disturbance, she was not at once able to lay aside her garments resplendent with gold, and she continued to attire herself in costly raiment.[41]

Heineken says that Agius does not mention the garb of the nun, but she calls attention to this statement from the "Vita Hathumodae" which might have been the source of Hrotsvitha's reference:

Gerberga at first does not enter into the community of the convent completely, for she still does not lay aside the shiny golden garments. By her dress only, the queen is distinguished from a nun. . . . For a special form of ecclesiastical bond or vow, whether it be a strict or light one, the uniform means nothing.[42]

Although Heineken makes little of the fact that Gerberga wore her royal robes for a time after her entrance into the Gandersheim monastery, the fact is, this privilege would never have been tolerated in a strictly monastic order. Since both the active and contemplative orders usually adopted as their uniform the simplest of the contemporary garbs, and since it is a matter of history that

as early as 814, Benedict of Aniane attempted to enforce uniformity in the quantity of food and drink, uniformity in the time of rising and going to rest, uniformity in their church services and their choir ceremonies, uniformity in the length and cut of the habit; in a word, absolute uniformity in everything,[43]

it would seem that all who professed vows as a way of life, wore some manner of distinctive garb. The very nature of the strictly monastic order would preclude any mitigation of rule in regard to dress. On the contrary, the less rigid regulations of the canonesses might have permitted it. The fact that such rich apparel was remarked by more than one chronicler of the canoness convent indicates a departure from the ordinary custom.

Thus, the externals of the Benedictines Regular and canoness rule reinforce the claim that there was considerable variance in the mode of living, and that Gandersheim could not have participated as freely and richly in tenth-century life if it had been a completely strict monastic institution. Just as Thomas Merton in his book, *The Silent Life,* differentiates between the more rigid Benedictine observance and "urban monasticism," or the life of the canon, by describing the former's labor, obscurity, and solitude and the latter's consciousness of his cultural function, so this study draws a similar corollary in the lives of the complementary women's orders.[44]

In reviewing the history of Gandersheim beyond 881, there are found occasional references which lead to the conclusion that Gandersheim housed both Benedictines Regular and canonesses at the same time. This may have been due to centralization of government, as well as support, or it may have happened because of the exigencies of the time.

The question as to whether Hrotsvitha was a canoness or a regular has seemed of little importance to the scholars disputing the theatricality of her dramas. That this might be a crucial point in determining the possibility or probability of performance has been for the most part, ignored. However, that Hrotsvitha was a canoness is one of the assumptions of this study. If Hrotsvitha were a Benedictine Regular, she would not have been in a position to write as she did; on the other hand, if she had been a canoness, every aspect of the canoness life would have contributed both to the writing of the plays and to their possible or probable performance.

Algermissen implicitly places Hrotsvitha in the canoness convent of Gandersheim when he says:

Only the daughters of the Saxon nobility were permitted to enter the *Kanonissenstifte* of Lower Saxony and Gandersheim was one of the most famous *Stifte* of the whole area. . . .Hrotsvitha has made the name of Gandersheim world-famous.[45]

He further places her under the abbess, Gerberga, whose place as the seventh abbess of Gandersheim has been historically documented. About Gerberga, Algermissen says:

She erected next to the new church of Mary, a second convent for 30 nuns, which was a Benedictine foundation. . . . While . . . Hrotsvitha was at work writing her poetry, the daughter of the already deceased Otto II, Sophia, entered the monastery at Gandersheim as a canoness.[46]

Algermissen speaks further of "her friendship with Gerberga" (*ihre Freundschaft mit Gerberga*) and he says in substance:

It is certain that Hrotsvitha's literary efforts fall within the reign of that capable Abbess Gerberga, and in that glittering epoch of the Ottonian Renaissance. She stands out in that period as Germany's greatest woman.[47]

In summary, relying primarily on the recent findings of the eminent archivist of the Braunschweig area, Goetting, and his endorsement by the scholarly historian of Hildesheim, Algermissen, it may be concluded that Gandersheim is rightly classified as a canoness convent which, at one and the same time, supported its own canonesses and, sometimes within the same monastery and again in a separate enclosure, a group of Benedictines Regular.

It may further be concluded that Hrotsvitha belonged to the canonesses. Several reasons are advanced to support this statement. Foremost, her association with the court and scholars of her time, which she mentions in her prefaces and letter, strongly indicates that she was living under the less rigid rule. She speaks familiarly of young Otto "looking at me with his bright clear eyes." [48] She consistently submits her writings to her abbess, Gerberga, to the archbishop, Wilhelm of Mainz, and to those who "know how to weigh things fairly." [49] She expresses her gratitude to certain scholars who admitted that she possessed "some little knowledge of those arts, the subtleties of which exceed the grasp of any woman's mind." [50]

Secondly, it is obvious that Hrotsvitha had every educational opportunity afforded to women of that time. It is an historical fact that there were great women scholars who wrote and who taught in the monasteries of the Middle Ages.[51] These writers and scholars were, by and large, religious whose *cursus honorum* was sponsored by noble patrons. According to Eckenstein:

Settlements such as Herford, Gandersheim, Essen, and Quedlinburg offered the companionship of equals, and gave a domestic and intellectual training which was the best of its kind. Later ages were wont to look upon the standard of education attained at Gandersheim and Quedlinburg as exemplary. The word college (*collegium*), which early writers often apply to these settlements in its modern sense of a learning and a teaching body, aptly designates their character. For the religious settlement was an endowed college where girls were received to be trained and where women who wished to devote themselves to learning and the arts permanently resided.

That Hrotsvitha was well taught is obvious; that she was allowed freedom and encouragement to pursue her intellectual activities is apparent; that she enjoyed royal sponsorship is equally apparent:

I was trained first by our most learned and gentle novice-mistress Rikkarda and others. Later, I owed much to the kind favour and encouragement of a royal personage, Gerberga, under whose abbatial rule I am now living. She, though younger in years than I, was, as might be expected of the niece of an Emperor, far older in learning, and she had the kindness to make me familiar with the works of some of those authors in whose writings she had been instructed by learned men.[52]

Finally, we point to Hrotsvitha's familiarity with the contemporary scene evidenced by her selections of subject matter in her dramas. She complains that

there are many, and we cannot entirely acquit ourselves of the charge, who, attracted by the polished elegance of the style of pagan writers, prefer their works to the holy scriptures. There are others who, although they are deeply attached to the sacred writings and have no liking for most pagan productions, make an exception in favour of the works of Terence, and fascinated by the charm of the manner, risk being corrupted by the wickedness of the matter.[53]

It is true, that if Hrotsvitha had been a Benedictine Regular, she might have known about the deplorable pagan tendencies of her day, but she would have had neither the opportunity nor the encouragement to do anything about them. Rather, she would have silently entrusted these ills to Divine Providence. As a canoness, however, she was free to exert her influence on her people. Löher refers to Hrotsvitha as the Saxon heroine, who through her enthusiasm for art and science made a strong impact on the people of her time, the records of which were lost to us through the brutality and destruction of the Thirty Years War.[54]

Thus, we find sheltered within the abbey walls a group of canonesses, a religious aristocracy, set apart from the world, yet closely connected with it. Here, in an atmosphere attuned to life at court with all its political, social, and cultural implications, yet tempered with a truly religious spirit, is a canoness convent in which a creative genius could come to full fruition. So lived Hrotsvitha, canoness of Gandersheim.

Chapter IV

HROTSVITHA OF GANDERSHEIM

The Woman and Nun

Most theatre historians admit that there is scant documentary evidence about Hrotsvitha's chronology and background. Three sources will be related here as representative of typical available data.

Magnin, relying on the *Hildesheim Chronicles, Monumenta Germaniae Historica,* and on the *Antiquitates Gandersheimenses* of Leuckfeld volubly states:

Hrotsvitha informs us that she was born a long time after the death of Otto the Illustrious, Duke of Saxony, father of Henry the Fowler, which event [the death of Otto] occurred on November 30, 912. In another source (the preface of her poetic works) she says she was a little older than the daughter of Henry, Duke of Bavaria, Gerberga II, the abbess of Gandersheim [consecrated] in 959, who was born, according to all indications, about the year 940. From these two events, it may be deduced that Hrotsvitha was born between 912 and 940, and much nearer the second date than the first, consequently, about 930 or 935. The date of her death is even more uncertain. One fact alone is beyond doubt—that her writing career extended beyond the year 968; since the fragment which still exists of the Panegyric to the Ottos, contains the events of that year and since subsequent to its completion, Hrotsvitha composed another poem to recognize the foundation of the monastery at Gandersheim. Casimir

Oudin says she died in the year 1001; she was in her sixty-seventh year, if we are right in our preceding calculations. Oudin bases his statement on the fact that Hrotsvitha wrote about the first three Ottos. True, the first book of poems, the only extant one, finished with the death of Otto I, but the very title of this work (*Panegyris Oddonum*), proves that we have only the first part. The second dedication addressed to Otto II, king of the Romans, probably served as the preface to the second book, devoted to the deeds of this prince. Let us add to this that in the *Hildesheim Chronicles* it states that Hrotsvitha had honored the three Ottos. If this were true, it would mean that Hrotsvitha was still living in the year 1002, which, incidentally, would only be most probable.[1]

Algermissen states more succinctly:

Neither her birth year nor the year of her death is historically documented; since the earliest year of her birth which could possibly be recognized is 932, and the earliest year of her death, 1003, therefore, she lived to be approximately seventy years old.[2]

St. John explicitly believes that Hrotsvitha's references to certain historical events and personages in her writings prove that she was born after 912 and before 940 and that she entered the cloister when about twenty-three years old.[3]

Aside from these express statements, there is the evidence within the works themselves. In speaking of Gerberga II, Hrotsvitha describes her as *aetate minor* though *scientia provectior*.[4] Blashfield places Gerberga's birth as approximately 940, alleging she was the daughter of Henry, Duke of Bavaria, who was married to Judith in 938.[5] This fortifies the preceding evidence that Hrotsvitha was born about 935.

Frequent references to contemporaries give further credence to the above-mentioned dates. Hrotsvitha refers to her tyrocinium as an author under *sapientissimae atque benignissimae Rikkardis magistrae* (ca. 950-970) and to Gerberga (955-1001) *cuius nunc subdor dominio abbatissae*.[6] She venerates the martyr of Cordova, Pelagius (d. *ca.* 921), in a tribute, the subject matter of which was told to her by an eyewitness. She defers to the Archbishop Willigis (975-1011) to whom Gerberga presumed to show Hrotsvitha's "unpolished lines." [7] She asserts her interest in the contemporary educational scene by including in "Pafnutius" and "Sapientia" impressive dialogue based on the trivium and quadrivium. She presents to Otto II (973-983) an account of the deeds of his illustrious father, saying, "If I were not urged by this dread command, under no circumstances should I have such self-assurance as to presume to offer to thy scrutiny this little book with its obvious lack of polish." [8] Such are the data which justify the statement that the brilliance of Hrotsvitha spanned the Ottonian Renaissance.

It has already been noted that the fourth abbess of Gandersheim, the first to assume ruling power over the monastery after the death of the last of Duke Liudolf's daughters, was a religious named Hrotsvitha, for "which learned lady," Blashfield says, "our more famous playwright [the second Hroswitha] of the same name is often mistaken; a pardonable confusion since the abbess was also an author and continued the literary traditions of the convent." [9]

Magnin, quoting from the Hildesheim sources, says that "some claim this Hrotsvitha, the fourth abbess of Gandersheim, came from the second branch of the ducal family of Saxony, and was the daughter of Duke Otto the Illustrious, the second son of Liudolf and father of Henry the Fowler." [10]

Whatever her family heritage, the first Hrotsvitha apparently had connections with a royal family. Algermissen supports this statement in his discussion of the Gandersheim foundation when he says "the nuns who entered the foundation convent were from noble families of the neighborhood." [11] "The fourth abbess," according to Algermissen, "was probably the aunt of our poetess; she was elected by the community in 916 and was installed by Bishop Walbert of Hildesheim (903-919)." [12]

64

It seems likely, therefore, that Hrotsvitha, the poetess, was of the same royal family as Hrotsvitha, the abbess. It has not been uncommon from the very earliest days for families to perpetuate the names of respected members through their use in succeeding generations. For example, Gerberga II, the ruling abbess of the monastery (955-1001) during the second Hrotsvitha's lifetime, was the daughter of Duke Henry and granddaughter of Otto the Illustrious, brother of the first Gerberga. It would not be an improbable assumption to assert that the younger Hrotsvitha honored in her name the memory of the abbess Hrotsvitha and might have been a relative.[13]

Little or no data are available about Hrotsvitha's immediate family either from historians or through allusions in her own writings. Numerous and unsubstantiated are the conjectures concerning her birthplace and parentage. Algermissen states that due to the conditions of the time, there are only two facts of which we can be certain, namely, that she was from the Eastphalian area of Lower Saxony and that she entered the *Kanonissenstift* of Gandersheim which was, at that time, the most famous monastery in the area. Since reliable sources have affirmed that this was a canoness convent, we have concluded that Hrotsvitha lived under the canoness rule rather than that of the stricter Benedictines Regular, and that her life was essentially freer, admitting of such privileges which afforded the canonesses contact with members of the court and with those who attended the monastery school.

However, regardless of the paucity of documented facts, a careful reading of the prefaces which she composed for each of her individual works, as well as an analysis of the content and style of her writing, reveals the character of the woman, her great stature as a religious, and her status as a writer.[14]

Of her character and experience before her entrance into Gandersheim much is inferred from her writings, for in them she shows an intimate knowledge of the world and its human conflicts. The fact that she does not suppress this knowledge, but uses it to advantage as a nun and as a littérateur, marks her as a person of integrity and courage.

She is conscious of her talents; and we do not object when she acknowledges the praise of critics to whom she submitted her works, undoubtedly, at the command of her superiors. Following the "Prefatio" there is an "Epistola Eiusdem ad Quosdam Sapientes Huius Libri Fautores," a letter to certain learned patrons of this book, in which she says in part:

> You have not praised me but the Giver of the grace which works in me. . . . I rejoice from the depths of my soul that God through whose grace alone I am what I am, should be praised in me, but I am afraid of being thought greater than I am. I know that it is as wrong to deny a divine gift as to pretend falsely that we have received it. So I will not deny that through the grace of the Creator I have acquired some knowledge of the arts. He has given me ability to learn— I am a teachable creature—yet of myself I should know nothing.[15]

Hrotsvitha in any era would have emerged as a woman of stature—noble in origin, learned in mind, great in heart, gentle in word—an honor to womanhood.

Concerning Hrotsvitha, the nun, her prefaces again are the definitive source from which her virtues may be divined. She exhibits sincere humility and industry when she says, "It must be remembered that when I began it [her writing], I was far from possessing the necessary qualifications, being young in both years and learning." Then she relates how she toiled secretly, writing, and rewriting, fearing to submit what she had done lest experts might discourage her because of the "crudity" of her style. She acknowledges the training of her novice mistress, Rikkarda—"most learned and gentle," and the "kind favor and encouragement of a royal personage, Gerberga. . . ."[16]

She again reveals her humility and her ready obedience, when she writes about the deeds of Otto in poetic form, as she had been requested to do by her superiors, regardless of the difficulty of the task. She begins the "Prefatio" to this work by addressing Gerberga thus:

Illustrious Abbess, venerated no less for uprightness and honesty than for the high distinction of a royal and noble race, Hrotsvitha of Gandersheim, the last of the least of those fighting under your ladyship's rule, desires to give you all that a servant owes her mistress. O my lady, bright with the varied jewels of spiritual wisdom, your maternal kindness will not let you hesitate to read what, as you know, was written at your command! It was you who gave me the task of chronicling in verse the deeds of the Emperor, and you know that it was impossible to collect them together from hearsay. You can imagine the difficulties which my ignorance put in my way while I was engaged in this work. . . . At present I am defenseless at every point, because I am not supported by any authority. I also fear I shall be accused of temerity in presuming to describe in my humble uncultured way matters which ought to be set forth with all the elegance of great learning. Yet if my work is examined by one who knows how to appraise things fairly, he will pardon me the more readily because of the weakness of my sex and my inferior knowledge, especially as I did not undertake this little work of my own presumption, but at your command.[17]

It was mentioned earlier that Goetting did not see mere coincidence in the fact that Hrotsvitha concluded her "Primordia" with the death of Christine. The subsequent history of the monastery reveals many administrative complications which resulted in the embarrassing Hildesheim controversy. Algermissen observes that her name does not appear among the nuns involved in the famous quarrel. Thus, Hrotsvitha, the nun, manifests her loyalty to her community.

The Poet

It has been shown that Gandersheim reached its highest point as a center of learning during the reign of the Abbess

Gerberga II, which was simultaneous with that rich cultural period of German history known as the Ottonian Renaissance. Since this was also the time of Hrotsvitha's literary endeavors, it seems that she is a figure of far greater importance than literary and theatre historians are wont to recognize.

To her credit are the following works, divided conveniently into three books. *Liber Primus* contains a prose introduction, a verse dedication to the Abbess Gerberga, eight legends—"Maria," "Ascensio," "Gongolfus," "Pelagius," "Theophilus," "Basilius," "Dionysius," "Agnes," and a prose conclusion. In *Liber Secundus* are found a prose introduction, the "Epistola eiusdem ad quosdam sapientes huius libri fautores," six dramas—"Gallicanus I and II," "Dulcitius," "Calimachus," "Abraham," "Pafnutius," "Sapientia," and a poem of thirty-five lines on a "Vision of St. John." *Liber Tertius* includes a prose introduction, verse dedications to Otto I and to Otto II, "Gesta Ottonis," a verse introduction, and the "Primordia Coenobii Gandeshemensis."

In evaluating these works and in an attempt to place them chronologically, Eckenstein says:

> Each kind of work has merits of its own and deserves attention. But while Hrotsvitha as a legend writer ranks with other writers of the age, and as an historical writer is classed by the historian Giesebrecht with Widukind and Ruotger, as a writer of Latin drama she stands entirely alone. . . . The first of her two sets of legends was put together and dedicated to Gerberg [*sic*] as abbess, that is after the year 959; she wrote and submitted part if not the whole of her history of Otto the Great to Wilhelm, Archbishop of Mainz, before the year 968, in which the prelate died. How the composition of her dramas is related in point of time to that of the legends and the historical poems cannot be definitely decided; probably the dramas were written in the middle period of Hrotsvitha's life. For the legends bear marks of being the outcome of early effort, while the historical poems, especially the one which tells of the early history of Gandersheim, were written in the full consciousness of power.[18]

Goetting claims that in the "Primordia," as well as in the

"Gesta Ottonis," Hrotsvitha is not objective in her writing; that she omits certain historical facts.[19] These observations are true, but it should be noted also that she was writing not only at the command of her superiors who were descendants of the royal founders, but without any objective chronicles for her source material, circumstances which certainly must have affected her writing.

In the preface which introductes the legendary poems, Hrotsvitha expresses the diffidence which she felt when she first began to write:

> Unknown to others and secretly, so to speak, I worked by myself; sometimes I composed, sometimes I destroyed what I had written to the best of my abilities and yet badly. . . . Writing verse appears a difficult and arduous task especially for one of my sex, but trusting to the help of divine grace more than to my own powers, I have fitted the stories of this book to dactylic measures as best I could, for fear that the abilities that have been implanted in me should be dulled and wasted by neglect.[20]

Actually, Hrotsvitha showed considerable skill in her use of the leonine hexameter, a form of verse popular with writers at that time. On the whole, her poetry is characterized by dignity and simplicity, and attests to her facile and sensitive powers of expression.

Hrotsvitha is rightly considered among the first of women poets after Sappho. She is rightly called the first woman dramatist, the only recorded playwright between the Romans and the writers of the medieval church drama of the twelfth century. Algermissen claims, "The first Christian poetess of lower Saxony and of our diocese, she was also the first German poetess. She was the first dramatic writer of the Christian world whose works represent an attempt to write Christian drama." [21]

Frequently, the dramas are classified as prose. However, since Hrotsvitha was instinctively a poet, there is a natural poetic quality evident in her dialogue. Fife calls attention to the "rhymed prose of her dialogue" which he terms "an undulating prose with its suggestion of a liturgical recitative, with a peculiar charm." [22]

Baldwin gives several examples of the use of tenth-century rhymed prose; and with reference to Hrotsvitha he says:

the use of rhyme and balance is most marked in passages of heightened emotional tone, particularly in the prayers. To one familiar with medieval hymnody, there is a rather striking similarity between these prayers and the 'transitional' sequences of the tenth and eleventh centuries, of which the most famous 'Victimae Paschali,' is the best example; and it seems possible that these passages may have been influenced to some extent by the church liturgy. [23]

Chasles says that, at first sight, one believes he is reading prose. All editors of Hrotsvitha's dramas have reproduced them in this manner without rhyme or rhythm. If one rereads the lines carefully, Chasles continues, one will be struck by the constant recurrence of assonance and incomplete rhymes which cut the sentence, sometimes in two, and sometimes in three unequal parts. The variety and irregularity of the dialogue suspends in vain this symmetrical movement. The rhyme reappears with tenacity. The following example shows how Chasles has rearranged the run-on text to reveal the assonance:

Abraham	*Abraham*
Hei mihi! O bone Jesu, quid hoc monstri est, quod hanc, quam tibi sponsam nutrivi, alienos amatores audio sequi.	Hei mihi! bone Jesu! quid hoc monstri Est quod hanc quam tibi sponsam nutrivi Alienos amatores audio sequi!
Amicus	*Amicus*
Hoc meretricibus antiquitus fuit in more, ut alieno delectarentur in amore.	Hoc meretricibus antiquitus fuit in more Ut alieno delectarentur in amore.

70

Abraham

Affer mihi sonipedem delica-
tum et militarem habitum,
quo, deposito tegmine religionis, ipsam adeam sub specie amatoris.

Abraham

Affer mihi sonipedem deli-
catum
Et militarem habitum,
Quo deposito tegmine religionis
Ipsam adeam sub specie amatoris.[24]

Chasles believes this love of the same sound offers a curious singularity and raises the question of the origin of the rhyme of the moderns:

One feels the balance and the soft cadence of the verse. It is, in effect, modern verse. One has only, to convince oneself, to follow step by step, the Latin of Hrotsvitha and trace verse by verse, the French verse of an equal number of feet and rhymes under the Latin lines:

Marie

Mon âme est toute à l'amour
Bien suprême!
Que celui qui n'aime.
Espère un doux retour.

Maria

Quicumque
me diligunt,
Aequalem amoris vicem
a me recipiunt.

Abraham

Un étranger, Marie,
Te prie,
Ah! veuille m'accorder
Un baiser!

Abraham

Accede,
Maria,
Et da mihi
osculum.

Marie

Mes bras, de leur douce ca-
resse,
Enlaceront ta tremblante
vieillesse;
Je baiserai tes cheveux
blancs.

Maria

Non solum dulcia oscula
libabo
Sed etiam crebris
senile
Collum amplexibus
mulcebo.[25]

71

Can one call this prose? Evidently, the religious has written in verse without knowing it.[26]

All of her works were written in the same poetic manner. And thus, Chasles affirms, here is a religious writer, creative and imitative of the time in which she lived, who passed on her impressions clearly. If she held to antiquity by her studies, to the middle ages by the form of style and depth of ideas, she touched, by essential points, the development of the poetry of a new people. Thus, a place is assured Hrotsvitha in the literature of the moderns, for here was a poet who believed she imitated Terence and who announced Racine.[27]

Such is the accolade Chasles accords Hrotsvitha, and in the same tradition, Magnin speaks of "this celebrated monastery which has been for Germany an intellectual oasis springing forth in the barbarian steppes,"[28] and to which Hrotsvitha brought literary immortality because in her poetical works are the origins of some of the great dramatic masterpieces of the centuries.

The Dramatist

Hrotsvitha's dramas have usually been treated in the light of literary and theatre history. It has been alleged that she lived in an age for which there are no established scientific data to prove the existence of a living theatre; thus, she had no immediate master. Drama was considered an alien literary form, one frowned upon by the Church and certainly not to be encouraged among scholars, much less in a woman, and far less in a nun. And so, literary and theatre historians have passed lightly over eight centuries, from the fourth to the twelfth, merely mentioning Hrotsvitha as the author of six short dramas; then they leave her in isolation with no link to the past nor impression upon the future.

Such casual treatment, based upon insufficient evidence, gives cause for serious concern. Research has proved, as shown above, that during these centuries, theatre existed in fluctuating emphasis in classical, mimetic, and liturgical forms; that the Church was, in turn, a friend and a foe to the theatre; that Hrotsvitha did not live in a vast dramatic wasteland since within her plays there can be discerned vestiges of the three forms of theatre existing during her day.

Her works were developed, of necessity, within the framework of medieval life. Realizing the impact of social, political, and religious institutions on the culture of the time, considerable space in this study has been devoted to the fusion of Graeco-Roman and Christian cultures; to the rise and significance of monasticism in general, and to Gandersheim in particular; to the tracing of the Carolingian and Saxon dynasties and Hrotsvitha's flowering within the latter; and to the waning relationship between Crown and Church and its repercussions on religious communities.

According to the Benedictine *Annales,* the rigidity and asceticism of the lives of the Regulars would have precluded the worldly contacts and freedom which, as a canoness, Hrotsvitha enjoyed. For this reason it seemed necessary to investigate as fully as possible the character of the canoness convent in order to understand the free and artistic climate within which she was inspired to write in the dramatic form, and to describe in detail the cloister-arcade which served as a background for much of the canoness' activity.

These data—a living tenth-century theatre, the cultural renaissance of the day, the canoness character, the natural cloister-stage—should not only clarify the problem under consideration, namely, the theatricality of Hrotsvitha's dramatic works, but should also justify the legitimacy of the problem and lend affirmative support to it. The remainder of the chapter will concern itself with Hrotsvitha's place as a dramatist. It will point out the rationale she used for selecting plot material; it will trace the development of the art form which she designed for the presentation of this material; finally, it will identify the dramatic influences which are evident in her plays.

73

Blashfield, quoting Magnin, says, "Hrotsvitha, like all play-wrights, 'elle prenait son bien ou elle le trouvait,' and her goods were the legends of the saints" [29]—the *Acta Sanctorum,* the *Apocryphal Gospels,* and the Christian legends of Greece. Hrotsvitha knew her authors and she knew her countrymen.

Köpke assures us that the library at Gandersheim contained not only the writings of Terence, but also the works of the outstanding Latin poets, historians, and essayists, as well as the writings of the Church Fathers.[30] Whether or not Hrotsvitha had access to the Greek legends in their original form is a matter of controversy. Ebert, in examining the sources of Hrotsvitha's dramas, contends that she read her Greek authors in Latin translations.[31] Barack, pointing to her use of words notably of Greek derivation, would argue her familiarity with that language.[32]

Regardless of the form of language in which Hrotsvitha found her sources, she apparently had the ability to use them in their entirety. As a member of the Gandersheim community, she had the accumulated wisdom of the ages at her disposal. She brought to this storehouse of knowledge a facility for learning, a creative flair, and a discerning eye. This combination impelled her to take material "wherever she found it," and to apply to it an artistic form which would appeal to a wide audience ("plures catholici"), an audience whose personal welfare was of vital concern to her.

The "plures catholici" of her day comprised almost all of the population. They were, for the most part, men and women of blunt candor, childlike in their needs and desires, whose entire way of life was oriented to the spiritual. The stories of the saints of the desert, of the early Christian martyrs, and of the miraculous conversion of the cruel pagan persecutors excited the imagination of the medieval mind just as the stories of the heroes and gods of the ancients exacted the homage of the pagan mind.

However, there is no need to appeal to secondary sources for a rationale to support Hrotsvitha's choice of subject mat-

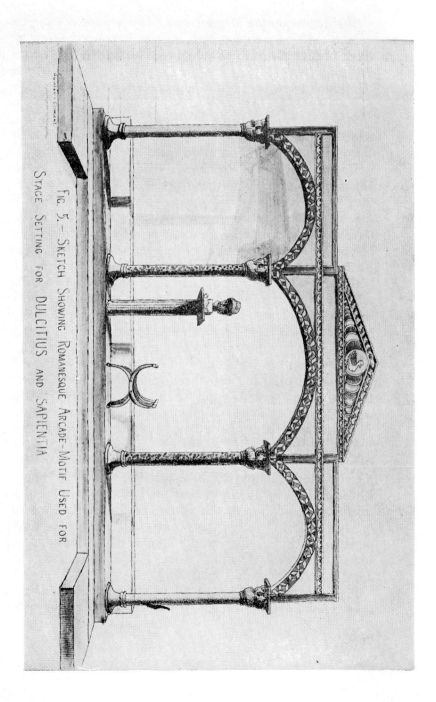

Fig. 5.— Sketch Showing Romanesque Arcade-Motif Used for Stage Setting for DULCITIUS and SAPIENTIA

Fig. 6.—Designs for the Costumes for Sapientia

ter and form. She supplies an authentic purpose in her own words:

There are many Christians, from whom we cannot claim to be excepted, who because of the charm of finished diction prefer heathen literature with its hollowness to our religious books; there are others who hold by the scripture and despise what is heathen, and yet eagerly peruse the poetic creations of Terence; while delighting in his flow of language, they are all polluted by the godless contents of his works. Therefore I 'the well-known mouthpiece of Gandersheim' have not hesitated in taking this poet's style as a model, and while others honour him by perusing his dramas, I have attempted, in the very way in which he treats of unchaste love among evil women, to celebrate according to my ability the praiseworthy chasteness of godlike maidens.

In doing so, I have often hesitated with a blush on my cheeks through modesty, because the nature of the work obliged me to concentrate my attention on and apply my mind to the wicked passion of illicit love and to the tempting talk of the amorous, against which we at other times close our ears. But if I had hesitated on account of my blushes I could not have carried out my purpose, or have set forth the praise of innocence to the fullness of my ability. For in proportion as the blandishments of lovers are enticing, so much greater is the glory of our helper in heaven, so much more glorious the triumph of those who prevail, especially where woman's weakness triumphs and man's shameless strength is made to succumb. . . . If anyone is pleased with my work I shall rejoice, but if on account of my unpolished language it pleases no one, what I have done yet remains a satisfaction to myself, for while in other writings I have worked, however insufficiently, only in heroic strophe, here I have combined this with dramatic form, while avoiding the dangerous allurements of the heathen.[33]

Many writers have paraphrased this quotation and many have fallen into the oft-repeated error of interpreting it from a contemporary point of view. Eckenstein, avoiding this fallacy, in a few brief paragraphs, has penetrated the essence of this rationale as stated by Hrotsvitha:

The keynote of her dramas one and all is to insist on the beauties of a steadfast adherence to chastity as opposed to the frenzy and the vagaries of passion. In doing so she is giving expression to the ideas of contemporary Christian teaching, which saw in passion, not the inborn force that can be applied to good or evil purpose, not the storage of strength which works for social advantage or disadvantage, but simply a tendency in human nature which manifests itself in lack of self-restraint, and the disturbing element which interferes with the attainment of calmness and candour. . . . For the nun does not disparage marriage, far from it; nor does she inculcate a doctrine of general celibacy. It is not a question with her of giving up a lesser joy for a greater, but simply of the way to remain true to the higher standard, which in accordance with the teaching of her age she identified with a life of chastity. Her position may appear untenable; confusion of thought is a reproach which a later age readily casts on an earlier. But underneath what may seem unreasonable there is the aspiration for self-control. It is this aspiration which gives a wide and an abiding interest to her plays. For she is not hampered by narrowness of thought or by pettiness of spirit. . . . In the plays we find ourselves in a variety of surroundings and in contact with a wide range of personalities. The transition period from heathendom to Christianity supplies in most cases the mental and moral conflicts round which centres the interest of these plays.[34]

To see how she presented this material in a variety of moods—tragic, comic, heroic, romantic, and didactic—one needs only to examine the arguments contained in the title-prologue of each.

In "Gallicanus," Part I, a woman's strategy results in the winning of a battle, the conversion of a would-be suitor, and his subsequent vow of celibacy. Part II retails his exile and martyrdom under Julian, the Apostate. John and Paul, who befriend him, also suffer death under the same tyrant and are thereby instrumental in converting their executioners.

In "Dulcitius," the supernatural elements confound Dul-

76

citius to his ridicule, and Sisinnius to his terror, when the virginity of the three maidens, Agape, Chionia, and Irena is preserved contrary to the merciless orders of Diocletian.

Calimachus' illicit and unwelcome love for Drusiana leads him to the brink of hell, when the intervention of John the Apostle restores him to life and grace.

Because of the prayerful influence of the holy monk, Abraham, Mary, his niece, turns from a life of sin and elects a life of penance and solitude.

The Thais legend lives again in "Pafnutius." At the exhortation of this saintly hermit, the courtesan, Thais, renounces unlawful wordly pleasures for eternal joys.

The three Greek virgins, Faith, Hope, and Charity, through the sustaining strength and wisdom of their mother, Sapientia, endure a cruel and prolonged martyrdom at the hands of Hadrian.

Thus, Hrotsvitha selected her material on the basis of accessibility of sources, appeal to the contemporary mind, and antidotal force. In her zealous apostolate for the Church, although she complains of some little embarrassment in writing on such subjects, she nevertheless felt compelled to use the "manner" of Terence as well as the "matter," thus, her use of the dramatic form.

Zeydel chides the six reputable German scholars who authored *Das deutsche Drama*[35] for their neglect of Hrotsvitha as a figure to be reckoned with in a consideration of the dramatic form:

Far from beginning their work with Hrotsvitha, although her plays may well represent a clear-cut and acceptable basis for our knowledge of literature in the dramatic form during the tenth century, these scholars first devote over one hundred large pages to a discussion of the liturgical drama of the period from the twelfth to the fifteenth century growing out of the Easter and Christmas services of the Church, and their *ex post facto* deductions therefrom. Then finally, on page 109, in the opening portion of their chapter on the neo-Latin plays of the sixteenth century, written by Rudolf

Wolkan, a short section is allotted to Hrotsvitha. The obvious reason for briefly disposing of her dramas thus belatedly derives from the feeling that, written in Latin and the sidetracked work of a recluse, these plays attained no significance until their publication by Conrad Celtes in 1501.[36]

Zeydel[37] further reports that the German humanists, Tritheim, Pirckheimer, and Dalberg, categorized the form used by Hrotsvitha as a later comedy of manners. Blashfield[38] supports this opinion but Magnin[39] reserves judgment on this point. However, he too, reproves Hrotsvithan scholars because they lack the courage to give this unique nun-dramatist her rightful place in the historical stream of drama.[40] Among literary historians, it is generally agreed that her plays are not liturgical in character, nor are they forerunners of the mystery, miracle, or morality plays. The majority of writers dismiss them as "pious exercises—intentionally didactic."

This art form as Hrotsvitha conceived it—a blend of religion, humor, and didacticism—was ideally suited to the Teutonic temperament. Blashfield notes this when she says:

Hrotsvitha's work is of the new, the modern epoch, for it shows the form the Latin drama assumes in Teutonic hands. . . . It is a rough new wine of a younger race, of a more childlike faith, that Hrotsvitha pours into the old amphora, and the shapely vessel is fractured by the stir and ferment of the spirit within.[41]

Unlike the impatient audience of Terence, "the practical Teuton wanted plenty of time to be edified as well as delighted; he liked to be sermonized." [42] At the same time he wanted to give full vent to his imagination, and his main concern was with "the thought conveyed by the diction, not the elegance of style." [43] The scenes might take place in the palace of a pagan Emperor, on the battlefield, or in the desert cell of a hermit, but the language was the same—that of educated tenth-century Saxony. Magnin, in speaking of Hrotsvitha's language says:

Strange thing! the language of the lover of the tenth century is as refined, as quintessential, as affected as that of the sixteenth and seventeenth centuries . . . only, in the poet of the Court of Elizabeth, the young lover is lost in the conceits of the Italian manner, while in Hrotsvitha, he exhausts himself in academic subtleties and distinctions of the doctrine of the Universals.[44]

This affectation of speech was as typical of the tenth century as euphemism was of the Elizabethan age. Blashfield, too, points out in the dialogue examples of "medieval courtesies" and of the "vernacular of the schoolmen of the tenth century."[45]

In her first work, "Gallicanus," Hrotsvitha occasionally used narration to advance the plot. According to Creizenach:

It took real inspiration to see that saints' legends which she and everyone else up to this time had handled in narrative form could be given as well, or better, in dialogue. And in adapting her material to the dramatic form, after the first awkward attempts, she shows a rare gift for seizing on the great moments of a story and presenting them strikingly.[46]

Thus in her later plays "she arranges the dialogue in such a manner that the advancing plot is completely absorbed within it."[47]

The strongest arguments offered to justify the inclusion of Hrotsvitha's works in dramatic anthology is the fact that her characters are authentic tenth-century Saxons. They are flesh and blood, three-dimensional, recognizable, not merely the personifications of vice and virtue.

Blashfield calls attention to male characters who are "the forerunners of the lovers, villains, and traitors of the Elizabethan drama," whose like, she says, "do not exist in the comedy of the ancients;" nor would we find "their counterparts among the cheats and rogues of Terence and Plautus."[48] Because of their modern blend of feminine dignity and dauntless spirit, the women characters are far removed from the soft, sweet, pagan heroines; they are "inhabitants of a different moral planet,"[49] representative of the mind which had not yet released itself from the chains of tradition, but which had gone far beyond to the freedom of inquiry. Hrotsvitha's characters, as it were, stood upon the crest of the millennium.

Blashfield, like many of the critics, accuses Hrotsvitha of violating the dramatic unities.[50] It is strange that so many theatre historians refer to this "famous neo-classic superstition." As for "unity of time," it finds support only in one brief passage of the *Poetics*. "Unity of place" is a deduction drawn by critics from the "unity of time." Should proponents of the "Three Unities" attempt to evaluate a Greek tragedy or even a later Greek comedy against this literary tradition, they would find more exception than adherence to the rule.[51] This study contends that Hrotsvitha does not violate the "one and only dramatic unity enjoined by Aristotle, the 'unity of action.'"[52]

Creizenach is one of the most vehement of the critics in his rejection of the dramas on this point. He claims that Hrotsvitha disregarded the limitations of stage presentation —"the distances, the spatial and temporal areas, in such a manner that her pieces would have been impossible upon the ancient stage."[53] This is not an acceptable thesis. The spatial and temporal disparities argued above do not present a problem in the actual staging of the plays. The scenes change in somewhat the same manner as the Elizabethan play of five centuries later. The opening lines of each scene set the time and place and create the mood; the closing lines provide the "curtain" as in the plays of both Terence and Shakespeare.

Throughout each play there is a "unity of action," which, according to Aristotle, is an "organic unity, an inward principle revealing itself in the form of an outward whole,"[54]—a dramatically constructed plot with a beginning, a middle,

80

and an end representing a coherent organism and producing the pleasure proper to it.[55] Clearly, this absolves Hrotsvitha from the perennial accusation that she "violates the three unities," and it supports the conclusion that it is her expert and intuitively dramatic handling of material that merits for her a place among the playwrights.

Finally, there are strong evidences of three contemporary dramatic streams within Hrotsvitha's writings—the literary tradition of classical antiquity, the mimetic influence, and the liturgical form—and the traces of their concomitant theatrical characteristics.

Numerous are the comments—from derogatory to laudatory—regarding these traces of classic authors:

Terence, the dear delight of the medieval monastery, was in the tenth century pruned of his pagan charm and naughtiness, and planted out in six persimmon comedies by a Saxon nun of Gandersheim, Hrotsvitha,—comedies of tedious saints and hircine sinners and a stuffy Latin style.[56]

A woman of the darkest of the dark ages, she pored over the pagan poets, and knew her Terence as well as she did Boëthius, or the New Testament.[57]

But though she might say of Terence as Dante did of Virgil, 'Tu duca, tu maestro, e tu signore,' she was moved by the greater master; indeed her convent-garden is fragrant with many grafts from antique groves, and the spiritual spouse of Christ was a child of the pagan poets as well.[58]

The fact that a nun was well aware and able not only to read and understand the poets, Horace, Ovid, Virgil, Plautus, and Terence but also set out to oppose these pagan authors and their works with a Christian work of art, was bound to attract the attention of everyone.[59]

The mimetic influence is strongly supported by Hermann Reich, a classical philologist, who edited Paul von Winterfeld's *Deutsche Dichter des lateinischen Mittelalters*:

81

Reich believes that Hrotsvitha's age was 'völlig dramenlos' and that although her dramas fairly cry for performance and she herself, with the blood of the theatre in her veins, would have welcomed their production, her superiors would have vetoed any suggestion to have such sacred materials presented by profane jugglers and mimes, the only possible media of representation before spectators of that time. But both von Winterfeld and Reich are convinced that as a writer Hrotsvitha is strongly under the influence of the contemporary mimes, and that her plays according to von Winterfeld are 'bühnensicher'.[60]

The scholar, Wilhelm Scherer, not only admits the influence of the mimes on Hrotsvitha's plays but goes so far as to suggest the possibility of their performance by the mimes of her day.[61]

Zeydel contributes to the plausible existence of the third dramatic stream in Hrotsvitha's work. He affirms that if the nun-dramatist knew Notker's sequences and, as von Winterfield believes, wrote her own, she would forge a link between her work and the liturgical drama.[62] That Hrotsvitha knew Notker is implied in Reich when he cites several instances which show similarities of style—devotion to detail, homely humor, terseness, anecdotal interspersions, insight into human behavior, and mystical elements.[63] These, as will be demonstrated, Hrotsvitha used in her dramas—some profusely, some sparingly. In addition, this study will identify passages which seem to contain the language of the liturgy.

Before proceeding with an examination of the text within the boundaries of these three influences—the classical, mimetic, and liturgical—some statement should be given summarizing the implications concerning Hrotsvitha's intention in writing in the dramatic form. Were the plays merely literary exercises intended for reading or were they genuine dramatic pieces intended for performance?

Whatever their subsequent disposition—reading or acting —one thing is clearly perceived, namely, Hrotsvitha's seriousness of purpose in writing them. "It is my object," she said, "to glorify virtue in the same medium as is used to glorify vice." [64] Again, "Modesty cannot deter me from using my pen to glorify the innocent to the best of my ability." [65] And again, "I strive only to use what talent I have for the glory of Him Who gave it me. Nor is my self-love so great that I would, to avoid criticism, abstain from proclaiming wherever possible the virtue of Christ working in His saints." [66]

Here are the words—strong and courageous—of a reformer. It is unthinkable that such clarity and singleness of purpose would be permitted to wither within a cloister cell. Hrotsvitha must have sought some means—quick and sure—to communicate her message. She found it in theatrical expression. Even though Reich believes that "Hrotsvitha's age was 'völlig dramenlos,'" here we have a playwright, a play, and an audience. Reich declares that her superiors would have vetoed any suggestion to use the mimes as actors. This is tantamount to declaring that the only legitimate theatre in existence during the tenth century was the theatre of the mimes. Since we know there was more than one type of theatre in existence, the problem of securing actors would not have been a serious one. Furthermore, it would have been highly inconsistent for her religious superiors to have spurred her efforts in the writing of this dramatic form and to have denied performance.

Further indications that the plays were meant to be acted, lie in the social structure of the day. The general public patronized the mimic shows and the liturgical dramas, leaving the more sophisticated plays of Terence to the educated class and to the nobility—either for viewing or reading. It was this group, the Terence admirers, that Hrotsvitha wished to reach. These people were frequently guests of the monastery. For their anticipated pleasure and subsequent edification, Hrotsvitha had no hesitancy in giving them the bitter pill of censure under the sweet cloak of drama, using the natural stage settings of the cloister and the natural talents of the canonesses.

Finally, the plays, in the words Zeydel, "fairly cry for performance." [67] The use of several dramatic devices within the dialogue—stichomythia, didascalia, oculia, and others—inherently require acting for effectiveness. Although, to the present, it has been impossible to marshal conclusive evidence for or against actual presentation, it should not prevent the acknowledgment that the plays themselves, the "spectacle-demanding" populace, and the talent and urgency of Hrotsvitha attest this intention.

Chapter V

THE THEATRICALITY OF THE DRAMAS

The introduction to this study demonstrates conclusively that there was a living theatre during Hrostvitha's lifetime. It further declares that this theatre existed in classical, mimetic, and liturgical forms with their complementary theatrics. In the subsequent chapters of the thesis, there is the recurring implication that the drama of this tenth-century canoness was not only a composite of the alleged dramatic forms of the first millennium A.D., but that it contained the germ of later dramatic forms.

Using these statements as a point of departure, this chapter will set forth evidence, both internal and external, proving that the plays of Hrotsvitha possess genuine theatrical qualities which admit of performance.

By *internal evidence* is meant all those elements which stimulate dramatic action because of their inherent emotional significance. Such evidence is manifested by characterization, dialogue, plot structure, plot development, and catharsis. Characters are strongly motivated, dialogue is familiar and meaningful, plot structure is acceptable, plot development is credible, catharsis is effective. Opposed to *internal evidence* is *external evidence* which is visual and aural, and includes all aspects of theatre which border on spectacle.

85

The German humanists of the sixteenth century are primarily responsible for the enduring interest periodically manifested in the classical influences found in Hrotsvitha. According to them:

Hrotsvitha reflects credit upon Germany, as Sappho upon Greece, and Terence, Vergil, and Horace upon Rome—the more so because she was a woman. . . . Her works may be compared favorably, they thought, with those of the ancient writers; . . . her Latin diction seemed to most of them praiseworthy and deserving of their attention. . . . The humanists thought of her not as a child of her particular age, but as a Latin author who happened to be a German by birth. Just as they regarded the Holy Roman Empire of the German Nation as a direct, unbroken continuation of the Empire of the Roman Caesars, so they looked upon Hrotsvitha as a mere continuator of the tradition of Sappho, Terence, and Vergil. They themselves felt a kinship with her not so much because she was German, . . . as because they looked upon themselves, too, as continuators of the classical tradition.[1]

The fact that Hrotsvitha herself says she elected to use Terence as her literarary model, would naturally seem to place the greater burden of proving the theatricality of the plays upon the classical. An analysis of the plays reveals that she solved many dramatic problems in this tradition.

Characterization.—Prominent among the internal evidence of classical influence in Hrotsvitha is characterization. According to Aristotle,[2] only certain types of characters "are capable of dramatic treatment." He describes the dramatic character as "a battling, energetic type, one whose emotions harden into will which expressess itself in action." Although the characters of Hrotsvitha will never be accorded the dramatic stature granted the characters of classical drama, nevertheless, in the following passage, there are some legitimate similarities.

Greek drama, in its most characteristic examples, dramatizes not the mere story of human calamities, but the play of great principles, the struggle between contending moral forces. The heroes are themselves the concrete embodiment of these forces. Religion, the State, the Family,—these were to a Greek the higher and enduring realities, the ideal ends for which he lived. Hence in the Greek drama, patriotism, wifely or sisterly devotion, all those elementary emotions which cluster round home and country, are the motives which chiefly impel to action and call forth the ardour of self-sacrifice. Seldom do passions purely personal animate these heroes: they are free from inward discord and self-contradiction: the ends they pursue are objective and rest on a belief in the abiding reality of the social organism. The characters hereby gain universal meaning and validity. They are not of their age and country only, but can claim kinship with mankind.[3]

Similarly, Hrotsvitha's characters are involved in moral conflicts. In all instances, the protagonist and antagonist are the embodiment of moral forces. The only worthwhile realities—God, family, country—motivate the protagonist to self-sacrifice and rest on the objective belief in the dual nature of man. Her characters, therefore, can claim kinship with universal man.

In her own words, as quoted previously, Hrotsvitha describes the moral conflict in which she involves her characters:

For in proportion as the blandishments of lovers are enticing, so much greater is the glory of our helper in Heaven, so much more glorious the triumph of those who prevail, especially where woman's weakness triumphs and man's shameless strength is made to succumb.[4]

Not only are her characters the embodiment of these contending forces in action and in dialogue, but frequently they are so in name as well. For example, there is Sapientia (wisdom), Constantia (constancy), Dulcitius (sensuousness), Calimachus (comeliness), Fortunatus (opportunism). Concern for one's fellowman ("Pafnutius"), constancy to a religious vow ("Dulcitius" and "Gallicanus"), fidelity to family and God ("Abraham," "Sapientia," and "Calimachus")—these realities motivate the chaarcters to self-sacrifice, even to death. In these similarities to classical drama rests the claim of her characters to validity and universality. To further support this claim, numerous references will be cited.[5]

In the plays, "Gallicanus," "Dulcitius," and "Sapientia," there are the antagonists, Julian, Diocletian, and Hadrian— all representing the pagan dictator, persecutor, or modern totalitarian ruler:

Gallicanus, II, vi, 135, 15.

IULIANUS: Vade, Terrentiane, sumptis tecum militibus, et compelle Iohannem et Paulum deo Iovi sacrificare; si autem obstinato restiterint pectore, perimantur, non palam, sed nimium occulte, quia palatini fuere.

JULIAN: Go, Terentianus. Take with you a few trusted soldiers and compel John and Paul to sacrifice to Jupiter. If they persist in their refusal, let them be put to death, not publicly but with the greatest possible secrecy, since they once held office in the palace.

Dulcitius, i, 140, 3.

DIOCLETIAN: Istae contumaces nostrisque decretis contraluctantes catenis inretiantur et ad examen Dulcitii praesidis sub carcerali squalore serventur.

DIOCLETIAN: Let these obstinate women who dare to defy our authority be laden in chains and thrown into a dungeon. Let them be examined by Governor Dulcitius.

Sapientia, i, 201, 25.

ADRIANUS: Et merito, ne reus maiestatis esse arguaris, si non celanda celaveris.

HADRIAN: Do you praise yourself for this? If you withheld such information, you would be guilty of treason to your Imperial Majesty.

Also typical of the tyrant, is the constant attendance of a henchman. In the early plays, Terentianus and Sisinnius servilely carry out orders. In "Sapientia," the last of the plays, the henchman has become the artfully-developed sycophant in the person of Antiochus:

Gallicanus, II, vii, 135, 19.

TERRENTIANUS: Imperator Iulianus, cui servio, misit vobis, Iohannes et Paule, pro sui clementia aureum simulachrum Iovis, cui tura gratis imponere debetis; quod si nolueritis, capitalem sententiam subibitis.

TERENTIANUS: Paul and John, the Emperor Julian, my master, of his clemency sends you this gold statue of Jupiter, and commands you to burn incense before it. Refuse, and you will be put to death.

Dulcitius, xi, 143, 26.

SISINNIUS: Deponite duritiam cordis et sacrificate. Sin autem: faciam vos interfectum iri iuxta praeceptum imperatoris Diocletiani.

SISINNIUS: Do not be obstinate. Unless you sacrifice to the gods I am going to put you to death. So it is decreed by my Emperor Diocletian.

Sapientia, i, 201, 13.

ANTIOCHUS: Tuum igitur esse, o imperator Adriane, prosperis ad vota successionibus pollere tuique statum imperii feliciter absque perturbatione exoptans vigere, quicquid rempublicam confundere, quicquid tranquillum mentis reor vulnerare posse, quantocius divelli penitusque cupio labefactari.

ANTIOCHUS: My Lord Emperor, what desire has your servant but to see you powerful and prosperous? What ambition apart from the welfare and peace and greatness of the state you rule? So when I discover anything that threatens the commonwealth or your peace of mind I try to crush it before it has taken root.

Sisinnius and Fortunatus might be classified as fanatical patriots defined in terms of brutality and bigotry. Even when confronted with extraodinary phenomena, they prefer to accept shame and death rather than deviate from the command of a tyrannical master:

Dulcitius, xiv, 147, 7.

SISINNIUS: Quicquid dedecoris accedit, levius tolero, quia te morituram haut dubito.

HIRENA: Hinc mihi quam maxime gaudendum, tibi vero dolendum, quia pro tui severitate malignitatis in tartara dampnaberis.

SISINNIUS: I accept the shame gladly, since now I am sure of your death.

IRENA: To me my death means joy but to you calamity. For your cruelty you will be damned in Tartarus.

Calimachus, ix, 159, 28.

FORTUNATUS: Si, ut asseris, Drusiana me suscitavit et Calimachus Christo credidit, vitam repudio mortemque sponte eligo, quia malo non esse quam in his tantam habundanter virtutum gratiam sentiscere.

FORTUNATUS: If it is as you say, if Drusiana has restored me to life and Callimachus believes in Christ, I reject life and choose death. I would rather not exist than see them swelling with grace and virtue.

Abraham and Paphnutius, who give titles to two other plays, exemplify the desert eremite of the early Church and the cloistered monk of today, who, despite their solitary way of life, never lose touch with the world around them:

Abraham, vii, 174, 15.

ABRAHAM: Nonne tui causa desiderabilem heremi habitationem reliqui omnemque regularis observantiam conversationis plene evacuavi, in tantum, ut ego, vetus heremicola, factus sum lascivientium conviva, et, qui diu silentio studebam, iocularia

ABRAHAM: What but love for you could have made me leave the desert and relax the strict observance of our rule? What but love could have made me, a true hermit, come into the city and mix with the lascivious crowd? It is for your sake that these

90

verba, ne agnoscerer, proferebam? Cur demisso vultu terram inspicis? cur respondendo mecum verba miscere dedignaris?

lips have learned to utter light, foolish words, so that I might not be known! Oh, Mary, why do you turn away your face from me and gaze upon the ground? Why do you scorn to answer and tell me what is in your mind?

Pafnutius, i, 184, 26.

PAFNUTIUS: Quaedam inpudens femina moratur in hac patria. . . . Sed prompta est omnes lenociniis suae formae illicere secumque ad interitum trahere. . . . Quid, si illam adeam sub specie amatoris, si forte revocari possit ab intentione nugacitatis? . . . Fulcite me interim precibus assiduis, . . .

PAPHNUTIUS: Brothers—there is a woman, a shameless woman, living in our neighbourhood. . . . She seeks to allure all men through her marvelous beauty, and drag them down with her. . . . What if I were to go to her in the disguise of a lover to try to persuade her to give up her diabolical intentions? I shall need your most fervent prayers.

To the casual reader of plays, the female characters may appear unimpressive. They may seem to be cast in the same mold, but such is not the case, for when brought to life on the stage,[6] these women become indisputably individual in their roles. They, too, may be classified as valid and universal in quality.

Constance is the incarnation of the woman-strategist. Her maneuverings not only motivate the entire action of the play, but guarantee the outcome:

Gallicanus, I, ii, 120, 31.

CONSTANTIA: Si meum digneris captare consilium, praemonstrabo, qualiter utrumque evadere possis damnum.

CONSTANCE: My lord, if you will deign to listen to my advice, I can show you how to escape this double danger.

Sapientia is the paragon of the valiant mother. Her words characterize her as familiar with the ways of the world as with the ways of heaven. She is learned, sophisticated, ingenious, witty, courageous, and maternal:

Sapientia, iii, 204, 24.

SAPIENTIA: Nullius alius rei nisi agnoscendae veritatis causa, quo fidem, quam expugnatis, plenius ediscerem filiasque meas Christo consecrarem. . . . Placetne vobis, o filiae, ut hunc stultum aritmetica fatigem disputatione? . . . O dulces filiolae, o carae pusiolae, nolite super carceralis angustia custodiae contristari, . . .

SAPIENTIA: For no reason than that we wish to know the truth. I came to learn more of the faith which you persecute and to consecrate my daughters to Christ. . . . What do you say, children? Shall I puzzle his dull brain with some problems in arithmetic? . . . Oh, my dearest ones! My beloved children! Do not let this narrow prison sadden you.

Her three daughters, Faith, Hope, and Charity, are the personification of the virtues for which they are named. Faith is sure, strong, and aggressive; Hope's apparent timidity is actually trust in the future; Charity is childlike, appealing, and unafraid. This seems to be a studied dramatic device:

Sapientia, iv, 208, 5.

FIDES: Pro ipsius amore sponsi promptae sumus mori. . . . v, 209, 16. Tui stultitiam irrideo, tui insipientiam subsanno. . . .

ADRIANUS: Mei?

FIDES: Tui.

FAITH: For His love we are all ready to die. . . . [To Hadrian] How can I help laughing? Such a lack of wisdom is ludicrous. . . .

HADRIAN: Whose lack of wisdom?

FAITH: Why, yours!

92

ANTIOCHUS: Imperatoris?

FIDES: Ipsius.

ANTIOCHUS: O nefas!

Sapientia, iv, 208, 8.

SPES: Praemitte nos ante tribunal iudicis et experieris, quantum eius amor nobis attulit temeritatis. v, 212, 4. O utinam admeruissem illam imitari patiendo, quo illi assimilarer in praemio! ... Depone taedium et tende ad praemium; non enim diu separabimur, sed ocius in caelo coniungemur.

Sapientia, iv, 208, 12.

KARITAS: Consertis palmulis incedamus et vultum tyranni confundamus. v, 214, 9. Taedet me vitae praesentis, taedet terrenae habitationis, quod saltim ad modicum temporis separor a vobis.

ANTIOCHUS: You dare to speak to the Emperor so?

FAITH: I speak the truth.

ANTIOCHUS: This is not to be endured!

HOPE: When we come before the tribunal you will see what courage our love will give us. . . . [To Hadrian] Would that I were worthy to imitate her [Faith's] sufferings, and so win a reward like hers. . . . [To Charity] Have courage! Stretch out your hands to the palm. We shall be separated only for a moment. Soon, very soon, we shall be together again in heaven.

CHARITY: Let us go hand in hand to the tyrant and make him feel ashamed. . . . I am weary of this earth. I do not want to be separated from you even for a short time.

Nor are these three daughters replicas of the three heroines in "Dulcitius"—Agape, Chionia, and Irena—who show a marked maturity in their words and in their reactions. These latter three stand as a united force in the plot.

Drusiana[7] is sometimes compared to Richardson's Clarissa, a timid soul beset with perplexities, who seeks escape rather than solution. True, the similarity may be extended to their common avoidance of conflict, but the motives which direct the actions of each are far different. In the case of Clarissa, it is personal—peace at any cost; whereas, Drusiana's prayer for death is impelled by her anxiety for her husband and their domain, by her contempt for her beauty which is unwittingly responsible for the impending condemnation of Callimachus, and by the threat to her virtue:

Calimachus, iv, 151, 12.

DRUSIANA: Eh heu! domine Iesu Christe, quid prodest castitatis professionem subiisse, cum is amens mea deceptus est specie? Intende, domine, mei timorem; intende, quem patior, dolorem! Quid mihi, quid agendum sit, ignoro: si prodidero, civilis per me fiet discordia; si celavero, insidiis diabolicis sine te refragari nequeo. Iube me in te, Christe, ocius mori, ne fiam in ruinam delicato iuveni!

DRUSIANA: O Lord Jesus what use is my vow of chastity? My beauty has all the same made this man love me. Pity my fears, O Lord. Pity the grief which has seized me. I know not what to do. If I tell anyone what has happened, there will be disorder in the city on my account; if I keep silence, only Thy grace can protect me from falling into the net spread for me. O Christ, take me to Thyself. Let me die swiftly. Save me from being the ruin of a soul!

Illustrative of Hrotsvitha's versatility in characterization are the Mary of "Abraham" and the Thais of "Pafnutius." With intuitive skill she has combined the wantonness of the courtesan with the despair of the compulsive sinner who is eventually restored to grace:

Abraham, vi 172, 21.

MARIA: Levi conpunctione permovebar, ideo talia fabar; sed epulemur et laetemur, quia, ut monuisti, hic non est tempus peccata plangendi.

MARY: A little thing moved me, and I spoke foolishly. It is nothing. Come, let us eat and drink and be merry, for, as you say, this is not the place to think of one's sins.

Pafnutius, vii, 193, 30

THAIS: Mens assueta lasciviae haut raro inpatiens est austerioris vitae.[8]

THAIS: I have long been so accustomed to pleasure and distraction. My mind is still a slave to my senses.

Equally ingenious is her caricature of Dulcitius, in the play of that name:

Dulcitius, ii, 140, 9.

DULCITIUS: Papae! quam pulchrae, quam venustae, quam egregiae puellulae!

DULCITIUS: Ye gods, but these girls are beautiful! What grace, what charm!

MILITES: Perfecte decorae.

SOLDIERS: Perfect!

DULCITIUS: Captus sum illarum specie.

DULCITIUS: I am enraptured!

MILITES: Credibile.

SOLDIERS: No wonder!

DULCITIUS: Exaestuo illas ad mei amorem trahere.

DULCITIUS: I'm in love! Do you think they will fall in love with me?

MILITES: Diffidimus te praevalere.

SOLDIERS: From what we know, you will have little success.

Dulcitius, iv, 141, 14.

HIRENA: Ecce, iste stultus, mente alienatus, aestimat se nostris uti amplexibus. . . . Nunc ollas molli fovet gremio, nunc sartagines et caccabos amplectitur, mitia libans oscula.

IRENE: O, look! He must be out of his senses! I believe he thinks he's kissing us. . . . Now he presses the sauce pans tenderly to his breast, now the kettles and frying pans! He is kissing them hard!

On the stage,[9] as well as in the lines, this ludicrous figure provides a striking contrast to the seriousness of the situation. Blashfield appreciates this "comic element which," she says, "is kept in abeyance in the *Acta Sanctorum* and which is here exploited with zest, and . . . mirth-provoking potentialities." [10] Fife goes so far as to say, "The play, 'Dulcitius,' contains comic elements worthy of Terence." [11]

Just as the classicist "seized upon a personality at some decisive moment of action—a small portion of life carved out of a human career," [12] so Hrotsvitha intuitively caught the personality at a strategic moment.[13] Of necessity, this classic device excludes complete character portrayal, but it does not exclude the optimum in character development within the scope of the plot.

One of the most frequent criticisms leveled at Hrotsvitha is her acceptance of static characters. Such a comment represents a truncated view of the author and her plays, for it ignores the fact that she had only one purpose in writing, and to this purpose, she ordered her plots and her characters. To the open mind, it is apparent that in each successive play, the *schema* becomes less structured, thus affording a more dynamic vehicle in which the action and the reaction of the characters become more self-determined.

From Julian whose lines mainly portray his almighty rule, to Hadrian who manifests not only despotic power but also the concomitant vices that so often accompany such power; from Abraham who uses a paternal chiding to move Mary, to Paphnutius who employs the impassioned language of the lover to attract Thais; from Terentianus who slavishly carries out his master's orders, to Antiochus who represents the ingratiating *alter ego* of Hadrian—all attest that the characters which this medieval nun created—whether comic or serious—have developed into three-dimensional roles. They go far beyond the scope of Terence, whose stage was peopled with amiable and amoral beings. Hrotsvitha's men and women, on the contrary, are endowed with souls within which the greatest conflicts of life take place.

Coulter supplies a rather extravagant, but conceivably merited compliment to Hrotsvitha in regard to her characterization when she says:

The sympathetic insight into the minds of her characters, and the deftness and sureness of the character-drawing in the best of her plays, are remarkable in one who had spent most of her mature years within convent walls.[14]

As is often the case, this quotation seems to underestimate the unusually liberal education that was available to the medieval scholar within the monastery. According to Steinhoff,[15] children of nobility, freedmen, and representatives of the court entered school at the age of five years and were educated in a manner which familiarized them with the total complex nature of man and of the universe.

To summarize, Hrotsvitha's delineation of character shows classical traces in its involvement with moral conflict, in its orientation to the universal type, and in the restrictions imposed upon it by the late point of attack. Further qualities of characterization will be discussed in connection with the mimetic, liturgical, and modern traces.

Dialogue.—Change of pace, passage of time, contrast, tragic irony, suspense, exalted passages—all classical devices —are represented in the dialogue and provide further internal testimony to the theatricality of the plays.

Stichomythia, a rhetorical device, designed by the Greeks, is a "cut-and-parry" or "cut-and-thrust" dialogue. Hrotsvitha used it frequently and effectively in each of her plays to change pace and to build emotional tension:

Gallicanus, I, i, 118, 22 through i, 119, 2.

CONSTANTINUS: Praemium scilicet nostrae adeptionem familiaritatis praecipuaeque inter palatinos dignitatis.

GALLICANUS: Fateor, sed id nunc haut molior.

CON: Si aliud expetas, oportet proferas.

CONSTANTINE: You enjoy the freedom of my court and the highest honor among those who surround me.

GALLICANUS: I know, but I am not thinking of that.

CON: If you have other ambitions, you must tell me.

GAL: Immo aliud.

CON: Quid?

GAL: Si praesumo dicere.

CON: Et bene.

GAL: Irasceris.

CON: Nullo modo.

GAL: Certe.

CON: Non.

GAL: Moveberis indignatione.

CON: Ne id vereare.

GAL: Dicam, iussisti: Constantiam, tui natam, amo.[16]

GAL: I have.

CON: What are they?

GAL: Dare I tell you?

CON: Of course!

GAL: You will be angry.

CON: Not at all!

GAL: You are sure?

CON: Quite sure.

GAL: You will be indignant.

CON: Your fears are groundless.

GAL: Since you command me, I will speak. I love Constance. I love your daughter.

It would almost seem that Hrotsvitha knew the modern rule of playwriting, that "a speech should not be over fifty words unless for a notable exception," since her speeches average approximately ten words. This makes her dialogue both brisk and fluid. To emphasize the pungency of speech even more, she occasionally interrupts the rhythm with the insertion of longer passages which take the form of so-called learned disputations and dialectics,[17] admonitions, prayers, and narration. The following example is a narrative passage:

Pafnutius, xi, 197, 25.

PAULUS: Videbam in visione lectulum candidulis palliolis in caelo magnifice stratum, cui quattuor splendidae virgines praeerant et quasi custodiendo astabant; at ubi iocunditatem mirae claritatis aspiciebam, intra me dicebam; 'Haec gloria nemini

PAUL: Father, I saw in my vision a splendid bed. It was adorned with white hangings and coverings, and a crown was laid on it, and round it were four radiant virgins. They stood there as if they were guarding the crown. There was a great brightness

magis congruit quam patri et domino meo Antonio!'[18]	round the bed, and a multitude of angels. I, seeing this wonderful and joyful sight, cried out, 'This glory must be for my master and father Antony!'

"A dramatist has to know when to stop," particularly in longer speeches arranged to achieve a climactic effect. Hrotsvitha exhibits a fine sensitivity to dramatic timing in the scene where Sapientia responds to Hadrian's simple question about the age of her daughters with a long involved scientific answer. The lines of this noble matron are so designed that they allow interjections which provide relief from tension and, therefore, change in tempo, yet do not interrupt the sequence of thought of the longer speeches. This technique also takes on the character of the dramatic pause leading to a laugh-line.[19]

In addition to *stichomythia,* variety in length of speeches, and the dramatic pause, Hrostvitha also used variation in mood, mental and verbal conflict, and introduction of new characters to effect change in pace in the dialogue:

Sapientia, v, 213, 16 (variation in mood).

ADRIANUS: Quid sentio novae dulcedinis? Quid odoror stupendae suavitatis?	HADRIAN: What is this strange sweetness in the air? If I am not mistaken a marvelous perfume fills the room.

Sapientia, v, 215, 13 (mental and verbal conflict).

ADRIANUS: Dic tantum: Magna Diana! et ego ultra ad sacrificandum te non compello.	HADRIAN: You shall say "Great is Diana." That is all. I will not compel you to sacrifice.
KARITAS: Percerto non dico.	CHARITY: I will not say it.
ADRIANUS: Quare?	HADRIAN: Why?
KARITAS: Quia mentiri nolo.	CHARITY: Because I will not

Ego quidem et sorores meae eisdem parentibus genitae, eisdem sacramentis imbutae, sumus una eademque fidei constantia roboratae. Quapropter scito nostrum velle, nostrum consentire, nostrum sapere, unum idemque esse, nec me in ullo umquam illis dissidere.

tell a lie. My sisters and I were born of the same parents, instructed in the same mysteries, and confirmed in the same faith. We have the same wish, the same understanding, the same resolution. Therefore, I am never likely to differ from them in anything.

ANTIOCHUS: O iniuria, quod a tantilla etiam contempnor homullula!

ANTIOCHUS: Oh, what an insult—to be defied by a mere doll!

KARITAS: Licet tenella sim aetate, tamen gnara sum te argumentose confundere.

CHARITY: Although I am small, my reason is big enough to put you to shame.

ADRIANUS: Abstrahe illam, Antioche, et fac, ut suspensa in eculeo, atrociter verberetur.

HADRIAN: Take her away, Antiochus, and have her stretched on the rack and whipped.

Gallicanus, I, iv, 122, 17 (introduction of new characters).

CONSTANTINUS: Sui primicerios, Iohannem et Paulum, tecum commoratum iri decrevit usque in diem nuptiarum.

CONSTANTINE: Then listen. She has given orders that her Almoners, John and Paul, shall stay with you until the day of your nuptials.

Not only did Hrotsvitha vary the change of pace by studied techniques, but she also consciously controlled the passage of time. Here, in particular, she seems to follow Aristotle and the classical tradition which maintains, "The whole play must be of such dimensions that the memory of the mind's eye can embrace and retain it. At the same time it should be of a magnitude sufficient to allow room for the natural development of the story."[20] Though in her plays, the span of time extends from a few days to many years, Hrotsvitha

controls its passage by such theatrical conventions as lapse of
of time between scenes, brief narrative references within
scenes, and the sheer use of imagination.

Sapientia, iii, 207, 15; iv, in toto; v, 208, 17 and 26 (lapse of
time between scenes).

ADRIANUS: In custodiam iuxta palatium ponantur, et triduanae induciae illis ad tractandum praestentur.	HADRIAN: Let these women be taken to the prison near our palace, and give them three days to reflect.

Scene iv indicates the duration of time.

ADRIANUS: Antioche, iube illas Italicas nobis repraesentari captivas. . . . Triduanas vobis inducias praestabat nostri serenitas; unde, si quid tractaretis utilitatis, cedite iussionibus nostris.[21]	HADRIAN: Antiochus, bring the Greek prisoners before us. . . . The three days' respite which of our clemency we granted you is over. If you have profited by it, obey our commands.

Abraham, i, 163, 1; i, 163, 12; iii, 165, 27 (references within
scenes).

ABRAHAM: Est mihi neptis tenella, . . . Si unius rotatus mansurni apponeretur, duas olympiades vitali aura vesceretur. . . . Maria, mis adoptiva filia, quam per bis bina lustra summa diligentia nutrivi, summa solertia instruxi! . . . Ei mihi! Periit.	ABRAHAM: I have a little niece of tender years. . . . At the end of this year she will be eight. . . . Mary! Mary! my adopted child! Mary, whom I cared for so lovingly and taught with all my skill for ten years! Mary— . . . Oh God! She is lost!

There are some striking examples where Hrotsvitha requires that the imagination accept a passage of time. For example, in "Sapientia" when Hadrian is frustrated at every turn in his attempt to conquer Hope, he commands Antiochus:

Sapientia, v, 213, 23.

ADRIANUS: Aeneum vas, plenum oleo et adipe, cera atque pice, ignibus superponatur, in quod ligata proiciatur.

HADRIAN: Put in the brazier a vessel full of oil and wax and pitch. Bind her and throw her in.

ANTIOCHUS: Si in ius Vulcani tradetur, forsitan evadendi aditum non nanciscetur.

ANTIOCHUS: Yes, she will not find it so easy to escape from Vulcan.

SPES: Haec virtus Christo non est insolita, ut ignem faciat mitescere, mutata natura.

HOPE: Christ has before now made fire grow mild and change its nature.

ADR: Quid? Audio, Antioche, velut sonitum inundantis aquae.

HAD: Antiochus, what is that sound? I seem to hear a noise like that of rushing waters.

ANT: Heu, heu, domine!

ANT: My lord! My lord!

ADR: Quid contigit nobis?

HAD: What has happened?

ANT: Ebulliens fervor, confracto vase, ministros combussit, et illa malefica illaesa comparuit.

ANT: The boiling fire has burst the cauldron! It has overflowed and consumed every man near it. Only the vile witch who caused the disaster has escaped unhurt.

The exit and reëntrance of Antiochus within these few lines present a definite problem in staging. A like situation occurs in the last scene of "Sapientia"[22] where there is a reference to a passage of time and no apparent opportunity for its occurrence. These two problems, apparently the only two of their kind, may be flaws in the writing or they may be the author's demand for the acceptance of some theatrical convention.

"Higher emotions are stirred by contemplation not of external events, but of how men react to those events in word and deed."[23] Hrotsvitha shows her awareness of the effectiveness of emotional elements in dialogue when she borrows from the classicists the practice of using contrast, dramatic irony, and exalted passages.

102

One has merely to recall her purpose in writing the plays, namely, "to glorify the virtue of chastity and to repudiate its opposing vice," to realize how prominent a part contrast has been given throughout. Not only is it the framework of the plot structure, but, consciously or unconsciously, it is embodied in every facet of the plays. At this point, some illustrations of the use of contrast in dialogue are cited:

Sapientia, v, 215, 33.

KARITAS: O iudicem inpotentem, qui diffidit se absque armis ignium octuennem infantem superare posse!

CHARITY: A mighty man! He cannot conquer a child of eight without calling in fire to help him.

Pafnutius, xii, 199, 14.

THAIS: O utinam mererer poenas evadere vel saltim clementius exuri mitiori igne! Non est enim hoc mei meriti, ut doner beatitudine interminabili.[24]

THAIS: To Paradise! I should be happy if I might be spared hell's torments and be mercifully cleansed in a gentle fire until my spirit is fit for the eternal happiness.

Dramatic irony was first used in Socratic dialogue for the purpose of confusing an opponent. In Hrotsvitha, it occurs in a modified or figurative sense, namely, as "a contradictory outcome of events as if in mockery of the promise and fitness of things." [25] It is included here in the discussion of dialogue, since the expression of the unexpected outcome serves to heighten the ironic effect.

Sapientia, vi, 216, 18.

ANTIOCHUS: Flamma erupit et quinque milia hominum combussit.
ADRIANUS: Et quid contigit illi? ...

ANTIOCHUS: The flames belched forth and five thousand men were burned to death.... And what happened to her? ... She ran to and fro,

ANTIOCHUS: Ludens inter flammivomos vapores vagabat et illaesa laudes deo suo pangebat.[26]

playing in the fierce whirlwind of smoke and flame, and sang praises to her God.

Just as the Greek and Roman plays abounded in soliloquies addressed to oneself, to an absent person or thing, or to the pagan gods, so, too, the plays of Hrotsvitha contain numerous passages of this kind:

Gallicanus, I, vi, 123, 23.

CONSTANTIA: Unum dominum habemus in caelis, cui debetur devotio nostrae servitutis, in cuius fide et dilectione condecet nos servata corporis integritate unanimiter perseverare, ut mereamur aulam caelestis patriae cum palma virginitatis introire.[27]

CONSTANCE: We have one Lord Who is in heaven. He alone should be served like that. We owe Him a love and fidelity which must be shown not only with whole hearts but with whole bodies. That is if we would enter His kingdom with the virgin's palm.

Plot structure.—Although the use which Hrotsvitha made of dialogue shows her intimate familiarity with classic models and her facility in imitating them, it would be presumptuous to assert that her plots conform to the structure of great classical drama as defined by Aristotle in his *Poetics*. This study maintains, however, that her dramas do simulate the classical in singleness of issue.[28]

In each of the plays there is the initial complication of events which provides the *beginning;* following this is the *middle* which flows with smoothly increasing tension of further complications to the climax; the rest of the play "unravels" to an accepted *end.* These three—*beginning, middle,* and *end*—provide the trinity required for an organic whole by Greek and Roman dramatists.[29] Within the restricted standards of the purely classical, Hrotsvitha approaches the single, non-episodic, non-subplot form—at times tragic, at times ethical, at times humorous.

Plot characteristics.—Although Hrotsvitha's handling of plot structure cannot conscientiously be aligned with the classicists, nevertheless, it is evident that her plots are marked by the characteristics frequently employed by classic writers. This study will conclude the exposition of the internal evidences of classicism found in Hrotsvitha with a consideration of such plot characteristics and, by this analogy, will implicitly support the theatricality of her plays. Two of the most powerful emotional elements of plot in classical drama are peripeteia and anagnorisis.

Peripeteia or *reversal of the situation*,[30] controls the changes of fortune within the plays and holds the action within the realm of probability and necessity. In "Abraham," Mary, the courtesan, arranges an assignation with Abraham only to discover that he is her former spiritual director come to save her. This discovery leads her first to despair, then to permanent incarceration in a desert cell.[31] In "Gallicanus," forfeiture of Constance, whom he loves, is the price Gallicanus must pay for a despaired-of victory in battle. His renunciation finally includes not only his love, but also his daughters, his wealth, and his freedom.[32]

Very often the complication is resolved by means beyond the range of human knowledge. The classicists ascribed such power to the gods and for the reversal of situation introduced the *deus ex machina*. In Hrotsvitha we find a corollary in her use of supernatural intervention through faith and prayer.[33]

Anagnorisis or *recognition*[34] denotes change from ignorance to knowledge engendering, in its wake, love or hate. Sometimes, it is coincidental with peripeteia as in the scene where Mary recognizes Abraham[35] and when Thais penetrates the disguise of Paphnutius.[36] This recognition of persons, according to Aristotle, is "the most intimately connected with the plot." [37]

Recognition is effected by signs (the least artistic), by contrived means of the writer, by memory, by reasoning, and by natural means (best of all).[38]

To Hadrian, Sapientia is a noblewoman because of her "appearance";[39] to Callimachus, the serpent is a curse upon him for his evil intent.[40] The author contrived to place the lecherous Dulcitius in a situation whereby he blackened his face and clothes, thus subsequently seeming to other characters as the devil or as one possessed by the devil.[41] When Mary weeps at the sight of Abraham, she is recalling the "time when I was good."[42] From the words addressed to her by Callimachus, Drusiana deduces his evil intentions toward her.[43] Of all recognitions, Aristotle believes the best is that which is least contrived and which rises spontaneously from natural means.[44] For example, it is natural that the grateful Gallicanus, after his conversion, visit the Church of the Apostles rather than the temple of the gods.[45]

Catharsis.—The final observation which this study makes in enumerating the internal evidences of the classical influence on Hrotsvitha concerns catharsis. The classical dramatist provided for the purification of the emotions of both the audience and performers through blind devotion to fate. It is not unreasonable, therefore, that Hrotsvitha might have, knowingly or unknowingly, provided a catharsis for her plays through reasoned faith. An audience unaware of the implications of Hrotsvitha's religion would refuse to accept some of the basic religious concepts which she employed within her plots—the renunciation of worldly pleasures and goods, apostolic zeal, the unity of the family, the power of prayer, and the desire for martyrdom rather than the denial of faith. Such an audience might consider the plays "merely pious platitudes" or the "conjurings of a dark mind in a dark age," thus failing to recognize the catharsis with which Hrotsvitha resolves the plays and the players.

The external evidences of classical influence in the plays are equally as numerous and are exhibited through costume, style and diction, the chorus, and structural facilities.

Costume.—Historically, the first and most significant feature of the classical costume was the mask, which "rendered in conventional forms an indication of age, station, and mood." [46] In both Greek and Roman drama, the masks became so numerous and specific in their representation that it was necessary for them to be catalogued. [47] A miniature preserved in the "Andria," a Terence manuscript, aptly illustrates this point, [48] for it sets up a series of masks for the characters in the play, differentiating them according to stock types. Since Hrotsvitha used Terence as her principal literary model, and since the masks were an integral part of the performance of his plays and appeared in many of the *aedicula* in the manuscripts which she studied with great care in anticipation of writing her own works in a similar style, it does not seem amiss to believe that Hrotsvitha conceived her characters as masked. Possibly most scholars of the theatre would not find this reference to masks convincing and would prefer to consider her use of the mask as a disguise technique rather than an integral part of the character as in Greek drama. The following lines are offered to demonstrate the medieval familiarity with masking:

Dulcitius, v, 142, 1.

MILITES: Vox senioris nostri; sed imago diaboli.

SOLDIERS: The voice is our master's voice, but the face is a devil's.

Abraham, vi, 171, 18.

ABRAHAM: Quae fiducia, quae constantia mentis mihi post haec, cum hanc, quam nutrivi in heremi latibulis, meretricio cultu ornatam conspicio?

ABRAHAM: O mind, be constant! Tears, do not fall! Must I look on her whom I brought up in the desert, decked out with a harlot's face?

Pafnutius, i, 185, 23.

PAFNUTIUS: Quid, si illam adeam sub specie amatoris, . . .

PAPHNUTIUS: What if I were to go in the disguise of a lover?

Abraham, vi, 172, 5.

ABRAHAM: Nunc, nunc est si-   ABRAHAM: On with the mask!
mulandum.[49]

Both directly and indirectly Hrotsvitha alludes to the dress
of the characters. She seems to depend on costuming as a
theatrical individuation. In fact, it is quite possible that she
employed the symbolism of the classical theatre which characterized not only by dress but also by color. For example, when
Abraham decides to go to the brothel to seek out Mary, his
niece, he speaks of *deposito tegmine religionis*.[50] The word
tegmen literally means the husk of a grain or a shield, thus
denoting either a brown or metallic color, indicating the
severity of the monk's garb. If Hrotsvitha did not consciously
use this word as color, then she must have meant it in a
metaphorical sense, "having set aside the protection of my
religious garb." This study prefers the former interpretation
based on the selection of words to denote color and presents
other indications.

In "Dulcitius," there are the words *nigellis panniculis*[51]
freely translated by St. John as "filthy rags." Literally these
words mean "somewhat black swollen tufts [of reeds used for
thatching]," symbolizing the worn thatching of a roof as it
yields to the gusts of a wind. The author evidently used it to
mean a "soiled turgid yellow." Since Dulcitius refers to his
usual attire as *nitidus*,[52] that is "shining" or "glittering,"
Hrotsvitha has apparently given much attention to the
selection of words to show the change in his appearance. The
Roman symbol for the courtesan was yellow. Its male comple-
ment, the seducer, might well wear gold. Following this line
of reasoning, the obese Dulcitius sees his garments change
from a shining gold to a dirty yellow.

In a scene of "Pafnutius," Antony refers to his confrere as
meus frater et cohermicola, that is, "my brother who not only
lives as a hermit but also dresses as one," since the word
colere means either "to inhabit" or "to clothe," so *coher-*

micola might well mean "dressed in the drab colors of the hermit."[53]

There are instances in which Hrotsvitha refers to "noble matrons," which would indicate that there are characters who wear long flowing robes either of a purple or a somber shade with a distinctively styled headdress featuring either a wig or a veil:

Sapientia, iii, 204, 11.

ADRIANUS: Videris esse summis natalibus orta.[54]

HADRIAN: I judge from your appearance that you are of a noble race.

Her soldiers, in particular, take on a classical aspect for she differentiates between *ostiarii* (doorkeepers)[55] and *milites* (guards);[56] between *tribuni* (tribunes),[57] *centuriones* (centurions),[58] *lictores* (flagellators),[59] *percussores* (executioners),[60] and *saggitarii* (archers).[61] Her apparitions, like the pagan gods, were *amictu splendidi, vultu admodum reverendi,* that is, "gorgeously dressed and of noble mien.[62]

Less frequent are allusions to the wearing of head coverings. In "Gallicanus," Paul uses the diadem in drawing a distinction between Christian and pagan rulers:

Gallicanus, II, v, 134, 2.

PAULUS: Deteriora imitaris. Qui ecclesias frequentabant et excusso diademate prostrati Iesum Christum adorabant.

PAUL: You follow worse examples. They frequented the churches and, laying their diadems on the ground, adored Jesus Christ on their knees.

Antiochus, in "Sapientia," commands Charity to bare her head to the executioner:

Sapientia, vii, 217, 1.

ANTIOCHUS: Detege duram, Karitas, cervicem . . .

ANTIOCHUS: Uncover that obstinate little neck, . . .

109

Abraham wears a felt hat to aid his disguise:

Abraham, iv, 170, 14.

ABRAHAM: Obsecro, affer et pileum, quo coronam velem capitis.	ABRAHAM: And I must borrow a felt hat to cover my tonsure.

Throughout the plays, Hrotsvitha apparently extends the conflict to the costuming, for there is implied the rich dignified raiment of the matron juxtaposed with the gaudy elegance of the ruler; the extravagant brilliance of the courtesan contrasted with the drab mantle of the monk, the flowing garments of the young maidens set against the austere armor of the soldier.

Style and diction.—Classical imitation is also evidenced in her style and diction. Coulter is of the opinion that her style was as nearly like that of Terence as was possible to achieve in her time:

To her as to the other readers of the Middle Ages, Terence's lines appeared in prose, but prose of a peculiar elegance; and she, therefore, chose for her dramas a particularly elaborate form of prose composition, in which short phrases are balanced against one another, with the ends of the clausulae marked by rhyme.[63]

Other writers hint of similarities to Terentian themes, namely, the use of the disguise-motif, the appearance of the courtesan, and the humorous elements. Coulter calls attention to some passages in "Abraham" which are strikingly similar to the style of Vergil as found in the *Æneid* and in the *Eclogues*.

The fact that her poetic works were written in leonine hexameter, a style and meter peculiar to the Latin epics read at that time, may also account for the natural poetic traits which are evident in the dialogue of the plays. It is this poetic quality in the dialogue which supports the dramatic and

110

facilitates the expression of certain classical devices, such as the expression of the "universal," the "aside," and the "elements of wonder."

The following passages are examples of Hrotsvitha's expression of the "universal":

Calimachus, ii, 148, 20.

AMICI: Aequum est, ut communicata invicem compassione patiamur, quicquid unicuique nostrum utriusque eventu fortunae ingeratur.

FRIENDS: It is right and proper that we share the outcome of fortune with a friend who has confided his miseries to us.

Abraham, iv, 170, 8.

AMICUS: Hoc meretricibus antiquitus fuit in more, ut alieno delectarentur in amore.[64]

A FRIEND: It comes naturally to harlots to yield at all times to the importunities of strangers.

The poetic quality in the dialogue admits of the "aside" wherein the actor shares his fugitive thoughts with the audience. Two illustrations are presented here:

Gallicanus, I, i, 119, 11.

GALLICANUS: Eh heu! dedignatur; praescivi.

GALLICANUS: Alas! I foresaw this. He scorns me.

Abraham, vi, 172, 5.

ABRAHAM: Nunc, nunc est simulandum, nunc lascivientis more pueri iocis instandum, ne et ego agnoscar prae gravitate et ipsa se reddat latibulis prae pudore.[65]

ABRAHAM: On with the mask! Chatter, make lewd jests like an idle boy! She must not recognize me, or for very shame she may fly from me.

111

The poetic quality also clothes the "exalted passages" and the "elements of wonder" which are threaded through the dialogue:

Gallicanus, I, xii, 128, 35.

GALLICANUS: Apparuit mihi iuvenis procerae magnitudinis, crucem ferens in humeris, et praecepit, ut stricto mucrone illum sequerer.

GALLICANUS: A young man of immense stature appeared before me carrying a cross on his shoulder. He bade me follow him sword in hand.

Dulcitius, xi, 144, 10.

MILITES: O novum, o stupendum miraculum! Ecce, animae egressae sunt corpora, et nulla laesionis repperiuntur vestigia? sed nec capilli, nec vestimenta ab igne sunt ambust, quo minus corpora.[66]

SOLDIERS: O wonderful, most wonderful! Their spirits have left their bodies, but there is no sign of any hurt. Neither their hair, nor their garments, much less their bodies, have been touched by the flames.

To explore adequately Hrotsvitha's choice of diction would require exhaustive treatment and lies beyond the scope of the problem under consideration. At this point, this study merely recognizes some general comments regarding diction and its relationship to the classical tradition.

Many Hrotsvithan scholars would add two further marks of the classical school which would strengthen the performance theory and support theatricality, namely, the presence of *didascalia* and *oculia* in the plays. According to Magnin:

The notes pointing out the action of the players, which Greek grammarians called *didascalia* are found, they say, very rarely in the ancient classics. These indications of *mise en scène* are equally rare in the plays of Hrotsvitha. However, we shall call attention to two instances in "Gallicanus" which have escaped Celtes. For our part we attach great

112

significance to these *didascalia* because they prove in the most explicit manner that these plays were not written to be read as M. Price asserts in his *History of English Poetry*.[67]

One instance in "Gallicanus" which Magnin cites occurs in scene v of Part I. "Introducuntur honorfice *(they are introduced with ceremony)*" appears in the Munich codex with a variant reading inserted just above it, namely, "introducantur honorifice *(let them be introduced with ceremony)*." This change from "u" to "a" is only one of many insertions made by a scribe in this manuscript. The Cologne codex, which in the opinion of some, may have been an earlier copy and a purer text, reads "introducantur."

On the other hand in Gallicanus, Part I, scene vii, both the Munich and Cologne manuscripts read "Precede (praecede) collectim comitantur ('Proceed.' *They go out together,)*" This is, in affect, a true *didascalia*. In his 1906 edition, Strecker changes "comitantur" to read "comitamur," basing his alteration on an erasure in the Munich codex. Zeydel believes this is an arbitrary alteration and notes that Strecker has retained the original form "comitantur" in his 1930 edition.[68]

In "Calimachus," scene viii, another potential *didascalia* is argued. The Munich codex would seem, in this instance, to support the production theory since it reads, "Expavete *(tremble)*," a form of direct address indicating an audience of more than one person whereas Andronicus is actually speaking to John, the only other character. All other verbs addressing John are in the singular form. However, the Cologne codex reads, "Expaveo *(I tremble)*."

If the above instances are true *didascalia,* they almost seem to intrude, because the dialogue throughout effectively assumes the task of directing. There is never a time in production when the actors need question stage movement and business.

Oculia, as seen in Hrotsvitha, is a variation of Celsus' ocular demonstration:[69]

113

It consists, first, in forming a clear conception of what we wish to say, secondly, in giving this adequate expression, and thirdly, in lending it additional brilliance, . . . for vivid illustration, or, as some prefer to call it, representation, is something more than mere clearness, since the latter merely lets itself be seen whereas the former thrusts itself upon our notice.[70]

Hrotsvitha might almost be considered extravagant in her use of *oculia*. Zeydel, the first to call attention to this characteristic of the plays, speaks of it as a "technique of immediacy which demands acting and stage business—a technique which is thoroughly characteristic of the ingrained dramatist." [71]

Chasles is convinced that Hrotsvitha selected her vocabulary from classical and the vernacular, artistically blending them into a diction to suit her own needs.[72] The following line from "Gallicanus" is offered as an example of a classic quotation "in reverse" expressed in the language of the tenth century:

CLASSICAL: Veni, vidi, vici.

CAESAR: I came I saw, I conquered!

HROTSVITHA: Promovimus, hostes impegimus, commisimus, victi sumus.[73]

GALLICANUS: We pushed on, we met the enemy, we engaged them in battle, and were defeated.

Typically classical—specifically Terentian—are such brisk exclamations as: *hercle, edepol, euax, pro dolor, hem*; and such idioms as: *non flocci facio* and *di te perdant*.[74] It may even be that Hrotsvitha patterned the conciseness of her six titles on those of the six plays of Terence, for the former exhibit the same exclamatory terseness as the latter, to wit: there are the "Gallicanus," "Dulcitius," "Calimachus," "Abraham," "Pafnutius," and "Sapientia" of Hrotsvitha as compared to the "Andria," "Timorumenos," "Eunuchus," "Phormio," "Hecyra," and "Adelphoe" of Terence.

114

Hrotsvitha's lines are shot through with the frequent use of the classical diminutive form: *puellulae, saepiuscule, tinnulae, tenella, clancula, cellula, filiolae, corpuscula, palmulis, craticula, tantillulae, sororculam, homullula, candidulos, corpuscula,* and *flosculos.* These are but a few of the many examples of the diminutive.

Chorus.—Another classical element which finds a homogeneous setting in the medieval plays of Hrotsvitha, and contributes to their theatricality is a remnant of the Greek chorus. There are the Lords and Soldiers in "Gallicanus"; in "Dulcitius," the weeping Ladies-in-Waiting; in "Calimachus," the Friends; in "Pafnutius," the Lovers and the Disciples; in "Sapientia," the Matrons. The main function of these groups, who speak and act in unison, lies in their supporting roles. In the play, "Dulcitius," [75] the weeping chorus not only contributes to a more complete portraiture of a main character, Dulcitius, but it also advances the plot. So, too, in "Gallicanus" [76] and "Pafnutius," [77] the soldiers and disciples perform a like function. The chorus also contributes considerably to the spectacle quality of the plays. For example, note the military escort in "Gallicanus" [78] and the funeral corteges in "Calimachus" and "Sapientia." [79]

Structural facilities.—Perhaps, the most conclusive argument supporting the theatricality of the plays, as evidenced externally under the influence of the classical, is found in the permanent structural facilities of Gandersheim. Highly reminiscent of the Roman street scenes, as provided for in Terence, are the settings implied in the action of Hrotsvitha's plays. They could reasonably have been staged in the Romanesque arcades of the cloister and garden. Nicoll observes that the best preserved examples of the typical Graeco-Roman theatre is that at Orange in France. It has an imposing architectural façade, broken by three doors, which serves as a background for the actors.[80]

The extensive treatment of the classical influence upon the plays of Hrotsvitha bears out a previous statement that herein will be found the most persuasive arguments for theatricality. From the internal evidences, involving characterization, dialogue, plot structure, plot characteristics, and catharsis through the external evidences of costume, style and diction, the chorus, and structural facilities, there are likenesses too pronounced to be accidental. They must have been predetermined and so structured.

Although this exposition of the classical influence cannot conclude with the evidence that the plays were put on the stage, it can assert that the potential for performance does lie within this evidence.

Traces of the Mimetic Influence

Contrary to the modern orthodox view which "involves a complete break in the dramatic tradition," this study uses the premise advanced by Nicoll [81] that certain features of the Roman mimic stage endured through the tenth century. The famous Vatican Terence (Cod. lat. 3868), a ninth-century miniature by Adelricus of Corvey, shows an amphitheatrical enclosure, a poet's reader, and a group of *ioculatores,* who, according to Hugutius, are identified with *mimi* as "imitators of human things." [82]

Nicoll summarizes the evidence thus:

A continuance of 'imitation' (the mime idea), a continuance of a fool tradition, with certain definite costume peculiarities and the continuity in the use of masks—all of these lead us to believe that at least some of the myriads of *jongleurs* with whom the Middle Ages are filled inherited part of the ancient mimic tradition. Dancing, gesticulating, they crowd in upon us, those *jongleurs* and those mimes.[83]

One of the most complete extant descriptions of the mime in its essence dates back to Chrysostom (d. 407):

What tumult! What satanic clamour! What diabolic dress! Here comes a youth, with hair combed back, who makes him-

116

self effeminate in look, in manner, in dress—aye, in every-thing takes on the shape and guise of a tender girl. Here comes an old man with his hair all shaved, who has cast off shame with his hair, and who stands there to receive slaps on the face and who is prepared for all that is said and done. And the women too! With uncovered heads, all shame lost, they stand talking to the people, aiming at unchastity, arousing the minds of the spectators to wantonness and obscenity. For these wanton words, these ridiculous manners, these foolish tonsures, these ways of walking, these dresses, these voices, that softness of limb, that winking of the eyes, these pipes and flutes, these dramas and arguments—aye, all are full of utter wantonness. Here are to be seen naught but fornication, adultery, courtesan women, men pretending to be women, and soft-limbed boys.[84]

There is no question but that Hrotsvitha knew the mime referred to by Chrysostom, as the writer will illustrate fur-ther in a discussion of "Dulcitius." However, according to von Winterfeld,[85] there was another pattern she might have followed, namely, the comic Christian mime, one of which resulted in the martyrdom of the mimic, Genesius, who was subsequently raised to the altars of the Church and called St. Genesius, patron of actors:

In his Mimus (I 82 ff. 566f.) he [Reich] spoke in detail of the christological mimes who abandoned the faith and the ceremonies of the Christians and their martyrdom to the mockery of the pagans. The typical example is the mimic art of Genesius. As a pagan, he had studied all the Christian practices, in order that he and his company could represent them realistically for the pleasure of the Emperor Diocletian. The substance of the mimic representation was this; Gene-sius collapsed in the open street and demanded baptism, as though he were seriously ill. We must now consider that many, even Constantine the Great, postponed baptism until they felt that their end was near; so Genesius gave an imita-tion of just such a half-Christian. Next scene: Genesius lies in bed; his friends are standing around him. He feels very heavy and longs for relief. His visitors answer, 'We are no cabinet makers to lay you on the carpenter's bench and plane a piece off you,'—typical coarse mimes' wit. He made it clear to them that he wanted to become a Christian. Loud applause from the Emperor at this splendid joke. They call the priest and the sexton; they come, ask about his wishes, and the baptism is performed it seems on the spot, with all the ceremonies. But soon a soldier comes to lead him before the Emperor. He confesses that he is a Christian—and then, of course, in the play, the condemnation and execution are about to follow. Then an unexpected incident occurs. The actor who was just now scoffing at Christianity, is suddenly inspired by the Spirit; he professes himself in earnest to be that which he had just then been declaiming in his role; in an enthusiastic speech he urges the Emperor and the public to be converted. So then the play becomes bloody earnest; they seize him, condemn and execute him. So the actor becomes a saint; and this occurrence is said to have taken place several times.[86]

In the hands of Hrotsvitha, however, the tables are turned and the pagan characters are subjected to satiric subtleties and are goaded delicately.

In enumerating the traces of the mime in Hrotsvitha's plays the title-prologue, character and costume, and gesticulation are classified under external evidences. Since by its very nature the mime is visual and aural, the external features are given priority of treatment. Under internal evidence, the comic and satiric elements of the mime are considered.

Title-prologue.—Reich notes that Hrotsvitha followed the practice of the mimes in her use of the title-prologue:

Hrotsvitha's dramas with their tables of contents in the title are perfectly valid examples of the practice of the mimes of that time: 'We will act out the wonderful history of the Duke Gallicanus; the Emperor Constantine promised him his daughter;' and so forth.[87]

118

He further points out the difference between her prologues and those of Terence, indicating that Hrotsvitha's purpose in using this mimic device was to entitle and summarize, whereas Terence used the traditional short title and a twofold prologue. The first Terentian prologue is similar to our current theatre program; it was used to announce the play, the actors and musicians, and theatre location; it was shorter than the second and served, to a certain extent, as a warning signal to quiet the audience. The second prologue was announced by the author, who referred to himself and the subject of his play, without, however, offering a summary. Reich offers the prologue of the mimographer, Laberius, as one of the few extant mimic illustrations of this latter type:

Necessity which many wished but few were able to escape, has brought me low. A flattering speech has captured me now that I am an old man, although in youth no ambition, no bribery, no fear of authority could have influenced me. Now sixty years of age, I set out this morning as a Roman knight; I shall return home as a mime. Truly I have lived by this one day longer than I should have lived. Like a sepulchre, I bear nothing but a name.[88]

However, in the second century A.D., Gaius Sulpicius Apollinaris, a critic, added a third type of prologue to the plays of Terence, called a *periocha* (summary). Reich claims that the mime also changed the character of its prologue at this time, and believes it was from this form that Hrotsvitha borrowed the pattern for her prologue:

Also the mime, especially in that time when the dramatic element was being limited by it, probably reduced the real prologue, which a player had to act (the *pronuntiatio fabulae*), to a prosaic summary, straightforwardly instructive to the listeners. This summary may be said to correspond to the oldest theatre playbills which did not always limit themselves to the bare title, but often explained what was to be presented in the comedy. Hrotsvitha's long titles, in the same artistic rhyming prose as the drama itself, are a substitute for the *periochae* of Terence and, indeed, in a form adapted to the mime as she knew it.[89]

The following, quoted from the play, "Gallicanus," shows conclusively how closely Hrotsvitha imitated the later form of the mime prologue:

CONVERSIO GALLICANI PRIN-CIPIS MILITIAE qui, iturus ad bellum contra Scythas, sacratissimam virginem Constantiam, Constantini imperatoris filiam, desponsavit, sed in conflictu praelii nimium coartatus, per Iohannem et Paulum primicerios Constantiae conversus, ad baptisma convolavit caelibemque vitam elegit, postea autem iubente Iuliano apostata in exilium missus, martirio est coronatus. Sed et Iohannes et Paulus eodem iubente clam occisi et in domo occulte sunt sepulti. Nec mora, percussoris filius, a daemonio arreptus, patris commissum et martirum confitendo meritum iuxta eorem sepulchra salvatus una cum patre est baptizatus.[90]

THE CONVERSION OF GALLI-CANUS, COMMANDER-IN-CHIEF. On the eve of his departure for a campaign against the Scythians, Gallicanus is betrothed to the Emperor Constantine's daughter, Constance, a consecrated virgin.

When threatened with defeat in battle, Gallicanus is converted by John and Paul, Grand Almoners to Constance. He is immediately baptized and takes the vow of celibacy.

Later he is exiled by order of Julian the Apostate, and receives the crown of martyrdom. John and Paul are put to death by the same prince and buried secretly in their own house. Not long after, the son of their executioner becomes possessed by a devil. He is cured after confessing the crime committed by his father. He bears witness to the merits of the martyrs, and is baptized, together with his father.

Character and costume.—Nicoll states that "the animal drama developed naturally out of mimic dances such as are depicted on a number of early Attic vases." [91] Since acts in which human beings represented animals are in the mimic tradition, it does not seem too strained to recognize the serpent in "Calimachus" as a mimic influence. [92]

The mimes also employed any styles of costume or couture which might be derogatory to those at whom their jests were aimed. One of their favorite disguises was the garb and tonsure of a monk. [93] Hrotsvitha, apparently knowing this, so apparels the seducer of Mary in "Abraham." [94] The devil mask, which is often exclusively associated with the later religious drama of the middle ages, actually stems from the mimes. Nicoll remarks this, "In a prohibition against festival merriment, pronounced by Concilium Nanetense in 890, there is a direct reference to *larvas daemonum*—'devils' masks.'" [95]

Gesticulation.—A manuscript, dated *ca.* 1000, calls attention to gesticulation, a uniquely mimetic practice:

This manuscript thus dates for us the dissolution of the antique iconography, for in its miniatures the old tradition is visible only as a norm from which the enterprising Romanesque draughtsman departs. . . . The literary reticence of the old cycle begins to give way to dramatic illustration with gestures and postures that are no longer classic. . . . The Graeco-Roman rule that one hand only should gesture is broken in favor of the mediaeval preference for two; the crossing of arms is introduced. [96]

Without doubt, this break with classical tradition relative to gestures had been coming to issue over a period of years. It seems to have crystallized in the general ferment of the tenth century. Hrostvitha's incorporation of this newly evolving dramatic feature adds considerably to the theatricality of her plays.

Comic element.—The fact that Hrotsvitha was not unfamiliar with the mime in its grosser aspects, is attested to by her facile, if sparing, use of comic and satiric elements, justified by internal motivation.

"Dulcitius" is frequently classed as a "farce." Could it be that the author intends to personify in this character the marks of vice—bestiality, lechery, lack of self-discipline—as a contrast to the virtue of the three maidens? If so, Hrotsvitha found the most refined weapon to use against vice, namely, ridicule. The antics of Dulcitius, who, in attempting to enter the prison cell of the young girls, gets mysteriously involved with the pots and pans, not only bring upon him the amusement of the girls, but also the jeering of the soldiers and the embarrassment of his wife.

Broad comedy, *per se*, in which the mimes excelled, apparently touched Hrotsvitha lightly. Her use of this element in "Dulcitius" is motivated by the need of a more graphic portrayal of the character, Dulcitius. The antics of the soldiers in the same scenes are intended, no doubt, to strengthen the farcical quality of this same character.[97] Hrotsvitha serves this ridiculous morsel to the audience, possibly as a diversion, but more likely, as a lesson.

One other scene carries the suggestion of this type of comedy when Abraham goaded himself with the words, "Chatter, make lewd jests like an idle boy!"[98] and later referred to this chatter as *"iocularia verba,"*[99] a term identified with the mime from its inception.

Satiric element.—Her satire is less obvious to a reader than to an audience. Contrary to the opinions of those who are acquainted with Hrotsvitha only on the page and not on the stage, there are occasions when the audience is delighted with her satiric wit. For example, the baiting of Hadrian by Sapientia is an excellent example of sophisticated subtlety. In answer to Hadrian's simple question regarding the age of her daughters, Sapientia launches into an involved mathematical answer which changes the Emperor's inquisition into the prisoner's disquisition. Hadrian's reaction is a mixture of surprise, bewilderment, and pique. Hrotsvitha adds to the humorous element through the delighted reaction of the girls and the utter stupefaction of Antiochus.[100]

More direct is the irony in the scene from "Gallicanus," in which John and Paul mock the power of Julian the Apostate. When the latter refers to his status as a priest, the two disciples willingly consign him to a chaplaincy in hell.[101]

Although there is substantial external evidence of the mimetic influence in the plays, it seems that more recent scholars have extended the issue when they have claimed that the "Stauferzeit recognized the dramas of Hrotsvitha as spirit of their [the mimes'] spirit." [102]

More attuned to the conclusion of this section is Reich's statement, "I mean, . . . that Hrotsvitha, when she began her first drama, envisioned indeed performance as a mime, even if only in her own mind." [103]

Traces of the Liturgical Influence

The tenth century was unique in many ways. One of its most significant movements was, according to Hunningher, the fusion of "the best of the mime" and the liturgical trope —a "fact which throws sudden light on the all too dim stage of the medieval theatre, . . . here was no longer commemorative recital, but an occasion for mimic portrayal and re-creation of an event from the past—here *was* a play, no longer symbolism—that was critical change." [104] While the trope was contributing its vast reservoir of scripture, hagiography, and legends as subject matter, the mime was furnishing the professional talent that was to endow the "new drama" with a comparatively fresh aesthetic quality.

Research has revealed few statements by Hrotsvithan scholars supporting the fact that she was a component part of the contemporary liturgical dramatic movement. Zeydel, in quoting von Winterfeld, suggests that she might have composed liturgical sequences similar to those of Notker.[105] To date,

123

however, no indications of such writings have been discovered.

This section will attempt to show that Hrotsvitha, a canoness, and furthermore, a Benedictine canoness, could hardly have escaped the pervasive influence of the liturgy which is the core of the Benedictine way of life. Her activity as a nun, in all its aspects—prayer, education, profession—must have been pregnant with liturgical overtones. Therefore, it is argued, the traces of this conservative fusion of the mime and trope, as well as the hallowed traditions of the Church, find both internal and external expression in her plays as subject-matter sources, as language, and as facets of style.

Subject-matter sources.—As regards subject matter, it is Magnin who supplies extensive research on the inception of each of the plays. He is quoted here in support of the source material.[106]

It has been argued by many scholars whether "Gallicanus" "forms deux pièces ou, du moins, une pièce en deux parties." Magnin believes it was originally two separate dramas, alleging as his main reason the inclusion of the word *amen* at the end of the first act[107] and, as a subsidiary reason, the fact that the two parts stem from entirely different sources. It is generally agreed that the first part is "la contrepartie de l'histoire du comte Bernhard et de l'abbesse de Gandersheim, Gerberge Ire."[108] The martyrdom of John and Paul, on the other hand, which forms the second part, is taken from the *Acta Sanctorum.*[109]

The *Acta Trium Sororum* supplies the subject matter for the play, "Dulcitius." This legend, according to Magnin, was popular in the Greek and Latin churches during the entire span of the middle ages.[110] The Bollandists list the martyrdom of the three sisters, Agape, Chionia, and Irena (under Diocletian at Thessalonica, 290 A.D.), under two dates, April third and fifth, one supplied by the Latin and Greek hagiographers and the other taken from the ancient records of St. Anastasia. An unusual feature of this play is the author's preoccupation with Dulcitius to the extent that Magnin refers to it as a religious farce which does not detract in any way from the heroism of the martyrs.[111]

It is believed that the original story of "Calimachus" dates back to the writings of a Babylonian bishop, which were translated into Latin at a later date by Julius Africanus. Fabricius later edited this romantic adventure which is now included in the *Apocrypha of the New Testament*.[112]

The *Vies des Pères de déserts* [113] is the source of the story of "Abraham." There is some diversity of opinion regarding the identity of the hermit, Ephrem, who might be a contemporary of Abraham or a later fourth-century inhabitant of Edessa. This is considered by scholars as one of the best, if not the best, of the dramas.

The story of "Pafnutius," similar in plot to that of "Abraham," comes from an unidentified Greek writer of the fourth century.[114] Latin and French versions of this theme have since appeared in the *Acta Sanctorum* and in the *Vies des Pères de déserts*.

The *Acta Sanctorum*[115] is the primary source for the material treated in "Sapientia." Comments on the martyrs are very brief in this collection and it is a credit to Hrotsvitha's ability that she has created such convincing characters from so little.

Reviewing the preceding sources it is clear that the plays have their undisputed origin in patristic and biblical literature. This, in itself, stamps their liturgical character. There are also numerous allegorical evidences taken from the Old and New Testaments.

The most recognizable allegory parallels the Passion and Death of Christ and is highly reminiscent of the Easter trope, which at this time was at its height under ecclesiastical auspices. It occurs in the play, "Sapientia." Christ was interrogated by Pontius Pilate; He was scourged and mocked by the soldiers; He died and was mourned by His mother and the three Marys; He arose from the tomb on the third day;

after forty days He ascended into heaven. Sapientia and her daughters are interrogated by Hadrian; the girls are scourged and mocked by the soldiers; they die and are mourned by their mother and the three matrons; they are carried to the tomb on the third day; after forty days Sapientia dies and her soul goes to join her daughters in heaven.[116]

There is another allegory in "Sapientia" worth noting. This is the episode where Charity walks through the fiery furnace untouched. Its similarity to the story of the three young men in the fiery furnace in the "Book of Daniel" is so closely drawn that it is quoted here:

Sapientia, v, 152.

HADRIAN: Then order a furnace to be heated for three days and three nights and let her be cast into the flames.

Daniel, iii, 20.

NABUCHODONOSOR: He would have the furnace heated seven times hotter than its wont and into this raging furnace he bade his chosen bodyguard throw Sidrach, Misach, and Abdenago.

Sapientia, vi, 153, 154.

ANTIOCHUS: Then I had her cast into a fiery furnace which glowed scarlet with the tremendous heat. ... The flames belched forth, and five thousand men were burned to death. ... She ran to and fro playing in the fierce whirlwind of smoke and flame, and sang praises to her God. Those who watched closely said that three men dressed in white walked by her side.[117]

DANIEL, iii, 20, 22-24, 49-50.

DANIEL: So fiercely was the furnace heated that those who threw them in were burned to death. Meanwhile these three fell fast bound into the heart of the fires that raged in it. And there, in the hottest of flames, they walked to and fro, singing to God their praises, blessing the Lord. ... But an angel of the Lord had gone down into the furnace and he drove the flames away from it, so that these three were untouched, and the fire brought them neither pain nor discomfort.[118]

Further allegorical traces are apparent. Abraham's solicitude for his niece, Mary, on their homeward journey, reminds one of the solicitude of Joseph for Mary on another journey. When Mary promises her uncle that she will follow in his steps, Abraham says, "Not so! I am going on foot, but you—you shall have a horse so that the stony road shall not hurt your delicate feet." [119] Representations of possession by the devil occur twice in "Gallicanus." When the soldiers are planning to confiscate the property and possessions of Gallicanus, they are suddenly stopped by an inexplicable incident which they rush to tell Julian, "No sooner did one of us set foot on the threshold than he was straightway stricken with leprosy or madness." [120] Again, after Terentianus has carried out the persecution of John and Paul, he notices the violent actions of his son and anxiously inquires the cause. He is told, "He grinds his teeth, foams at the mouth, and rolls his eyes like a madman. He is surely possessed by a devil." [121]

A final episode merits a remark. The revenge which Dulcitius attempts to inflict upon the three Greek maidens—exposing them naked to the public gaze—resembles the indignity imposed upon the virgin martyr, Agnes.[122]

Language.—Scholars, if they admit her existence, uniformly accept the fact that Hrotsvitha read and wrote in Latin. This gave her unlimited access to the literary treasures of the Christian, as well as pagan, writers, When reading her lines, one recognizes her frequent use of the Scriptures. Yet so smoothly are these biblical allusions incorporated into the text, they seem to lose their lofty identity and become the expression of the author. For example, in the play, "Abraham," Hrotsvitha uses the language of the Parable of the Good Shepherd in describing the joy of Abraham after he has reclaimed Mary, the "lost sheep." One of the most touching excerpts of this parable, "There is more joy in heaven over one sinner who does penance than over ninety-nine just who need not penance," is aptly fitted to the denouement of the play:

Abraham, ix, 177, 33.

ABRAHAM: Et merito, nam fa-
langes angelicae gaudentes dominum laudant super pecca-
toris conversione.

EFFREM: Nec mirum; nullius
namque iusti magis delecta-
tur perseverantia quam impii
poenitentia.

St. Luke, xv, 7.

JESUS: Dico vobis, quod ita
gaudium erit in caelo super
uno peccatore poenitentiam
agente, quam super nonagin-
tanovem justis, qui non indi-
gent poenitentia.[123]

Direct quotations from the Scriptures are inserted skill-
fully in the dialogue. The following verse, "God has chosen
the foolish things of the world to confound the wise," serves
one of the disciples when he expresses to the philosopher,
Paphnutius, his wonder at the ways of God:

Pafnutius, i, 183, 35.

DISCIPULI: Congratulamur tu-
ae benignitati, sed terremur
sententia apostoli, dicentis:
'nam stulta mundi elegit deus
ut confunderet sophistica.'

Corinthians, I, i, 27.

PAUL: ... sed quae stulta sunt
mundi elegit Deus, ut confun-
dat sapientes.[124]

Frequently, an overflow of emotion is expressed in the
form of a lamentation or prayer with biblical overtones.
Thais, despairing of salvation as her death approaches, complains that she is not worthy of forgiveness. To this Paphnutius answers in the words of the psalmist, "If the Lord takes
heed of our iniquities, who has the strength to bear it?"

Pafnutius, xii, 198, 24.

PAFNUTIUS: Si deus iniquitates observabit, nemo sustinebit.

Psalm, cxxix, 3

PSALMIST: Si iniquitates ob-
servaveris Domine, Domine,
quis sustinebit?[125]

Consoled by his words, Thais, in a sudden upsurge of hope,
utters a prayer recalling the psalm of Alleluia:

Pafnutius, xii, 199, 20.

THAIS: Unde laude illum caeli concentus omnisque terrae surculus, necnon universae animalis species atque confusae aquarum gurgites, quia non solum peccantes patitur, sed etiam poenitentibus praemia gratis largitur.[127]

Psalm, cxlviii, 4, 9-10, 14.

PSALMIST: Laudate eum coeli coelorum, et aquae omnes, quae super coelos sunt. . . . Montes, et omnes colles; ligna fructifera, et omnes cedri. . . . Bestiae et universae pecora. . . . et altum tribuit cornu populo suo.[126]

The language of the liturgy is really the language of song. It would seem that Hrotsvitha, who spent some hours each day chanting the Divine Song, would not be insensitive to its dramatic quality. She does not hesitate to introduce song wherever it can be used effectively:

Dulcitius, iii, 140, 30.

DULCITIUS: Quid agunt captivae sub hoc noctis tempore?

MILITIS: Vacant hymnis.[128]

DULCITIUS: What are the prisoners doing at this hour of the night?

SOLDIERS: They pass the time singing hymns.

Style.—To attribute to the liturgical influence an important part in the development of Hrotsvitha's style would presuppose a dominant motif existing in the dramatic tropes of the time. Such a premise would be contrary to historical fact. Nicoll says that the liturgical drama was hardly recognizable as a drama since its origin, its substance, its participants, its locale were basically untheatrical.[129] What impact, then, did the liturgical spirit of the time have upon Hrotsvitha and her plays? It imparted to her a spiritual vitality which found expression in her writings, and marked them with detail, reserve, and apostolic significance.

The dramatic trope of the tenth century is admittedly founded on detail. Every incident in the liturgy was seized upon, expanded and embellished to capture the spirit of the

129

participants and the attention of the audience. The processions—seasonal, festival, ferial, ceremonial; clerical installations and investitures; household and family consecrations; triumphal and passional feasts—each contributed of its essence and accidents to the liturgical drama. This devotion to detail is reflected in all of Hrotsvitha's dramas.

Nothing is too insignificant for her studied and embarrassing elaboration. She went into battle with Gallicanus; she explored the greasy cavern of a pantry with Dulcitius; she suffered the pangs of unrequited love with Callimachus and the ravages of unsolicited love with Drusiana; she entered the brothel with Abraham and Paphnutius and the inhuman desert cell with Thais and Mary; she suffered every refinement of the tortures with the martyrs and went with them to their death. In a climate of scholarly discipline and liturgical fullness, Hrotsvitha could not have done otherwise.

Often in the tropes, Hrotsvitha obviously heard and saw the efficacy of well-placed narration, but in her plays she uses it sparingly and never at the cost of theatrical effectiveness. In "Gallicanus," her neophyte attempt, which some critics describe as "halting" and "patched-up," there is an intelligent use of narration which offers relief from the fast-moving action preceding it.[130] It is also used to advantage in "Abraham" to cover an unusually long span of time.[131]

When the "best of the mime" brought to the dramatic trope a "gentle humor," the Church, fearful of innovations and levity, provided a strict censorship over the spectacles under its patronage. This statement does not wholly agree with Hunningher, who claims, "The clerical supervisors did not oppose the addition of comic scenes, for they increased the attractiveness of the Church-plays, making them a more effective weapon against the worldly mime."[132] The Church did exercise moderation on the scenes designed to afford comic relief.[133]

Hrotsvitha must have known the mind of the Church in

this matter, consequently the occasional humor, which relieves the earnestness of her lines, is usually sophisticated and perceptive:

Gallicanus, I, v, 134, 13.

IULIANUS: Frivola; ego quondam stultus talia exercui et clericatum in ecclesia optinui.

JULIAN: Absurd! Once I too was fool enough to believe in these meaningless practices. I was a priest of your Church.

IOHANNES: Placetne tibi, o Paule, clericus?

JOHN: Do you hear, Paul? How do you like this priest?

PAULUS: Diaboli capellanus.[134]

PAUL: Very well—as the devil's chaplain.

Finally, the fullness of the liturgy imposed upon Hrotsvitha an apostolic mission. She writes, "I have been compelled to apply my mind and my pen to glorify the innocent to the best of my ability." [135] Just as the Church seized upon the trope as an opportunity to carry out its apostolic mission, namely, "to teach and to preach," so, too, Hrotsvitha found in her ability to write drama a most potent and pliable instrument "to teach and to preach." That she could do so without offence and unostentatiously is clear from the following excerpts:

Calimachus, ix, 154, 18.

ANDRONICHUS: In hoc tamen illud est vel maxime admirandum, cur huius, qui pravum voluit, resuscitatio magis, quam eius, qui consensit, divina sit voce praenuntiata, nisi quia forte hic, carnali deceptus delectatione, deliquit ignorantia, iste autem sola malitia.

ANDRONICUS: What astonishes me most is that the Divine Word should have promised the resurrection of him who had planned the crime, and not of him who was only an accomplice. Maybe it is because the one, blinded by the passion of the flesh, knew not what he did, while the other sinned of deliberate malice.

131

Abraham, iv, 174, 30.

ABRAHAM: Peccata quidem tua sunt gravia, fateor; sed superna pietas maior est omni creatura. Unde tristitias rumpe datumque poenitendi spatiolum pigritando noli neglegere, quatinus superhabundet divina gratia, ubi, habundavit facinorum abominatio.

ABRAHAM: The mercy of heaven is greater than you or your sins. Let your sadness be dispersed by its glorious rays. O, Mary, do not let apathy prevent your seizing the moment for repentance. It matters not how wickedness has flourished. Divine grace can flourish still more abundantly.

Sapientia, v, 209, 22.

FIDES: Quid enim stultius, quid videri potest insipientius, quam quod hortatur nos, contempto creatore universitatis, venerationem inferre metallis?

FAITH: What is it but folly to tell us to insult the Creator of the world and worship a bit of metal!

Thus, not only did Hrotsvitha use her literary talent in the service of the liturgical tradition, but because of the very nature of her life, she exemplified in her dramas the characteristic marks of this tradition—familiarity with the official writings of the Church, in particular, with the Scriptures, the use of Latin, perfection of detail, restraint in humor, devotion to the parable, and, finally, manifestation of a personal obligation to extend and advance the kingdom of God on earth.

Traces of the New Drama

Hrotsvitha was "la religieuse, imitatrice à la fois et créatrice," said Chasles.[136] There seems to be a remarkable accord among writers that Hrotsvitha contributed something new to drama both by presenting old elements in a new guise and by introducing new ones.[137] The final section of this chapter will briefly summarize these innovations, some of which find a surprising parallel in the new forms and practices of recognized drama in the second millennium. As in the previous sections of this chapter, these anticipatory traces will be considered under internal evidences—motivation, characterization, and handling of plot; and under external evidences—poetic meter, treatment of torture scenes, and descriptive dialogue.

Hrotsvitha's purpose in writing has been discussed previously in this study, and in large part, has been attributed to the apostolic character of the liturgy, which ideally compels man, under its influence, to extend the boundaries of his interest—to become his brother's keeper. Such samaritanism would imply not only interest in, but involvement in, the problems of others. There is evidence in Hrotsvitha's preface that she was concerned about the moral impact of Terence on the people of her time.[138] She assayed her abilities to deal with this contemporary situation and, diffidently, she produced the first "problem" drama. Not until the latter half of the nineteenth century do we again meet the "problem" drama, as it appeared, first, in the mechanical and superficial art of Sardou and later in the sculptured greatness of Ibsen.

The most favorable remarks advanced by scholars on "the general dramatic excellence" of the plays of Hrotsvitha concern the realistic nature of her characters. Never before her day had the emotions been so frankly portrayed in subject matter drawn from sacred sources. For example, even though Mary is first introduced to us as an innocent child, the words which Hrotsvitha places in her mouth are pert and naïvely sensual, and presage her moral lapse.[139]

It is evident that every word and action of the characters are the result of stress of feeling under the duress of both natural and supernatural law. In no instance do they maintain passive neutrality. The realism of the classical dramatists characterized man as "good" or "evil" to arouse the audience on a humanistic plane to admire the former and scorn the latter; the mimic writers depicted "good" and "evil" as completely amoral on a naturalistic plane;[140] Hrotsvitha's realism portrays "good" and "evil" on a supernatural plane, which by its very essence, is built upon the natural and gives a moral and psychological coloring to her characters. The claim made here for Hrotsvitha is that her characterization, though far less impressively viewed in dramaturgy, is an isolated but amazing phenomenon lying in the path of the realistic and psychological drama between Euripides and Ibsen.

A third trace of modernism is evident in the manner in which Hrotsvitha handles her plot. Fearlessly, she selected material which, in her day, was forbidden. She found it necessary to modify the prevailing classical dramatic form in order to adapt it to her plot which she develops within the boundaries of good taste, producing a new blend fittingly described in the words of Chasles:

The nuances in the unfolding of the heart's desires, the fusion of voluntary chastity and devoted love, the moderate expression of strong passion, the metaphysical in the emotional, all these characteristics of modern civilization are found in Hrotsvitha in their first traces, and, as it were, in their virginal form.[141]

Externally, the juxtaposition of opposites within the plot is expressed consciously by a change in poetic rhythm, a device employed constantly by modern writers to differentiate moods. Chasles illustrates this variety in meter:

When the hermit reveals himself to Mary and reproaches her for her misconduct, the meter, which we see as erratic and as undulating as the action of a harlot, becomes heavy, regular, and as constant as the impressiveness of a dogmatic tract.[142]

One of the most frequent objections to the performance of the plays is the prominence of the torture[143] scenes and the

134

use of miracles.[144] Classical drama "generally avoided violent physical action, deaths occurring off-stage and being related by a character known as a messenger." [145] Nicoll offers documented data showing that the mimes went beyond the classical conventions and presented scenes of unbridled violence and ruthless sadism before the audience.[146] Hrotsvitha presented allegedly gory scenes of persecution on the stage, a theatrical convention justified by the mimic tradition. However, the spiritual aura surrounding her portrayal of torture removes from it a revulsion of feeling on the part of the audience. These scenes, together with her use of divine intervention, antedate the acceptance of these realistic conventions as similarly used in the miracle and mystery plays of a few centuries later.

Descriptive dialogue completes the enumeration of external evidences of theatricality which find a parallel in later drama. In this respect, dialogue reclassifies itself under two aspects; the first deals with words and phrases which seem to demand visual and aural representation. The second concerns the stage directions inherent in the dialogue. Both of these features reveal Hrotsvitha's keen discernment and seem to be derived from her natural poetic ability.

The following illustrations exemplify her facility with expressive words and phrases. When the Scythians "boldly resist our power," a period of history unfolds before the eyes ("Gallicanus," I,i,117,18, *resistere paci nostrisque temere*). Constantine refers to his daughter as a "reward," thus implying that Gallicanus expects no small gain for his constant and devoted service ("Gallicanus, I,i,119,9, *non leve appetit praemium*). Irena, reproaching Diocletian when arguing with him against the superiority of the pagan gods, says, "What could be more shameful baseness, what baser shame than to venerate slaves as if they were lords?" ("Dulcitius," i,139,26, *quae inhonestas turpior, quae turpitudo maior*). Then asked to explain her use of the word "slaves," she replies, "A god who can be bought cheap in the marketplace, what is he but a slave?" ("Dulcitius," 1,139,30, *Nonne is est cuiusvis ser-*

135

vus, qui ab artifice pretio comparatur ut empticius?). Abraham, anxious to reach Mary as quickly as possible, asks for a charger ("Abraham," iv,170,10, *sonipedem*—a horse with sounding feet). Sapientia refers to the words of Hadrian as "the satanical flattery of a serpent" ("Sapientia," iii,204,6, *serpentinis huius satanae lenociniis*). These are but a few of the visual and audible words and phrases crowding the pages of Hrotsvitha, which foreshadow the sensuous significance of the romantic writers.

The second aspect, stage directions inherent in the dialogue of the dramas give a decided impetus to the argument that the plays may have been performed. As late as 1945, Zeydel remarks that heretofore, attention does not seem to have been focused, to any considerable extent, on the theatrical qualities inherent in the dialogue. He points particularly to the stage directions therein when he says:

> The dialog is much enlivened by numerous explanations which almost demand acting and visual representation. . . . This technique of immediacy, as we might call it, is thoroughly characteristic of the ingrained dramatist. It makes the action so vivid that we constantly see the performers acting it out before our eyes. Especially should Hrotsvitha's frequent use of 'ecce' be noted, a demonstrative which points out a visible object or person with emphasis. If Curtius is correct in believing that this word is related to the root *oc-* in *oculus* (cf. the article on 'ecce' in the Harper unabridged Latin dictionary): . . . Hrotsvitha's fondness for it is particularly significant.[147]

Stage directions are verbalized over and over again denoting entrances and exits, stage movements, posturings, and handling of properties. A few examples from the many in the text will be offered to substantiate this statement.

Entrances and exits are suggestive of the ebb and flow of Shakespearean movement and cover extension of time and identification and change of locale. Had Hrotsvitha followed

Shakespeare in time, this theatrical device would not merit consideration here. However, since she preceded him by several centuries, and since there seems to be no evidence of the dialogue having been used consistently in this precise way prior to her time,[148] it may be concluded that Hrotsvitha's sensitivity to the dramatic impelled her to use dialogue in this manner. In presenting the technical illustration below, this study by no means implies a qualitative comparability between the authors:

Sapientia, iii, 141.	*Hamlet*, I, ii, 1011.
(Throne room of Hadrian.)	(Room in Castle.)
HADRIAN: Let these women be taken to the prison near our palace, and give them three days to reflect.	HAMLET: . . . So, fare you well. Upon the platform, 'twixt eleven and twelve, I'll visit you.
ANTIOCHUS: Soldiers, see that these women are well guarded and given no chance of escape.	ALL: Our duty to your honor. Farewell.

Scene iv of "Sapientia" and scene iii of "Hamlet" intervene to permit passage of time and change of locale:

Sapientia, v, 142.	*Hamlet*, I, iv, 1012.
(Temple of Diana in palace of Hadrian, three days later.)	(The Platform, that night.)
HADRIAN: Antiochus, bring the Greek prisoners before us. . . . The three days' respite which of our clemency granted you is over.[149]	HAMLET: . . . What hour now? HORATIO: I think it lacks of twelve. MARCELLUS: No, it is struck.[150]

Further illustrations are given below of verbalized entrances and exits as they mark the beginning and end of scenes, appear within scenes, and serve as announcements for succeeding scenes:

Gallicanus, I, vi, 124, 7 (Entrance at the beginning of scene).

IOHANNES: Praesto sumus, hera quos vocati.

JOHN: You sent for us, Highness. We are here.

Gallicanus, I, iv, 122, 29 (Exit at end of scene).

GALLICANUS: Statis, milites? currite, abite!

GALLICANUS: Are my soldiers still there? Come, fellows, hasten!

Gallicanus, I, ix, 125, 30 (Entrance within scene).

HOSTES: Heus, rex Bradan, sperandae fortuna victoriae illudit nos; en dextrae languescent, vires fatiscent, sed et inconstanti pectoris cogit nos discedere ab armis.

ONE OF THE ENEMY: Woe to us, King Braden! Fortune, who but now promised us victory, was mocking us. Our men are weakening, their strength is exhausted—they have lost heart and are giving up the struggle.

Dulcitius, i, 139, 8 (Exit within scene).

DIOCLETIANUS: Ista insanit; amoveatur.

DIOCLETIAN: The girl raves. Take her away.

CHIONIA: Mea germana non insanit, sed tui stultitiam iuste reprehendit.

CHIONIA: My sister does not rave. She is right.

DIOC: Ista inclementius bachatur; unde nostris conspectibus aeque subtrahatur, et tertia discutiatur.

DIOC: This maenad seems even more violent than the other! Remove her also from our presence, and we will question the third.

Pafnutius, vi, 192, 2 (Entrance announced in preceding scene).

PAFNUTIUS: Ecce, abbatissa occurrit. Admiror, quis illi nos adesse tam cito retulerit.

PAPHNUTIUS: But look! The abbess has come out to meet us. I wonder who can have told her so promptly of our arrival.

138

Sapientia, iv, 208, 5 (Exit announced in preceding scene).

FIDES: Pro ipsius amore sponsi promtae sumus mori. . . .

FAITH: For His love we are all ready to die. . . .

KARITAS: Consertis palmulis incedamus et vultum tyranni confundamus.[151]

CHARITY: Let us go hand in hand to the tyrant.

Lines indicating the movement of characters from one acting area to another are numerous:

Gallicanus, I, ii, 119, 24.

CONSTANTINUS: Huc ades, o filia Constantia, paucis te volo.

CONSTANTINE: Constance, my daughter, come nearer. I wish to speak to you.

Gallicanus, I, v, 123, 18.

CONSTANTIA: State, state, ne procidatis, sed libate mihi osculum amoris.

CONSTANCE:. Stand up, stand up! No, do not kneel. Salute me rather with a loving kiss.

Dulcitius, ii, 140, 6.

DULCITIUS: Producite, milites, producite, quas tenetis in carcere!

DULCITIUS: Soldiers, produce your prisoners.

MILITES: Ecce, quas vocasti!

SOLDIERS: The ones you want to see are in there.

Dulcitius, iv, 141, 11.

HIRENA: Lustrabo. Accedite, quaeso, per rimulas perspicite!

IRENA: I will go and look. Come quick and peep through the crack of the door.

Calimachus, iv, 151, 20.

ANDRONICHUS: Vae mihi infortunato! ex inproviso mortua est Drusiana. Curro sanctumque Iohannem advoco.

ANDRONICUS: Drusiana, Drusiana! Christ, what blow has befallen me. Drusiana is dead.

Sapientia, iii, 203, 18.

ADRIANUS: Huc ades, Antioche.

HADRIAN: Are you there, Antiochus?

ANTIOCHUS: Praesto sum domine.

ANTIOCHUS: At your service,
my lord.

Sapientia, v, 208, 19.

ANTIOCHUS: Procede, Sapientia, teque cum filiabus im-
peratori repraesenta.

ANTIOCHUS: Step forward, Sapientia, the Emperor has
asked for you and your
daughters.

SAPIENTIA: Pergite mecum, filiae, constanter, . . .[152]

SAPIENTIA: Walk with me
bravely, children, . . .

So, too, are posturings numerous, a term which covers the
bodily reaction to an emotional impact:

Gallicanus, II, viii, 136, 9.

CHRISTICOLAE: Stridet denti-
bus, sputa iacit, torquet in-
sana lumina; nam plenus est
daemonio. . . . Humi provol-
vitur seque ipsorum precibus
torqueri fatetur.

CHRISTIANS: He grinds his
teeth, foams at the mouth,
and rolls his eyes like a madman. He is possessed by a
devil. . . . he writhes on the
ground and cries out.

Dulcitius, ii, 140, 9.

DULCITIUS: Papae! quam pulchrae, quam venustae, quam
egregiae puellulae! . . .
Captus sum illarum specie.
. . . Exaestuo illas ad mei
amorem trahere.

DULCITIUS: Ye gods, but these
girls are beautiful! What
grace, what charms! . . . I am
enraptured. . . . I'm in love!
Do you think they will fall
in love with me?

Calimachus, iii, 150, 31.

DRUSIANA: ... sed te ipsum penitus sperno. . . . Nihil aliud nisi indignationem.[153]

DRUSIANA: Your love disgusts me; ... it moves me to indignation.

The handling and disposition of properties is always indicated in the lines:

Gallicanus, II, vii, 135, 19.

TERRENTIANUS: Imperator Iulianus, cui servio, misit vobis, Iohannes et Paule, pro sui clementia aureum simulachrum Iovis, cui tura gratis imponere debetis; . . .

TERENTIANUS: The Emperor Julian, my master whom I serve devotedly, sends you this gold statue of Jupiter, and commands you to burn incense before it.

Dulcitius, iii, 141, 2.

DULCITIUS: Observate pro foribus cum lucernis, . . .

DULCITIUS: Take your torches, and guard the doors.

Dulcitius, xiv, 147, 1.

SISINNIUS: Quisquis es meorum, strenue extende acrum, iace, sagittam, perfode hanc maleficam.

SISINNIUS: Take a bow, one of you, bend it as far as you can, and loose a shaft that shall pierce this devilish witch.

Sapientia, v, 209, 33.

ADRIANUS: Duodecim centuriones alternando scindant flagris eius membra.

HADRIAN: Let ten [sic] centurions take turns in flaying her with scourges.

141

Sapientia, v, 210, 24.

ADRIANUS: In craticulam substratis ignibus assanda ponatur, quo vi vaporis enecetur.[154]

HADRIAN: Put her on a gridiron, and let fire be placed beneath so that she may be roasted to death.

No dialogue ever worked so hard in the service of theatricality as did Hrotsvitha's. Nor is there evidence of any drama preceding hers that depends so completely on the significance of the lines for stage directions and does not find them wanting. What needs to be done for continuity and theatrical effect is stipulated in the dialogue; what can be done on stage is clearly apparent in the lines; what can not be done is provided for by exit lines. Since in this respect she ceases to belong to the past or to her present, she must, of necessity, be linked to the future, even though remotely.

In a casual reading or analysis of the plays, it would be difficult to predict that such a mass of evidence could be collected in defense of their theatricality. Though the classical traces are most numerous, they do not overshadow the mimetic and liturgical influences. Rather, all three work together in an artistic blend to characterize the "new drama," the product of this inimitable medieval playwright.

Chapter VI

TWO DRAMAS IN PRODUCTION

This chapter presents the experimental approach to the problem under discussion. In order to test the thesis that Hrotsvitha's plays are theatrical and to prove that they contain within this theatricality the potentiality for performance, the writer submitted two of the plays to the criteria of production, namely, significance, structure, and spectacle. The experiment was so designed as to give the writer the opportunity to face the actual problems encountered in presentation, and to appraise reaction to the plays.

The use of the word *theatricality* in this study has not been confined to the purely technical meaning of the word. It has been maintained that a drama, to be a "theatre piece," must have significance as well as structure and spectacle. Artistically, a play must have a qualifying experience if it is to be accepted as an art form of the period in and for which it was written. Morally, it must admit of some universal experience if it is to be accepted as drama in any period. If the plays of Hrotsvitha admit of this universal experience, then the fact that she wrote her dramas for the tenth century should make no more difference to a present-day audience than the fact that "Antigone" was written for the ancient Greeks or "Henry V" was written for the Elizabethans. This study believes that the plays of Hrotsvitha do admit of that universal experience that plays must have to make them timeless.

The poetic dramatist is capable of writing much that the peoples of different philosophies can accept as true, even though they reject the belief, since the theatrical merit of a play also rests on the ability of the playwright to present the "truly human and essentially pure, in the midst of inhumanity and impurity." [1] Such a poetic dramatist was Hrotsvitha.

The German humanists of the early sixteenth century, the German historians of the eighteenth and nineteenth centuries, the French scholars of the nineteenth century, and the English and American studies of the twentieth century— all give testimony to the ever-increasing interest in the dramatic value of Hrotsvitha's plays. Aside from possible performances in Germany during these centuries and aside from the marionette plays which delighted Anatole France in the nineteenth century, there is no record of Hrotsvitha productions until the English and American Hrotsvithaphiles dared to put her plays into performance in the twentieth century in England and the United States with surprisingly favorable reaction.

In selecting two of Hrotsvitha's plays for production, the choice was made in favor of "Dulcitius" and "Sapientia," which seemed to have no record of production in English. Although they appeared to have similar plot ideas and characters, a careful scrutiny revealed so many differences that it was decided to present them as companion pieces. The plot structures were enough alike, however, to admit of the same kind of stage space, but unlike enough in dramatic situations to maintain audience interest throughout.

With no prior opinions as to whether the plays were stageworthy, other than it seemed that there should be no purpose, on the author's part, for writing in the dramatic form if she had not intended them for performance, plans for production were formulated.

Casting.—In casting the plays, it was decided that one would be acted with a mixed group and the other with an all-female cast in which the male parts would be taken by

144

women. If there had been any performance in Hrotsvitha's day, it would have admitted of either possibility—the mixed cast, if mimes or members of the court took part, or the all-female cast, if her sister canonesses or the canoness school pupils performed. For this experiment, a group of selected college students, with some theatre interest and experience, met to read the plays for the purpose of orientation before putting them on the stage.

Reading.—In reading a well-written play, one of the first theatrical effects to be noted is its *simultaneity*,[2] that is, the reader should be aware that more than one thing is happening on the stage at the same time—characters becoming involved in action, interaction, and by-play. This awareness heightens dramatic reading and is best experienced in Shakespeare. Although Hrotsvitha's plots are simple rather than complex like those of the "great dramatist," they do show an innate sense for simultaneity. In reading her plays, the members of the cast, with little effort, were able to identify themselves emotionally with the action and interaction of the characters, as well as to visualize the stage setting in which the plot might develop. As Molière advised, one should read "with eyes that uncover all the stage action." [3] To read in this manner, is to uncover the drama as a whole—the plot, character, and setting—through the dialogue. The cast discovered that Hrotsvitha was provocative reading from this approach.

Characterization.—To insure as legitimate an interpretation of the characters as was possible, the director and the cast studied the problem of transporting historical facts typical of the early Roman Empire to the culture of the Holy Roman Empire of the German Nation. For it appears that Hrotsvitha Saxonized all but the story-line. To lift an episode from second-century tyranny and place it in the newly decentralized freedom of the tenth century required not only an understanding of the facts and characters involved in the episodes, but also a knowledge of its chronicler, its subsequent playwright, and the culture of the time in which the play was written. This insight was developed through research and discussion. Broad rather than specific features of Saxon life which overcast the Roman culture, were agreed upon by the players as background for the development of the characters. They considered that it was a turbulent age of revolution and rehabilitation. They saw man as a product of this age which started out in a brilliant, violent, and blustering pageant and ended in a "vital and ecclesiastically-colored civilization." [4] Consequently, they believed the male characters had to be developed as adventurous, vigorous, and masterful, and the women characters, fearless, intelligent, and dramatic.

After this research analysis, there was an almost unanimous response from the players to go into action. They sensed the immediacy of the scenes. They remarked the ease with which the characters moved and reacted to the dialogue. The awareness that the characters were typical human beings, capable of development within actual situations, created an excitement among the players. Here was relationship, inter-action, juxtaposition, alternation—all the traits of the theatre trade. [5]

Setting.—It is axiomatic that real drama can be staged not only anywhere and any time, but even any place; that is, it can be brought to life in any acting area or stage space conceived by the director for his actors. Hrotsvitha's dramas can be acted in as plain or as elaborate a stage-setting as one may wish to use. Her dialogue suggests what is necessary.

The next step then was to determine a kind of stage for performance. For this purpose, tenth-century illuminated manuscripts were examined from the Bernward School of the Ottonian Renaissance and from the contemporary Reichenau School. [6] It was noted that the Romanesque arcade-motif was used repeatedly to frame the subjects of the miniatures therein. This striking architectural resemblance to the monastery cloister-bay determined the setting (see Fig. 5). Presuming performance, such a background would be credible inside or outside the monastery.

Thus, the stage setting for "Dulcitius" and "Sapientia" was

constructed from a design patterned on the architectural features of two miniatures, namely, *St. Matthew in Ecstasy* and *Adoration of the Magi*, Reichenau (*ca.* 1000).[7] This design attempted to capture the feeling of the miniatures as described by Swarzenski:

The architecture seems to float in space, and has assumed a new and purely decorative compositional function, reduced to a mere framework, or to a series of arcades uniting whole groups or single figures—a principle which is to find its fullest development in the baldaquin-statues of Romanesque art.[8]

When the scenes were blocked, it was discovered that all interior action could be handled in three locales arranged in a definite pattern, one that would fit both plays, or for that matter, all six of Hrotsvitha's plays. These locales were supplemented by a neutral area in front of the arcade closely resembling the Roman street scene of Terence. The neutral area was to be used for all exterior action.

Three Romanesque arcades supported by pillars represented the interior locales. They measured twenty-two feet in length, twelve feet in height, and nine feet in depth, and were centered on the stage, leaving the foreground for the neutral area. The center bay was slightly larger than the side locales and its arcade extended into a complex roof. The decorative scheme of the framework and roof was characterized by a symmetrical and rhythmic design of late Romanesque art. It was dominated by a bird symbolizing immortality. Since colors were used in the illuminations for symbolic value only, the gold and green used on the set symbolized heaven and earth, and the violet, royalty.

Costumes and Properties.—The miniature of Otto II, Trier School (*ca.* 983), provided the pattern for Hadrian's royal robes, crown, and sceptre.[9] From the *Christus bei Maria und Marta* illumination, Aachen (*ca.* 985), was derived the design for the tunics and mantles of Sapientia and her three daughters (see Fig. 6).[10] *The Otto III Surrounded by Ecclesiastical and Secular Dignitaries* illumination, Reichenau (*ca.* 1000), was used for Diocletian's robe and crown, for Dulcitius' tunic, mantle, and crown, and for the robe and mantle of Sisinnius.[11] The *Verkündigung* miniature from the Codex Egberti of Reichenau (*ca.* 980) provided the pattern for the costumes and head veils for Agape, Chionia, and Irena.[12] The tunics, cloaks, shields, and weapons of the soldiers, guards, and attendants were copied from *Besiegung des falschen Propheten,* Bamberg (*ca.* 980).[13]

Suggestions were taken from the *Miniatures of the Manuscripts of Terence* for properties used in the torture scenes in the play, "Sapientia."[14]

The Production of "Dulcitius"

Dramatic Structure.—The legend of "Dulcitius" concerns three young women who suffered torture and death during the reign of Diocletian about 290 A.D. The first part of the play is a religious farce—the misadventures of the erotic Dulcitius. The comic element, which Hrotsvitha inserts in the dramatic form, does not appear in the original legend. According to Magnin:

This work, although it is written in a mood of piety and edification like all the works of this author, nevertheless fulfills the indispensable requirements imposed on the writer of comedy, that is, to provoke laughter and delight. One can even say that, in this respect, *Dulcitius* goes somewhat beyond the boundaries of this genre. This play is more than a comedy; it is a religious farce, a pious buffoonery, a holy burlesque, which unfolds, astonishing thing! without any disparagement to the martyrdom of the three sisters, Agape, Chionia, and Irena. In this play, in which illusions and the miraculous dominate, the persecutors are not simply represented, according to custom, as fierce and bloody executioners, but as incompetent men, simpletons, exposed to the

148   ,

most ridiculous illusions, delivered to the mystification of an unseen hand which makes sport of them.[15]

The opening scene shows the young Christian girls, Agape (Love), Chionia (Purity), and Irena (Peace), being examined by the Emperor Diocletian who tries by flattery and the promise of royal marriage to induce them to offer sacrifice to the pagan gods. When his efforts prove vain, he orders them bound in chains and cast into prison where they are to be held until Dulcitius decides their fate.

Dulcitius, amazed at the beauty of the young girls, has them placed in a room where he may have easy access to them. He approaches their room intending to seduce them; they pray to God to watch over them. There is a great noise, and the girls peering through the crack in the door, see Dulcitius clasping the grimy cooking-utensils to himself and kissing them. Black with soot, he returns to the soldiers who do not recognize him, but only cry out, thinking he is some emissary of the devil. At this point, Dulcitius, ridiculed and repulsed, retires from the scene.

Diocletian then orders Count Sisinnius to put the maidens to death. The two elder, Agape and Chionia, are placed on a pyre and burned. Neither their garments nor their bodies are consumed by the flames. Not to be outdone by mere girls, Sisinnius commands Irena, the youngest, to be taken to a house of ill fame, but she is rescued by supernatural beings who take her to a hilltop. Sisinnius, in trying to reach her, seems to be held back by some mysterious force. Finally, he orders a soldier to loose an arrow from his shaft. Uttering a triumphant prayer, Irena dies (see Table 3).

The plot structure apparently indicates one of Hrotsvitha's earlier attempts with the dramatic form. For example, Diocletian appears only in the early part of the play. Although his speeches establish him as the antagonist who has power over the fate of the girls, he has no opportunity for full character development. It is clear that Hrotsvitha used Diocletian only as a symbol of the highest earthly power opposing the

149

Christians. When he had completed the purpose intended by the author, he is perpetuated only as a figurehead in the lines of the other characters. So, too, Dulcitius, after whom the play is oftentimes titled,[16] is an unfinished character. Where he appears in the earlier farce scenes, the episodes are well rounded and serve as delightful contrast to the other situations. However, at a high point, Dulcitius falls into oblivion and another character, Sisinnius, completes the role. This makes Sisinnius, a cruel, ruthless creature, of little dramatic interest. Thus, the play has three partially delineated characters who serve as the antagonist.

On the other hand, the three young maidens evince enough intelligence and appreciation of their situation to stand as full-bodied characters. True, the play is didactic in its emulation of the virtue of purity. For this reason, some critics complain that it lacks "sweetness and fortitude," that is, the more human touch on the part of the women characters. Such criticism does not consider motivation. Hrotsvitha's heroines, faced with death, have put aside all thought of the "softness and sweetness" of life for themselves and exhibit excessive fortitude at the hands of their persecutors rather than surrender their faith. The victims of modern totalitarianism are not considered "lacking in sweetness and fortitude" because, when put to the test, they prefer persecution to apostasy.

This story is significantly dramatic because the theme embodies a subject of universal interest and because the lines contain the potentiality for visible and audible representation.

"Dulcitius" concerns itself with *religion,* one of the three great subjects, which, by their very universality, appeal in all ages to all people. Although a modern audience may find the style of language unfamiliar, the structural surorundings quaint, and the strength of devotion unnatural and excessive, none can deny the integrity of the basic theme, the defense of one's convictions.

Blashfield's unfavorable commentary [17] on the theme is based not only upon a complete misunderstanding of the religious belief underlying the preservation of chastity, but also upon a distortion of the position of the early Christians regarding the dignity of womanhood. Her statement referring to the impropriety of "publicly lauding chastity as a virtue" savors of the Victorian era and strikes at the very core of the plot. A further remark, "their lack of human interest, which removes the sufferings of the saints from the sphere of our sympathies, makes these girls literally puppets in God's hand; they do not really live or suffer," flagrantly denies a principle of literary criticism requiring intellectual integrity of the critic. Did Mrs. Blashfield's opinion rule the drama desk today, plays based on the theme of Joan of Arc, namely, the execution of God's will in the face of insurmountable odds and the safe-guarding of chastity at all costs, a theme frequently and aesthetically explored, would never have endured.

Of all Hrotsvitha's plays, none more than "Dulcitius" can be better described as a series of artistically and thematically connected pictures. From the pageantry of the throne room in the opening scene to the glimpse of heaven on the mountain top in the last scene, there is a constant kaleidoscope of picturesque action. Dramatic effect is intensified by the symbolic use of the "corps noirci" of Dulcitius as representing the "noirceur de son âme," [18] and the use of fire to show the unalloyed purity of the young maidens, by the unusually undecorous reactions of the king's military retinue and the weeping household, by Sisinnius' use of a charger in the pursuit of Irena,[19] and by the employment of archery, which personifies grace both in its appearance and use.

Nor are aural effects neglected. Music has its place, as well as laughter—ribald, scornful, and joyful. Anger erupts and lamentations sound.

Practical staging.—The controversy over performance has always carried in its wake numerous lesser contentions, one of which concerned the probable composition of the cast. Earlier in this study, it was mentioned that, presuming performance, the *dramatis personae* might have consisted of

151

mimes, which fact would admit of both male and female participants; the pupils of the canoness school, all female; or the canonesses themselves. To cover this question, it seemed necessary to experiment with both types of casts. Of the two plays, "Dulcitius," because of its farcical element, seemed to lend itself more readily to a mixed cast.

This group, while reading, was particularly sensitive to the dramatic potentiality inherent in the lines, and considered the play one of action rather than of psychological interest. They believed that the action aimed toward one final end and that each character moved consistently in this direction. They were well aware of the limitations in the scope of the plot, but agreed that there was enough in the dialogue to create definite characterizations.

The most difficult role was that of Dulcitius. To achieve sincerity, it was necessary to avoid, on the one hand, a ludicrous over-simplification and, on the other, a false complexity of characterization. Too often in this play the element of mystification has been obscured by the comedy, whereas the latter seems to have been introduced to accent the former. For example, Dulcitius contrives an assignation with the three Greek maidens; an unseen force dulls his senses to the point of idiocy. He has recourse to the soldiers and to the Emperor; again a strange malady presents him as alien and revolting. Finally, blaming his embarrassing predicament upon the girls, he orders them stripped and exposed to the public; to his appropriate disposition, he is thrust into a senseless sleep.

It required deft handling to give to these episodes their proper dramatic emphasis. The fact that the occult phenomenology had to receive priority did not detract from the potentiality for farcical excellence. In fact, the one was intended to point up the other.

When Dulcitius sees the beautiful girls for the first time, he reacts in the manner of the mimes who used the *mimica licentia*.[20] The audience responded with the expected "*risus mimicus*, no small thing to provoke," according to Petro-

152

nius.[21] Dulcitius' next scene, however, is not one of comic ribaldry, but rather one of comic hallucination. His antics were silhouetted on a translucent screen by backlighting. They would have been revealed much more effectively, merely by the dialogue of the girls, punctuated by the noise when Dulcitius incredibly mistakes the pantryware for his innocent victims. Had the technical director not resorted to the anachronism of silhouetting on a translucent screen, and left the burden of reporting the scene to the dialogue, the good theatrical sense of Hrotsvitha would have been underscored by the production and the comic element would have come through as *paradoxus*.[22]

The same type of unaccountable idiocy characterizes Dulcitius when he returns to the stage and meets the soldiers and ushers. Here the comic element was induced by his unexpected appearance and by their frantic antics in their efforts to escape him. The spell is broken when he meets his weeping wife and realizes how he has been duped. This respite from the farce is momentary. When Dulcitius decides to punish the girls for his mishap, he is again overcome by a strange force which casts him in public into another ludicrous position—the sleep of a snoring stupor.

In no other place does Hrotsvitha show more clearly the influence of the mimic style on her works, for here we see both the freedom of the mimic form and the ways in which it can be utilized:

The freedom of the mimic drama is something which cannot be over-emphasized. Basing their art upon an 'imitation of life,' the mimes retained perfect liberty to interpret life according to its widest significance. The mythological element testifies to this, and we must endeavour, in the forming of our mental picture, to take into due account the fantastic element which met with the realistic. The mimes were sometimes called *paradoxi* (literally, 'strange beings'), and the mimic art was an art of hallucination (*mimus hallucinatur*, according to Apuleius). They could introduce the most startling contrasts.[23]

Diocletian, like most of the Caesars, was wont to enhance his court with the best of knowledge, talent, and beauty. His summons bringing Agape, Chionia, and Irena to an audience was the typical gesture of a self-indulgent tyrant. Thus he was portrayed. In the two scenes in which he appeared, the player was amazed to find that, in this apparently brief role, he had the opportunity to portray haughty insolence, astonished incredulity, contemptuous impatience, pained pride, and brutal finality. This fitful exhibition of emotional reactions was particularly pointed up in scene ix which contains only three sentences, each one a capsule of emotion:

DIOCLETIAN: [Comic irony attended by raucous laughter] I grieve to hear of the outrageous way in which the Governor Dulcitius has been insulted and hoaxed! [Outrage] But these girls shall not boast of having blasphemed our gods with impunity [still smarting from the refusal of the girls to obey his commands, he vows revenge] or having made a mock of those who worship them. [Scheming] I will entrust the execution of my vengeance to Count Sisinnius.[24]

The students who portrayed the feminine roles selected one characteristic which seemed to envelop the whole personality of each character and elaborated it to the exclusion of any other. Consequently, Agape was portrayed as the oldest and spokesman in the presence of authority;[25] Chionia, as less vocal but showing a touching interest in her sisters and in the executioner;[26] Irena, as the youngest with an appealing gaiety,[27] who, as the most fully developed character of the three, exhibited a delighted appreciation for the pantry mime and at the same time a matter-of-fact steadfastness in her own convictions.

There are those critics who would characterize the fearlessness and outspokenness of the maidens as disrespectful to authority and unfeminine, but such critics should also remember that these young women believed they were being intimidated by an authority that was usurped from God.

It was evident in the finished characterizations that the

preliminary research and discussion undertaken by the members of the cast had, to a great extent, avoided the oft-repeated fallacy of presenting characters out of time and place. These were people of the tenth century, portraying the second century, not the twentieth century; they were Saxons portraying Romans, not Americans portraying Romans; they were medieval, not primitive nor modern.

As previously mentioned, a three-bayed structure, together with the forestage, accommodated the action. Three major problems required some adaptation of this permanent setting.

The first one was concerned with the pantry scene. According to the dialogue, it was necessary that "the passage where the pots and pans were kept" adjoin the inner room in which Dulcitius had ordered the girls held. The locale on stage right was designated as the inner room. It was finally decided to provide this locale with a backdrop consisting of an extended translucent screen through which the entanglement of Dulcitius with the pots and kettles could be observed in silhouette. As mentioned before, this device did not effect the desired contrast and this action should have been interpreted through sound effects and dialogue. This also substantiates the suggestion that if the play had been performed in the cloister, this scene could have been played with Dulcitius out of sight. It would not have been necessary to arrange an acting area somewhere in the vicinity of a pantry.

The second problem involved the simulating of a mountain crest. To stay within the confines of the unit-staging and still achieve distance required some sort of stage convention. Since the center bay was used only for the throne scenes which occurred early in the play, it was decided to use the area behind this locale, and by means of a slight elevation, indicate a mountain top. Distance and height were effected through lighting. Although lighting is considered a strictly modern convention, Nicoll reports its use by the mimes in the fourth century.[28]

155

The most difficult problem concerned the susceptibility of the modern audience to a medieval convention. The director was well aware of the narrow line between the serious and the ridiculous in the presentation of the pyre scene. Historically, the medieval mind was conditioned to stark realism. The decision had to be made in favor of such realism or in favor of stylization. Since it seemed that the latter would be more acceptable to a present-day audience, a painted backdrop was contrived for the pyre scene which appeared to grow in brilliance under artificial light and shadow.

Another convention which the audience accepted with imaginative participation involved the slaying of Irena by an archer. Here again distance had to be contrived. Sisinnius ordered one of the soldiers standing in the neutral area down left to simulate the loosing of a shaft from a drawn bow.

There was one convention in "Dulcitius," however, which would not lend itself to the modern stage, namely, Sisinnius' use of a charger in his pursuit of Irena. Hrotsvitha's use of animals followed the custom of medieval entertainment. Magnin actually describes how this might have been done:

> We might think, perhaps, that it would be difficult for the novices of Gandersheim to portray the Count Sisinnius shouting for his horse, as Richard III in Shakespeare, and following on his restive mount the innocent Irena. We need only to remember that the horse had only to turn about as in a riding-school, which considerably simplifies the matter. Besides, the presence of animals in ecclesiastical entertainments was not at all rare in the middle ages. . . . We see, then, that the *mise en scène* of "Dulcitius" does not go beyond what could be done in the hieratic drama of the tenth century according to rule.[29]

An outdoor presentation would very likely admit of this interesting and highly dramatic use of the horse.

The fact has been mentioned that spectacle, full of sound and color, played a prominent part in the life of the tenth century.[30] It seemed appropriate, therefore, to capture this vital quality of spectacle through emphasizing costumes, the chorus, and music.

The art relics which furnished the designs for the costumes[31] attribute much of their significance to the strong, rich colors of the liturgy. Just as the illumination featured a monochromatic background in order to accent the main figure, so, too, the dark *siparium* of the arcade accented the the brilliant façade and the harmonizing liturgical colors of the costumes. Considerable attention was given to the grouping of the main characters and the attendants to maintain this spectacle effect. In her constant use of attendants—soldiers, guards, doorkeepers, household retinue—Hrotsvitha adds to the variety of the spectacle and, thereby, foreshadows the brilliant court scenes of the Elizabethans.

"The use of the chorus," says Gassner, "greatly enriched the spectacular qualities of the Greek stage and introduced a musical component into the theatre." [32] There was a suggestion of the Greek chorus in two scenes of "Dulcitius." Therefore, this device was employed. In scene iii,[33] Agape, Chionia, and Irena moved in accord with the liturgical hymns which they sang in unison. Their movements were appropriate to the spirit of their song. The second chorus appeared in scene vii.[34] Although the chorus had no lines nor song, they followed with stylized movement the emotional content of the meeting of their weeping mistress with her husband, Dulcitius.

Since "Dulcitius" appeared as a companion-piece to "Sapientia," both plays will be evaluated together at the close of the chapter.

The Production of "Sapientia"

Dramatic Structure.—" Sapientia" seems to be a later play and, without doubt, the result of a more developed craftsmanship. The story line is taken from the Greek legend of

157

Faith, Hope, and Charity, three maidens, and their noble Christian mother, Sapientia, who come to Rome to learn more about the Christian faith and to dedicate themselves to Christ's service. It is during the reign of the Emperor Hadrian, persecutor of the Christians. In spite of his many endeavors "to save" them by flattery and promises, the girls remain firm in their belief in the Christian God. Hadrian first subjects them to cruel tortures which they do not feel because of divine intervention. They are finally put to death by the sword. In the last episode, which is not only reminiscent of the funeral scene of the early Greek tragedy, but also of the burial rites of Ophelia, Sapientia is seen with her friends, Roman matrons, carrying the bodies of her three daughters to a prepared sepulchre. There, after a long prayer, she joins them in death (see Table 4).

There are many characters and incidents in "Sapientia" similar to characters and incidents in the earlier plays, but "Sapientia" is better playwriting. For example, the complexity of the characters, Hadrian and Antiochus, and their personal impact on the plot throughout the play, help to make "Sapientia" a better play structurally and dramatically. Through them, Hrotsvitha shows a broad and intimate knowledge of the world in which she lives, and the capacity for projecting real people into her characterizations.

Compared with Diocletian in "Dulcitius," Hadrian is an arresting character. He has all the arrogance and consequential bearing of a dictator. In the opening scene with Antiochus, his adviser, he shows the characteristic frankness of a ruler with a confidant, encouraging free interchange of opinion but always maintaining the upper hand. He is dazzled by the youth and beauty of the Christian maidens, and can see no reason for sacrificing them if he can save them for himself. He offers them his patronage, arrogant in his presumption that they will join him in an act of worship to the gods. Consequently, he is shocked and baffled at their uncooperative attitude. Attracted by their beauty, thwarted by their courage, and chagrined by their superior intelligence, he tries in turn, patience, flattery, and a show of affection. When none has the desired effect, he resorts to the utmost cruelty and, finally, puts each of the daughters to the sword. He believes he has saved the most refined torture for Sapientia by permitting her to live on in sorrow and loneliness after the death of her daughters.

Antiochus, confidential aide to the Emperor, is a sophisticated Dulcitius and Sisinnius in one. He combines the comic buffoonery of the former with the sadistic tendencies of the latter. He is fawning yet impudent, fearful yet greedy. He has a small mind consistently acting on generalizations and false premises.

The women characters in "Sapientia" are named for the virtue each most strongly exemplifies. Sapientia, generally speaking, means good sense, discernment, and prudence; in particular, it means wisdom, that is a deeper insight into the nature of things by learning and meditation. The Sapientia of this play has a brilliant intellect developed through learning, and an insight not only into the nature of things, but also into the nature of man through meditation on the ways of God. Strangely enough, it is her manifestation of wisdom that seems to confound the critics of this play. Her subtle and delightful taunting of Hadrian by means of a numerical discourse has invited the unflattering epithets of "heavy-handed fanaticism," "fatiguing formalism," and "plain boredom." Without doubt these opinions were formed from the point of view of a reader, rather than of an audience. Sapientia is an excellent example of Hrotsvitha's ability to delineate character consistently, for throughout, Sapientia shows herself a woman of intelligence, forthrightness, and courage. These qualities, together with her wit and sparkle, would make her an appealing character, even in the current theatre.

There is a strong companionable bond between Sapientia and her daughters; they apparently enjoy one another's company. This may account for the fact that the girls seem so mature for their years.

Faith, in her youth, has developed the same qualities as her mother; she has a keen sense of humor and takes great delight in her mother's ability to confound the Emperor and his dull-witted prefect. In choosing torture and death, rather than sacrifice to pagan gods, she is sure, strong, and aggressive. She is loyal to her beliefs; her strength is in her faith; her trust is in her God; her powers of endurance prevail even to the block on which the executioner's sword falls.

Hope, the second sister, always speaks with the desire of expectation. She is shy and retiring almost to the point of apparent diffidence. Where Faith seems aggressive and pert, Hope is submissive; even when she assures Hadrian that she will not conform to his wishes, she is respectful. At this point, she seems to struggle within herself—the struggle is not against Hadrian but against the lifelong habit of respect for authority. She gains strength through Sapientia's prayers and endures the tortures. She even faces the executioner joyfully, exhorting her mother to "laugh, not weep, to see me die for Christ." [35]

Charity is love. Though she is the youngest of the three girls, Charity is completely dominated by her sisters' virtues of faith and hope; she expresses herself as not likely to differ from them in any respect. This child of only eight years is not tricked by the blandishments of the Emperor. Standing before her and making dire threats, Hadrian is a symbol of the hatred he bears for all Christians. Charity, the symbol of love, makes Hadrian appear the more ludicrous when, in childish simplicity, she says to him, "Although I am small, my reason is big enough to put you to shame." [36] She submits to the tortures with meekness, she kisses her mother, and she goes before the executioner.

In all her dramatic writings, Hrotsvitha displays the ability to keep her characters at cross purposes, but never better than in "Sapientia." Even the characters, who are essentially in agreement, come to grips, if only in verbal conflict.

The general excellence of the structure of the play is presaged by the opening lines, which not only initiate conflict,

160

reveal character, and provide local color, but also encapsulate the theme. Antiochus' first speech with Hadrian establishes the mood of intrigue and sets the plot into immediate action:

Sapientia, i, 201, 13.

ANTIOCHUS: Tuum igitur esse, o imperator Adriane, prosperis ad vota successionibus pollere tuique statum imperii feliciter absque perturbatione exoptans vigere, quicquid rempublicam confundere, quicquid tranquillum mentis reor vulnerare posse, quantocius divelli penitusque cupio labefactari.[37]

ANTIOCHUS: My Lord Emperor, what desire has your servant but to see you powerful and prosperous? What ambition apart from the welfare and peace and greatness of the state you rule? So when I discover anything that threatens the commonwealth or your peace of mind I try to crush it before it has taken root.

After a give-and-take of only four speeches each, the tension precipitates the conflict into the major question concerning religious differences, showing again that Hrotsvitha selects the "universal" for her theme and thus meets the first requirement of dramatic significance:

Sapientia, i, 202, 3.

ADRIANUS: Sed profer, si quid scias novi.

HADRIAN: Come, if you have discovered some new danger, make it known to us.

ANTIOCHUS: Quaedem advena mulier hanc urbem Romam nuper intravit, comitata proprii faetus pusiolis tribus.

ANTIOCHUS: A certain alien woman has recently come to this city with her three children.

ADR: Numquid tantillarum adventus muliercularum aliquid rei publicae adducere poterit detrimentum?

HAD: And you think that a handful of women threaten danger to the state?

ANT: Permagnum.

ADR: Quod?

ANT: Pacis defectum.

ADR: Quo pacto?

ANT: Et quod maius potest rumpere civilis concordiam pacis, quam dissonantia observationis?

ADR: Nihil gravius, nihil deterius; quod testatur orbis Romanus, qui undiquesecus christianae caedis sorde est infectus.

ANT: Haec igitur femina, cuius mentionem facio, hortatur nostrates avitos ritus deserere et christianae religioni se dedere.[38]

ANT: I do, and very grave danger.

HAD: Of what kind?

ANT: A disturbance of the peace.

HAD: How?

ANT: What disturbs the peace and harmony of states more than religious differences?

HAD: I grant you that. The whole Roman Empire witnesses to the serious troubles they can cause. The body politic is infected by the corpses of slaughtered Christians.

ANT: This woman of whom I speak is urging the people of this country to abandon the religion of their fathers and embrace the Christian faith.

This ability to inject conflict, characterization, local color, and delineation of theme into dramatic exposition in the opening lines of a play is indicative of the imaginative playwright and gives strong support to Hrotsvitha's preference for the dramatic rather than the narrative form.

The plot structure of "Sapientia" also illustrates the dramatist's fidelity to unity of action despite one apparent deliberate excursion. The mathematical problem, for example, described by some critics as of dubious value to the plot, is actually designed to contribute to it. It provides a needed contrast to a seriously developing theme. It gives opportunity for character development, thus contributing to the clarification of motives which dominate future action.

"Sapientia" meets the second requirement of dramatic significance through its dialogue which provides for a wealth of visual and auditory representations. There are the *scowling Emperor*, the *crafty fox* and *cunning chameleon*, the *pert child*, and the *mere doll*. Pictures are painted when the characters speak of the *fierce whirlwind of smoke and flame*, the *powerful and prosperous Empire*, the *alien woman*, the *slaughtered Christians*, the *drawn sword*, and the *fiery furnace which glowed scarlet*. Sounds parallel the words which announce the *rushing waters*, the *song of praise*, the *flaying with scourges*, the *funeral dirge*, and the *laughing girls*. The passage of time is telescoped into a few well-chosen phrases: *the day has passed, night is falling, supper is ready*, and *your three days' respite is over*.

There is spectacle in "Sapientia," but it does not have the brash quality of the spectacle in "Dulcitius." The theme seems to demand action that is, for the most part, classically styled. Mimetic remnants are called for only in the action of Antiochus. Its movement is generally dignified and fluid. It does not deserve Blashfield's comment that the "play betrays a lack of spontaneity, has a sombre tone, and is unrelieved by any gleam of humor." [39] The stage presentation showed considerable animation. It is possible that this *élan vital* does not carry over in a mere reading of the script, but on the stage, the play demonstrated many facets of good theatre.

Practical Staging.—"Sapientia" was presented by an all-girl cast. To offset the unnatural representation of the male parts by females, the most gifted dramatic students available, possessing suitable physical and vocal qualifications, were assigned to these roles. They were students who had an intelligent approach and a serious respect for the art of stagecraft.

For them, this play was a psychological study in which Christianity, in the person of Sapientia, and paganism, represented by Hadrian, struggled for supremacy. They understood that, paradoxically, the victor could be either or both, depending upon the point of view of the reader or viewer. "Offer sacri-

163

fice or die," gave the non-Christian the victory, whether the Christian capitulated or was decimated. "Offer sacrifice or die," gave the Christian victory, either temporally or eternally.

They identified the basic conflict—virtue struggling with vice. They also identified sub-conflicts ranging from the most refined subtleties of the mind to the cruelest tortures of the body. Even between Hadrian and Antiochus, who were apparently in sympathy, they saw conflict—Antiochus offering adulation, Hadrian accepting, yet scorning it; Hadrian commanding, Antiochus obeying, yet condescending. To capture these psychological nuances in each character taxed the ingenuity of the cast to the utmost.

Sapientia has been described by some commentators as an "old patrician," [40] as "cette vieille mère," [41] and as "venerable." [42] These were misleading cues to the student who was preparing to portray the part. Even if, as Magnin says, the play has, as its secondary purpose, the glorification of Oda, the *vieillesse* co-foundress of the monastery of Gandersheim, who dedicated five of her daughters to God and then lived to see four of them die,[43] nevertheless the spirit of the character, Sapientia, is one of vigor and acuity, a person in the prime of life. The fact that Sapientia's daughters were only eight, ten, and twelve years old[44] would strongly argue for this latter point, despite the translation of St. John which places these words in the mouth of Sapientia, "Give thought to the mother who gave you life even when the years had exhausted her strength.[45] Magnin, referring to the same passage, offers this meaning, "Remember your mother who gave birth to you when your elder sisters had already exhausted her strength." [46] To clarify the apparent disagreement of these translations, the Munich Codex was consulted:

memto matr̃ıſ.ıammatr-ona effecta tr parıentıſ· [5]

Clearly, the implication here is to the fact that Sapientia was already a mother and had borne children before giving birth

164

to Charity, her youngest daughter. St. John's allusion to "the years which had exhausted her [Sapientia's] strength," may be due to either of two facts: that she used a Latin text which read *iam patrona effecta*[48] rather than *iam matrona effecta*; or that she translated the word *effecta* as a participial adjective meaning "exhausted" or "tired out" instead of treating it as a gerundive in the ablative absolute construction, "a mother who had already given birth." The word *patrona* might well carry the connotation of age, since it presumes a kind of sponsorship that flows from wisdom and affluence. On the other hand, *matrona* which means "married woman" or "matron" has only two accessory meanings neither of which implies age; namely, moral and social dignity or rank.[49]

Consequently, it was agreed that Sapientia would be portrayed as a mature, but not an old, woman—motherly, well-adjusted, spirited, in command of the situation at all times, spiritually refined, and sensitive. This decision in favor of a matron younger than is commonly admitted by most critics was not based on ease of interpretation, but on the compatibility of this kind of character with the spoken lines, all of which contributed to a more appealing and dramatic characterization.

The most brilliant facet of this role occurs in the numbers scene. To give the characterization herein just the right ingredients of learned simplicity, subtle mockery, and valiant intrepidity in order to effect a sort of peripeteia within the scene was a challenge to the player. The comments regarding this scene by some scholars are the criticism of readers, not viewers.

Eckenstein, generally very well disposed towards the dramatic quality of Hrotsvitha, has this to say about the numbers scene:

The learned disquisitions of the play 'Sapientia' are presented in a form still less attractive. The Lady Sapientia, who speaks of herself as one of noble stock, and as the descendant of Greek princes, dilates on the relative value of numbers to the emperor Hadrian till he tires of it and commands her to be gone.[50]

Blashfield speaks of the "learned quibbling with the patient monarch" as "hairsplitting."[51] Magnin believes this mathematical dissertation the natural result of the educational system of the day:

Hrotsvitha here falls into one of those learned digressions wherein she enjoys the scholarly pursuit of exploration into traditional fields of knowledge. These are not threads of scholastic philosophy as in *Calimachus* nor is it a technical exposition of musical science as in *Pafnutius*. Willingly or unwillingly, we are present at a class on the theory of numbers. It seems that Hrotsvitha was compelled to prove herself adept in nearly all the branches of the *trivium* and *quadrivium*. Besides, she states this ambition in the preface of her plays under the semblance of a modest acknowledgement, 'So that my negligence,' she said, 'may not contribute to the atrophy of my God-given talents, at all opportunities I have introduced in my work some threads or scraps from the ancient mantle of philosophy.' She certainly carried out her intention. In effect, this scholarly nun missed no occasion to don her doctoral bonnet, or, in other words, to be carried away, at the least occasion as she was in this instance.[52]

Just as the attention of the modern audience is drawn, not by the words themselves but by the artistry of the actor, to the significance of classical soliloquies and learned disputations of the dramatic literature of the past, so the student who played this role attempted to interpret its psychological significance.

The three girls who enacted the daughters of Sapientia believed their characterizations should be marked with childlike candor. It was agreed that all should reflect the courage and intelligence of their mother and that each, in addition, would exemplify the virtue for which she was named.

Some disagreement exists among critics as to the attitude

166

of Faith, Hope, and Charity toward Hadrian. St. John commenting on this spirit, says:

Many may find the impertinence of Sapientia's daughters to their imperial persecutor as trying as the real thing must have been. These slips of girls defy 'law and order' in the person of the Emperor Hadrian much as in our own day [1923] youthful suffragettes used to defy the British magistrates.[53]

More uncomplimentary is Blashfield's statement, "In spite of his (Hadrian's) amiable endeavors to save them, Sapientia and her girls persist in denying the gods and in reviling the Emperor." [54] Any assertion that the girls were disrespectful to Hadrian limits the play to one of chronological report and neglects the psychological impact. The adjective, "impertinent," is not justified. Theirs was a natural reaction of brave young individuals who find their basic security threatened. So, they were portrayed.

The character of Hadrian[55] was conceived as a typical villain type. The student who took this role realized that the character would need to be overdrawn to offset her natural femininity. Since she was tall and commanding in appearance, with a deep resonant voice, the credulity of the audience was not overtaxed to a marked degree. The role was played in such a way as to echo the pages of history which placed Hadrian in a most uncomplimentary light.

The problems of a female player attempting to impersonate Antiochus were not so exacting, since this role incorporated reflections of some of the alleged weaknesses of womanhood rather than of manhood, namely, proneness to gossip, flattery, and inventive spite. To these were added the unmannerly traits of a boor, the morbid enjoyment of a sadist, and the peevishness of a lout. In brief, the role of Antiochus was interpreted as an unpleasant mixture of the typical Roman mercenary and the mimic *bucco*.[56]

Thus, the director and cast developed characterization on the keystone of inner conflict. Too often, this aspect of the play is overlooked in favor of an allegorical emphasis and

167

interpretation. Time and again, a purely symbolic character has been ascribed to the women.[57] This is disputed by the reliable account of the martyrdom of this brave mother and her daughters as reported by the Bollandists in the *Acta Sanctorum,* as well as by a large number of Greek and Latin authors.[58] The fact that Hrotsvitha assembled this material in the dramatic style and wove into the fabric of her play an allegory representing the sequential events of the life of Christ gives substance to these allegations. But all the characters in "Sapientia" are historically real.

St. John confirms the statement made in this study that "'Sapientia' is the best constructed of the 'martyrdom' plays, and is singled out for special praise by most of the Roswitha commentators."[59] No doubt, this greater skill in craftsmanship is primarily responsible for the fact that it was easier to block the action of "Sapientia" than that of "Dulcitius." "Sapientia" utilized the same three connected cloister-bays and the same neutral area, as were used in "Dulcitius." However, because of its longer scenes, its psychological nature, and the many and varied physical properties involved in the torture scenes, the presentation of "Sapientia" was more difficult.

As in "Dulcitius," the center locale was reserved for the palace scenes. Those on the right and left were designated as the prison and the torture chamber. The neutral area, or street scene, was used only once.[60] In "Sapientia," Hrotsvitha also makes use of off-stage action.[61]

Scene iii contains one of the longer episodes in the play,[62] namely, the mathematical discourse. It involved the problem of covering the lengthy speeches of Sapientia. This scene, as mentioned earlier, performed a twofold purpose. It contributed a dramatic pause at a strategic point in the play by inserting an intellectual conflict; and it foreshadowed the physical conflict of the ensuing scenes and prefigured the ultimate victory of Sapientia. This psychological character of the scene determined its interpretation.

Hrotsvitha, apparently wishing to change the pace in the

168

action of the play inserted this meaningful pause. On a smaller scale, Hadrian performed the same service by contributing the dramatic pauses within the scene. He interrupted the lines of Sapientia, but, in no instance, did he violate continuity of thought. Herein Hadrian was interpreted as an apparently benevolent monarch who, in reaction to the psychological overtones of Sapientia's intellectual baiting, reverted at the end of the scene to his familiar role as a persecutor.

Antiochus, who in the play was developed in the mimic tradition of the *bucco*,[63] although he had no lines in this scene until the very end, still his mind ran footloose and revealed his constantly increasing boredom in characteristic pantomime. His mere actions served a purpose: they revealed another facet of his character, they underlined the superiority of Sapientia intellectually, and they pointed up the questionable wisdom of Hadrian's political appointments.

The question which Sapientia addressed to her daughters, "What do you say, children? Shall I puzzle his dull brain with some problems in arithmetic?" [64] gave a clue to the reactions expected of Faith, Hope, and Charity in this scene. With the most exquisite subtlety, Sapientia intended to point out to her children her lack of fear of Hadrian and her defiance of his ability to harm them. To his simple question, "How old are the girls?," she launched into a complicated discussion of diminished and augmented numbers and their relation to the "perfect" numbers. She further confuses her thesis by using contradictory words in profusion, such as, "evenly even" and "evenly uneven," "major" and "minor," and "quantity" and "quotient." [65]

In typical childlike fashion, the three daughters reflected their mother by overt enjoyment. From this episode, the players of these three parts informed their characterization as fearless and scornful throughout the remaining scenes. Thus the numbers scene justifies its inclusion in the play.

Scene v, also longer than ordinary, contains much business that might easily have degenerated into deadly repetition. To give to each episode within this torture scene its distinct character required careful planning. According to hagiographers, "the only instrument which had an immediate fatal effect on the martyrs was the sword." [66] This statement is truly verified in "Sapientia."

All three of the sisters submitted to scourging, two of which took place on the stage. These did not require identical props nor business. The scourging of Faith was executed by centurions using the traditional leather-thonged lash; lictors flogged Hope with heavy rods.[67] Each of these soldier-groups was handled as a quasi-chorus with stylized movement. This technique made it possible to reduce the number of centurions and lictors required by the text. The synchronous movements symbolizing the lashing differed from the movements representing the use of the rods. In both cases, a divine force intervened with varying visual results: Faith was not harmed but the centurions showed extreme exhaustion; the lictors, after inflicting a few strokes, were rendered powerless, unable to move, and Hope felt not a twinge of pain.

In the next torture—the mutilation of the body—to which the two elder girls were subjected in turn, it was necessary to rely on modern stage conventions. Even though the miraculous outcome of these two episodes might have rendered the preliminary gore palatable to a medieval audience, it was difficult to preserve the realistic effect of this scene for a modern audience. Consequently, stylized movement was again resorted to.

To simulate the mutilation of Faith's breasts with the miraculous flow of milk instead of blood and to depict the laceration of Hope's body, from whose torn shreds of flesh emanated a "heavenly fragrance," stylized movement was used inside the torture chamber with the complementary reaction on the part of the other characters on the stage. For these lancinations, a sword and a rod spiked with nails[68] were symbolically handled.

For the gridiron and cauldron episodes involving Faith, the action was more realistic. A Terence miniature appearing in the "Adelphoe" suggested the pattern for the gridiron,[69] and the kettle on the brazier in this same miniature provided the idea for the cauldron. A primitive cultivation instrument on wheels in a miniature of the "Timorumenos" supplied the design for the portable cradle bearing the cauldron.[70] Although the involvements with these torture instruments seemed in some respects naive and gauche, they were generally acceptable to the audience.

The dialogue required that the remaining tortures, with the exception of the beheading, be performed off-stage. These were of such a nature as would not admit of performance on stage, namely, the immersion of Hope in a boiling cauldron from which she escaped unhurt, but which destroyed all those nearby when it burst, and the casting of Charity into a fiery furnace in which she joyfully walked with "three young men in white" while the flames consumed five thousand men standing near. The narrative report of these episodes appeared to be a conscious variation used by Hrotsvitha for a greater dramatic effectiveness.

The final ordeal to which Faith, Hope, and Charity were subjected was the executioner's ax.[71] This, in each case, was performed in the torture locale. The movement was contrived so that the kneeling victim would fall away from the audience, thus the head could not be seen. The action was further covered by the brooding figure of Sapientia.

In the sequence of tortures, those inflicted on Faith and Hope were generally similar in nature and effect: the scourging, the mutilation of the body, the immersion in boiling pitch, and the final beheading. However, Faith, as the oldest, was exposed to one more cruelty than Hope, and Charity, as the youngest, to one less than Hope. It appears that one particular torment, different from the rest, was reserved for each: for Faith, the gridiron; for Hope, the boiling oil; for Charity, the fiery furnace.

In the torture scene Hrotsvitha shows a complete break with the classic tradition when she makes use of the *scène-à-faire* or obligatory scene. Unlike the ancients who never permitted horror and death to be enacted on the stage, she has the torture and death scenes performed before the audience. For those episodes which are physically impossible to do on stage, she provides for their legitimacy off-stage without destroying the unity of action. In this treatment of horror and death, Hrotsvitha seems to have conformed to a gross realism which was not unknown to the medieval audience. In the mimic tradition, on occasion, the stage "ran with blood" not always artificial.[72] It was not uncommon for mimic themes to concern themselves with a *Dianam flagellatam, a sacerdotem templi crucifixum,*[73] a *hominem emasculatum*[74] as well as with the *mimici naufragii*[75] and the *mimos obscaena iocantes,*[76] and later the *oxyrynchus* mimes reminiscent of the realistic tragicomedy of Beaumont and Fletcher.[77] Both the Christian and the anti-Christian mimes were enacted with cruel fidelity. That these mimic types expressed in dialogue were still popular in the ninth and tenth centuries is clearly verified in the letters and documents of kings and bishops.[78]

The second chapter of this study suggests another justification for this realistic touch in the plays of Hrotsvitha. The constant infiltration of the Slavonic and Scandinavian barbarians throughout the ninth and tenth centuries brought a new realism to civilization. For these peoples carried on a vigorous and destructive piracy throughout western Europe, and exerted a strong pagan influence on the Teutonic peoples which partially explains their readiness in the tenth century to countenance inhumanity and cruelty. There are startling episodes of noble women developing the flogging of their servants as an artistic accomplishment; of husbands dealing out mortal punishment to their wives for infidelity; of shameless crudities and public intrigue.[79]

Such realism is not uncommon today. The modern audience is treated to its fare of physical violence on the stage and on the screen. John Steinbeck's dramatized novel, *Of Mice and Men,* which presents four episodes of extreme violence, is offered as an example of legitimate stage realism.

172

The modern motion picture offers an even greater vehicle for realism. One of the most representative of this style is *The Vikings,* whose essence is violence and terror, and which is, coincidentally, geared to the century of Hrotsvitha.[80]

Two further problems were faced in the staging of the torture scenes. The first involved characters leaving to perform off-stage action. During this interim the text provided neither dialogue nor business for the characters on stage:

Sapientia, v, 213, 23.

ADRIANUS: Aeneum vas, plenum oleo et adipe, cera atque pice, ignibus superponatur, in quod ligata proiciatur.

HADRIAN: Put on the brazier a vessel full of oil and wax and pitch. Bind her and throw her in.

ANTIOCHUS: Si in ius Vulcani tradetur, forsitan evadendi aditum non nanciscetur.

ANTIOCHUS: Yes, she will not find it so easy to escape from Vulcan.

SPES: Haec virtus Christo non est insolita, ut ignem faciat mitescere, mutata natura.

HOPE: Christ has before now made fire grow mild and change its nature.

ADR: Quid audio, Antioche, velut sonitum inundantis aquae?

HAD: Antiochus, what is that sound? I seem to hear a noise like that of rushing waters.

ANT: Heu, Heu, domine!

ANT: My lord! My lord!

ADR: Quid contigit nobis?

HAD: What has happened?

ANT: Ebulliens fervor, confracto vase, ministros combusit, et illa malefica illaesa comparuit.

ANT: The boiling fire has burst the cauldron! It has overflowed and consumed every man near it. Only this vile witch who caused the disaster has escaped unhurt.

ADR: Fateor, victi sumus.[81]

HAD: It seems we are worsted.

Between the lines of Hope, "Christ has before now made fire grow mild and change its nature," and Hadrian's speech,

"Antiochus, what is that sound?" it is evident that the following incidents take place: Antiochus and a guard of soldiers take Hope some distance to a torture which has to be prepared and which subsequently overflows and consumes all the persecutors nearby; then there must be time for Antiochus and Hope to return to the stage. The problem was solved in the following manner. The lapse of time was minimized to an almost negligible extent. Interest was focused on Sapientia and Charity, who by posture and movement indicated they were offering supplication for Hope's perserverance. Hadrian remained motionless in the position of his last speech looking toward the off-stage action. He was alerted to the reëntrance of Antiochus and Hope by the sound of the bursting cauldron.

A subsequent study of this incident suggested another interpretation which would completely remove from Hrotsvitha the blame of retaining an apparently awkward passage. It is possible that the torture instruments including the "cauldron of boiling fire" used previously for Faith would be already available and that its shattering could be the result of Hadrian's voiced intention to use it. Thus the "sound of rushing waters" could have interrupted the dialogue on the stage and the narration of the "burning of all around the cauldron" could have been reported by Antiochus rushing back and forth from Hadrian to a vantage point on the stage from which he could easily have seen the off-stage catastrophe. This would have lent itself with considerable effectiveness to the mimetic actions characteristic of Antiochus, who more than ever throughout this scene recalled the "garrulous busybody" of the mimes.[82] Such an interpretation, at all events, is not denied by the dialogue.

The three-day intervals occurring between scenes iii and v and between scenes viii and ix presented no problem. In the first instance, the intervening scene with appropriate allusions to time and place in the dialogue took care of the time interval. Between scenes viii and ix, the time lapse and change of locale were simulated by contriving a stylized funeral procession in the manner of the Greek chorus.

The second problem concerned the initial entrance of the characters and their final exit. The director resorted to the conventional opening and drawing of the modern stage curtain. An alternative would have been both desirable and possible. Provisions for entrances and exits might have been made in the manner of the classical *paradoi*. This device could have been used to particular advantage in both "Sapientia" and "Dulcitius" for the aesthetically acceptable disposition of the lifeless bodies. Exits and entrances on the Elizabethan stage were actually made in this manner.

One final convention needs to be mentioned. The Roman stage of the first four centuries was not too different from the modern stage in its use of automatic devices, such as trapdoors, swinging guy wires, revolving platforms, and machines which could produce startling effects with water and fire.[83] How much of this realism the mimes retained and transmitted in the West after the fifth century has been questioned, since they seem to have relied much on their words to create the atmosphere about them. However, Nicoll suggests that, since their characterizations tended toward the spectacular, they would hardly have overlooked such mechanical contrivances as would make their acts more attractive to the spectacle-loving audience. To use such devices, however, would necessitate a permanent stage. That there were theatres producing full mimetic drama in both the East and the West as late as the ninth century is a matter of record.[84] Therefore, since these mechanical contrivances were probably known to Hrotsvitha through the mimes, it is not surprising that the dialogue of her plays suggests the use of similar devices,[85] such as a fire machine in the torture scene,[86] and the possibility of a trapdoor to serve as a tomb for the interment of the bodies of the girls in "Sapientia." This would eliminate the necessity of carrying them off-stage.[87] In "Dulcitius," since the dialogue makes no provision for the removal of the bodies of Agape and Chionia or for burial rites,[88] and since the use of an *aulaeum,* or curtain, is questionable, the bodies might have been carried off by attendants.

Evaluation of the Experiment

After performance,[89] the plays were subjected to an evaluation from the point of view of the director, the cast, and the audience. Comments are presented in this order. The director:

First, it was clear that the values of the playwright shone through with a clarity of purpose. Motivated by a doctrinal impulse and prompted by a social problem of her time, Hrotsvitha wrote her six plays. It would seem then that, limited to their proper purpose, the presentation of the plays would have been justified.

Second, it has been said that "the best theatre for the dramatist is the theatre of his own day when it has joined hands with the past, thus giving it fresh needs and stimuli.[90] Hrotsvitha apparently knew the theatre of her day. She borrowed the most appropriate from the past and colored it with the best of the present. Her unique contribution resulted from the new needs and stimuli which arose from this union.

Third, as a drama of heroism, which lies between comedy and tragedy,[91] "Dulcitius" and "Sapientia" were marked by a mood of earnestness, which, if it did not move to action, at least provoked to thoughtfulness. The characters harmonized with the situations and the dialogue prepared for them, thus resulting in sincere characterizations.

Finally, the director believed these two plays met the challenge as "institutions of continuity," for by helping to restore a facet of theatrical history, they brought to life a record of the past.

As for the members of the cast, they believed participation in these plays was one of the finest theatrical experiences

176

they could have as students. The fact that these plays were a part of an experimental project added to their appreciation.

They were strongly affected by the denouement of both plays which moved from the death scene through the purification of prayer to eternal life. Magnin courageously speaks of the last scene of "Sapientia" as one having "an impressive spiritual quality which recalls somewhat, if I dare to say it, the denouement of Oedipus at Colonus." [92] The catharsis of this latter play moves from misery to release. There is surprising parallel here, for the catharsis of "Sapientia" is also effected by release from sorrow.

Many critics of the plays suppose that it takes a fairly sophisticated audience to accept them. These critics believe that a modern audience would not find them as interesting as one that is limited and specialized. Of such a nature was the select audience which witnessed the performance of these two plays. In commenting on the staging and its conventions, the casting, atmosphere, stageworthiness of the dramas, and the value of the experiment as a whole, the following reactions were observed.[93]

As for staging and its conventions, the consensus of opinion, derived from the medievalists and classicists in the audience, was that the plays were rightfully presented as works of antiquarian art. To have attempted a modernized version, they believed, would have been literarily and dramatically unsound since the medieval art form, very interesting in its own right, deserves to be preserved. Plays like those of Hrotsvitha, they claimed, afford an excellent means for its preservation.

The majority of the audience preferred men in men's roles and women in women's roles, but all agreed no great violence was done to the validity of the play performed by an all-girl cast. Some expressed surprise at the ease with which the human mind accepts a character on the stage for whatever he purports to be, and almost immediately disregards the fact that a supposedly male character is speaking with a female voice and vice versa. The audience realized it was seeing a very specialized kind of performance and so, with imagination, entered into the spirit.

An eminent Shakespearean scholar said that the plays were very successful in creating an atmosphere of devotion. He believed this called for really sincere acting since it would be so easily possible to make the presentation excessively tedious or even comic without sincerity in the actors. Another critic likened the atmosphere, created by the quaintness and color of the setting and costumes, to a medieval illumination. To another, a philologist, the symbolic and simple settings and properties seemed quite right and were in large part responsible for success in creating an atmosphere of fervor, piety, and naïveté.

On the most important considerations, the stageworthiness of the plays and the value of the experiment as a whole, the audience, in general, believed that these performances had, at least, succeeded in making it impossible to deny outright either the potentiality or the probability of original performance.

Chapter VII

CONCLUSION

Hrotsvitha lived in one of the most revolutionary periods of the middle ages—in a culture that is now considered the matrix of modern civilization, a culture rooted in spiritual energy and marked by intense social and political changes, a culture that spanned the fall of Rome and the glory of the Renaissance.

Contrary to traditional opinion, a theatrical vacuum did not exist during this period. It can be proved that Hrotsvitha wrote in an age in which there have been found traces of three distinct dramatic streams—classical, mimetic, and liturgical—all of which left an impress on her plays. Chambers calls attention to the continual issuance of prohibitive banns by the Church against the secular theatre from the seventh through the tenth century. Nicoll enumerates these pronouncements, which vehemently attacked the degraded remnants of classical and mimetic theatre, in some detail.

The indisputable traces of the *comoediae elegiacae* and other classical models appearing from the first through the twelfth centuries, are evidence that the classical writers never lost their appeal to the popular imagination. In the *Concordia Regularis* of Ethelwold (963), there appeared specific directions for the enactment of the Easter trope. Hunningher, in his thesis supporting the mimetic origin of the theatre, argues the influence of the mimes on the tropes before the tenth century, and offers, as proof for his position, a *troparia* demonstrating mimetic participation in the tropes. Thus, it can be stated conclusively that these three distinct dramatic streams were existing at the time Hrotsvitha was writing her dramas. To understand her position as a playwright, it was necessary to define her place historically and then to substantiate it experimentally.

Documentation attests to the fact that Gandersheim was a canoness cloister, that is, a monastery with a unique blend of asceticism and worldliness. Like most monasteries of the age, it had an enviable tradition of sanctity and a vast number of holdings and wealth-producing enterprises. However, these latter in no way detracted from the poverty of spirit and renunciation of will expected of those who lived under the cloister rule. Actually, this fusion of world and spirit equipped the canonesses to assume the leadership demanded of them in every aspect of medieval life.

Invariably, these corporate houses were founded upon the gratuity of the reigning nobility to serve many purposes, among which, one of the most significant was the establishment of ecclesiastical holdings which would give to the ducal owner a balance of power within the Church as well as within the State. In turn, the canoness cloister served the royal household not only as a religious sanctuary but also as an educational and cultural center. The ducal daughters, in many instances, became abbesses by right of succession, and as recipients of the royal patrimony and feudal tithes, enjoyed unlimited powers and privileges.

Gandersheim was founded by the noble Liudolfian family and was administered by its royal daughters. Its "members were, for the most part, from noble families of the neighborhood," all of which leads to a logical conclusion that Hrotsvitha was a canoness of noble origin.

Having established from the data thus far that Hrotsvitha lived in an age of social, political, and intellectual inquiry; that as a canoness of Gandersheim, she enjoyed a certain freedom of experience and routine; that she probably shared in the distinction of a noble parentage—all of which would have been conducive to the flowering of a courageous and creative dramatic genius—the writer then directed attention to the possible existence of an acting area for Hrotsvitha's theatre pieces. Such an area was found to exist in the inherent architectural pattern of the cloister-arcade of the tenth-century monastery. Thus, a natural creative milieu was set for Hrotsvitha to which she might bring the intuitive talent of a dramatist.

One may wonder why a playwright of this calibre left no apparent imprint on her immediate posterity, why her plays received no recognition for five centuries and little attention for ten centuries. This study places the cause for Hrotsvitha's enforced isolation and oblivion on the religious and political turmoil that flooded the culture of the eleventh and twelfth centuries, particularly in her own monastery. Perhaps, some day, dramatic historians will recognize that the span of time covering the theatre of Hrotsvitha is significant enough to complete the bridge of theatre history.

A survey of the Hrotsvithan literature, restricted to the dramatic works of this tenth-century nun, reveals an arresting fact. In the perennial controversy, as to whether she wrote her plays to be acted or read, the arguments both *pro* and *con* have been based on literary rather than on theatrical criteria. There does not seem to be a single instance in which scholars, interested in the problem, have argued their position from the practical-theatre standpoint.

Since there are apparently no documents which affirm or deny performance in Hrotsvitha's day, and since it is unlikely that such verification may now be uncovered, this controversy will probably never be resolved conclusively. What can be determined conclusively, however, is the potentiality of the plays for performance—the issue in this study.

Relative to Hrotsvitha's purpose in writing in the dramatic form, differences in the past have taken the perspective of literary and quasi-religious arguments. In a critical approach to the theatricality of the plays, the writer advances the hypothesis that the plays were given some kind of theatrical expression. One major assumption supports this view, namely, that Hrotsvitha would not have used such visual dialogue in her plays if she had not intended them to be acted. Her subject matter, already in narrative form, was well known to her audience. Her purpose, therefore, was not merely to acquaint her contemporaries with the message embodied in the legends, but to arouse attention and to attract to virtue. The dramatic form served her purpose best. In the light of this form, plot material, adherence to organic unity, and characterization, her facility in writing drama is analyzed. The following conclusions are reached:

The dramatic form in which she invested her subject matter, as well as the matter itself, is characterized by features specifically theatrical. It is the mark of a truly creative genius to foresee the effectiveness of the traditional narrative legends of the saints and martyrs in a new form. According to Creizenach, she "shows a rare gift for seizing the great moments of a story and presenting them strikingly" with highly dramatic dialogue—dialogue which informs the director, constructs the set, prompts the sound effects, dictates the blocking, suggests the action and interaction of the performers, and invites the reaction of the audience. Its poetic quality, strikingly apparent in the Latin text, translates easily into colorful rhetoric which thereby adds to the emotional impact. Its appropriateness makes no illogical demands for stage action. Its compatibility with the temper and tempo of the age gives it credibility and sincerity.

The subject matter has two qualities which recommend it to a theatre audience, namely, universality of theme and specific appeal to the age in which it was written. So concretely is the basic theme conceived—virtue in conflict with vice—that its timeliness is assured in any age for any people. This theme has always been and always will be legitimate theatrical fare.

In using the legends from the *Acta Sanctorum*, the *Apocrypha*, and from the Fathers of the Church, Hrotsvitha shows a knowledge of the Teutonic mind which wanted to be

182

"edified and sermonized as well as delighted." When her plays appeared, the liturgical movement was just beginning to make a strong impact on the populace. This provided a receptive climate for the religious subject matter. The Saxon, who was a paradoxical blend of Christian humanism and barbaric aggressiveness, must have found these plays with their classical, liturgical, and mimetic traces, surprisingly satisfying.

Hrotsvitha does not violate in her plot structure the "one and only dramatic unity enjoined by Aristotle, the unity of action." She adheres to the principle of limit and thus her plays are individual and intelligible, characterized by a concreteness that assures their universality.

Her characterizations are as sharply and briefly drawn as cameos. They are honed on the cross of both inner and outer conflict. Even when involved in identical themes and episodes not too dissimliar, the characters achieve a distinct individuality. All this is effected through the dialogue. In this efficacy lies Hrotsvitha's chief claim to the title of playwright.

The ability to humanize her characters so sincerely indicates a thorough knowledge, not only of the culture of her time, but also of the culture of the past. The character of her life, as a Benedictine canoness, admitted of the demands made upon a playwright with a socio-religious purpose—demands which imply familiarity with the ways of common man and nobility, time and freedom to read and write, access to sources such as the Terence manuscripts at Corvey, and the patronage of superiors and prominent friends.

That part of the research problem which treated of the three dramatic streams existing throughout the middle ages assembled considerable evidence in support of the theatricality of the plays.

Under the influence of the classical tradition, the characters assume universal appeal because of their involvement in moral conflict; the dialogue manifests classical proportions in its expression of change of pace, passage of time, irony, suspense, and exalted passages; the plot structure conforms to the classical pattern marked by singleness of issue and shows traces of anagnorisis, peripeteia, and catharsis. Externally, the plays are characterized by a poetic quality of style and diction, by a concern for costuming, and by the use of such dramatic devices as the chorus, the procession, and song. The use of a permanent façade for many acting locales is strongly reminiscent of the classical theatre.

It was readily apparent that there is an amazing spectacle quality inherent in the form and subject matter of the plays that makes them truly theatrical. Hrotsvitha achieved this by relying primarily upon the mimetic tradition. From it she borrowed mimic character types, satirical and farcical elements, gesticulation, and animal impersonation. From the mime she also derived the title-prologue in the form in which it appears in her plays.

The liturgical influence shows itself naturally in the selection of subject matter, in the use of the Latin and Biblical language, and in the narrative dialogue which contains much detail and didacticism. As a Benedictine canoness, there would have been no studied attempt on the part of Hrotsvitha to incorporate within her plays those liturgical elements which were so much a part of her way of life.

The writer concludes with the declaration that, despite the lack of historical records supporting performance, the potentiality for performance exists in the traces of these three dramatic streams as they impress the plays of Hrotsvitha.

To further support this declaration in favor of theatricality, an experimental project was designed and executed, namely, the production of "Dulcitius" and "Sapientia." These two plays were subjected to practical criteria involving dramatic significance, spectacle quality, and staging. It was agreed that the presentations were dramatically significant, not only in their own right as drama, but as art forms of the tenth century. Visual and aural representation, aesthetically profuse, insured the spectacle quality of both plays.

The staging, for the most part, followed a natural sequence of movement and was admittedly convincing.

The generally restrained reaction of the audience to this experimental production was due to its uniqueness, to the employment of several unfamiliar stage conventions, and to the respect accorded by scholars to tradition and to Hrotsvitha in particular. The effort made to capture a composite of theatrical qualities as they appeared in this "new" tenth-century drama production, characterized by a social motivation, a supernatural significance, a refined realism, and an expressive dialogue, was significantly achieved.

NOTES

Chapter I

1. *Speculum,* XX (1945), 443-456. (Hereafter cited as Zeydel, "Hrotsvitha's Dramas.")

2. *Ibid.,* p. 443.

3. Trans. Henry Schaefer-Simmern and Fulmer Wood (Berkeley: University of California Press, 1949), pp. 12-14.

4. M. Le Compte de Douhet, *Dictionnaire des Mystères, Moralités, Rites Figurés et Ceremonies Singulières* (nouvelle ser., t. unique XLIII of J. P. Migne's *Nouvelle Encyclopédie Théologique,* Paris: 1845), cols. 9-16 with special reference to col. 13. "Les preuves positives ne manquent pas, qui établissent d'une manière sûre qu'en effet les représentations scéniques n'ont pas cessé après la chute de l'empire romain; que la société chrétienne a accepté le théâtre, et que l'esprit dramatique a été transporté alors des monuments publics destinés au drame païen, dans l'intérieur des basiliques."

5. J. D. Mansi, *Sacrorum Conciliorum et Decretorum Nova et Amplissima Collectio* (Leipzig: Wetter, 1901), XI, cols. 943-975.

6. Sancti Isidori Hispalensis, *Etymologia,* a storehouse of all knowledge and terminology used as a source book throughout the Middle Ages (LXXXII of J. P. Migne's *Patrologiae Latinae;* Paris: 1850), tomi tertius et quartus, liber xviii, capita xlii-xlix, pp. 658-659. "Caput xlii.*De theatro*—Theatrum est quo scena includitur, semicirculi figuram habens, in quo stantes omnes inspiciunt. Cujus forma primum rotunda erat, sicut et amphitheatri, postea ex medio amphitheatro theatrum factum est. Theatrum autem a spectaculo nominatum ἀπὸ τῆς θεωριας quod in eo populus stans desuper atque spectans ludos contemplaretur. . . . Caput xliii. *De scena*—Scena autem erat locus infra theatrum in modo domus instructa cum pulpito quod pulpitum orchestra vocabatur, ubi cantabant comici, tragici atque saltabant histriones et mimi. . . . Caput xliv. *De orchestra*—Orchestra autem pulpitum erat scenae, ubi saltator agere posset, aut duo inter se disputare. . . . Caput

xlv. *Tragoedi* sunt qui antiqua gesta atque facinora sceleratorum regum luctuoso carmini, spectante populo concinebant.... Caput xlvi. *Comoedi* sunt qui privatorum hominum acta dictis atque gestu cantabant, atque stupra virginum et amores meretricum in suis fabulis exprimebant.... Caput xlvii. *Thymelici* autem erant musici scenici, qui in organis, et lyris et citharis, praecinebant. ... Caput xlviii. *Histriones* sunt qui muliebri indumento gestus impudicarum feminarum exprimebant: ii autem saltando etiam historias et res gestas demonstrabant. Dicti autem histriones, sive quod ab Istria id genus sit addictum, sive quod perplexas histroiis fabulas exprimerent, quasi histriones.... Caput xlix. *Mimi* sunt dicti Graeca appelatione, quod rerum humanarum sint imitatores. Nam habebant suum auctorem, qui antequam mimum agerent, fabulam pronuntiaret."

7. Allardyce Nicoll, *Masks, Mimes, and Miracles* (New York: Harcourt Brace, 1931), p. 136. (Hereafter cited as Nicoll, *Masks*.) Benj. Hunningher, *The Origin of the Theater* (Amsterdam: E. M. Querido, 1955), p. 76.

8. *Ibid.*, p. 146.

9. *Ibid.*, p. 145.

10. Mansi, Canon li, col. 967. "Omnino prohibet haec sancta & universalis synodus eos, qui dicuntur mimos, & eorum spectacula; deinde venationum quoque spectationes, atque in scena saltationes fieri. Si quis autem in praesentem canonem contempserit, & se alicui eorum quae sunt vetita, dederit, si sit quidem clericus, deponatur; si vero laicus segregetur."

11. *Ibid.*, Canon lxii, col. 971. "Kalendas quae dicuntur . . . in primo Martii mensis die . . . saltationes . . . nullus vir deinceps muliebri veste induatur, vel mulier veste viro conveniente. Sed neque comicas, vel satyricas, vel tragicas personas induat; . . ."

12. *Ibid.*, Canon lxvi, col. 974. ". . . Necquaquam ergo praedictis diebus equorum cursus, vel aliquod publicum fiat spectaculum."

13. *Ibid.*, Canon lxxi, col. 975. "Eos qui docentur leges civiles . . . nec in theatrum induci, . . . Si quis autem deinceps hoc facere ausus fuerit, segregetur."

14. Douhet, "Sentiments de l'Eglise relativement au Théâtre," *Dictionnaire des Mystères,* col. 19, Lettre I du Pape Zacharie (entre 726 et 742), "Canon vi. 'Quant aux Calendes ou Januaires . . . pratiquées à Rome . . . comme, par les efforts du diable, ces pratiques recommençaient . . . prédécesseur de pieuse mémoire, et notre maître, le seigneur Grégoire Pape.' (Labbé t. VI, col. 1500, c, d, e.).''

15. *Ibid.*, col. 20, Second concile de Cloveshow, en Mercie (Angleterre), "Canon xvi. 'Il est recommandé . . . de célébrer, selon la coutume de nos aïeus, les trois jours qui précèdent celui de l'Ascension de Notre Seigneur, en jeûnant jusqu'à none chaque jour, et en disant la messe: mais on s'abstiendra de ces vaines coutumes trop répandues parmi les gens de peu de foi ou ignorants, telles que les jeux (*ludis*), les courses de chevaux, et les festins extraordinaires.' (Labbé, t. VI, col. 1578, a, b.)."

16. Douhet, "Écrits des Saints Pères," *Dictionnaire des Mystères*, col. 63. (Lettre du Saint Jean Damascène dans le iiie des *Parallèles*, chap. 47).

17. Nicoll, *Masks*, p. 147.

18. *Monumenta Germaniae Historica*, Epistolae Karolini Aevi, ii, t. IV, Epistola 124, 181. Alcuin to Higbald of Lindesfarne, 797, "Melius est pauperes aedere de mensa tua, quam histriones vel luxoriosos (luxuriosos quoslibet)."

19. *Ibid.*, Epistola 189. Alcuin to Adalhard, abbot of Corbie, de Angelberto, 799, ante Jul. 10. "Vereor, ne Homerus irascatur contra cartam prohibentem spectacula et diabolica figmenta. Quae omnes sanctae scripturae prohibent, in tantum legebam sanctum dicere Augustinum. 'Nescit homo, qui histriones et mimos et saltatores introducit in domum suam, quam magnos inmundorum sequitur turba spiritum.' . . ."

20. Douhet, "Sentiments," *Dictionnaire des Mystères*, col. 20, Concile de Mayence, "Canon x. '. . . C'est pourquoi le saint concile a trouvé bon de mettre en lumière les règles propres aux clercs. Que ceux donc qui ont quitté les coutumes des laïques et se sont séparés de la vie ordinaire, s'abstiennent des plaisirs du monde; qu'ils n'assistent ni aux spectacles, ni aux fêtes publiques, et qu'ils fuient les festins déshonnêtes.' (Labbé, t. VII, col. 1244, b, c.)."

21. *Ibid.*, col. 21, Second concile de Châlons, "Canon ix. 'Les prêtres doivent s'abstenir de tous les divertissements des oreilles et des yeux; ne s'occuper ni de chiens, ni d'éperviers, ni de faucons ou d'autres choses semblables; et non seulement repousser loin d'eux, mais engager les fidèles à chasser de même ces jeux indécents ou obscènes des histrions et des bateleurs.' (Labbé, t. VII, col. 1274, c, d.)."

22. *Ibid.*, Concile d'Aix-la-Chapelle, "Canon lxxxiii. 'Les prêtres ni les clercs ne peuvent assister aux spectacles ni sur les théâtres ni dans les noces; mais avant l'entrée des acteurs, ils devront se lever et s'en aller.' (Labbé, t. VII, col. 1361, a, b.)."

23. *Ibid.*, col. 22, Quatrième concile de Paris, "Canon xxxviii.

'Tous les Chrétiens ayant pour loi, selon textes de l'Apôtre (*Ephes.* v), d'éviter les vaines paroles et les bouffoneries, à plus forte raison les prêtres de Dieu, qui doivent à autrui l'exemple et le fondement du salut, ont à y prendre garde. Les personnes appartenant à l'Église repousseront donc les jongleries, les sots discours et les jeux obscènes, et les autres vains amusements qu'offrent les histrions, moins propres à donner à rire qu'à pleurer, à cause de l'amollissement où ils plongent l'âme chrétienne la plus vigoureuse.

'Il n'est donc pas convenable, et il est défendu aux prêtres de Dieu de polluer leurs yeux de spectacles de cette sorte et d'abandonner leur esprit à ces vains, plats, et honteux jeux de la parole. ...' (Labbé, t. VII, col. 1624, a, b, c, d.)."

24. *Ibid.*, col. 23, Constitutions de Gaultier, archevêque de Sens, "Canon xiii. 'Nous avons décrété que les clercs ribauds, surtout ceux dont on dit vulgairement qu'ils sont de la *famille de Golias,* ne pourront recevoir la tonsure des mains des évêques, archidiacres, officiaux ou doyens ecclésiastiques; ils seront même rayés des tableaux matricules des clercs, et on ne leur laissera pas la tonsure ecclésiastique; et en cela, on s'efforcera d'éviter le danger et le scandale.' (Labbé, t. IX, col. 578, d.)."

25. *The Works of Liudprand of Cremona,* trans. F. A. Wright (London: George Routledge, 1930), pp. 126-127.

26. *Ibid.,* p. 253.

27. E. K. Chambers, *The Mediaeval Stage* (2 vols.; Oxford: University Press, 1903), II, 306-307 (edited by W. S. Logemann in *Anglia,* xiii, 1891, 365, from *Cotton MS. Tiberius A. III, Regularis Concordia,* saec xi).

28. Cf. p. 5.

29. *Ibid.,* pp 6-7.

30. *Ibid.*

31. *Liudprand,* pp. 235-277.

32. Cf. Reigns of Charlemagne, Alfred the Great, Otto I; cf. also *infra,* p. 8.

33. Hunningher, p. 7.

34. Louis Marie Duchesne, *Christian Worship,* trans. M. L. McClure (New York: Macmillan, 1931), pp. 490-491.

35. *The Drama of the Medieval Church* (2 vols.; Oxford: Clarendon Press, 1933), I, 79-178.

36. Hunningher, p. 50.

37. *Ibid.*

38. *Ibid.,* p. 82.

39. *Ibid.*

40. *Ibid.*

41. *Ibid.,* p. 84.

42. *Ibid.,* p. 85.

43. *Deutsche Dichter des lateinischen Mittelalters in deutschen Versen,* ed. Hermann Reich (Munich: C. H. Beck, 1913), p. 449. (Hereafter cited as Winterfeld-Reich, *Deutsche Dichter.*)

44. Leslie W. Jones and Charles R. Morey, *The Miniatures of the Manuscripts of Terence: Prior to the Thirteenth Century* (Princeton: University Press, 1931), text, pp. 212-213.

45. This was undoubtedly the tradition to which Hunningher refers when he speaks of the well-developed dramatic form found in *Jeu de la feuillée (ca.* 1250), for it has the characteristic techniques and craftsmanship of the earliest recorded European drama. p. 8.

46. Young, p. 2.

47. Jones and Morey, text, pp. 28, 33-35, 212-213.

48. Christopher St. John [Christabel Marshall], *The Plays of Roswitha (*London: Chatto & Windus, 1923), p. xxvi.

49. Karl Mantzius, *A History of Theatrical Art,* trans. Louise von Cossel (6 vols.; London: Duckworth & Co., 1903), II, 1.

50. *Théâtre de Hrotsvitha* (Paris: Duprat, 1845), pp. v-vi.

51. Young, p. 5.

52. Aristotle, *Theory of Poetry and Fine Art,* trans. S. H. Butcher (New York: Dover Publications, 1951), p. 288. (Hereafter cited as Aristotle *Poetics* when referring to the text, and as Butcher when referring to the commentary on the text.)

53. *The Times* (London), December 30, 1913, p. 8, and January 12, 1914, p. 10.

54. *Plays of Roswitha* (London: The Faith Press, 1923).

55. *The New York Post,* December 17, 1934.

56. *The College News,* May 7, 1952. Presented in honor of Lily Ross Taylor, retiring Dean of the Graduate School and Head of the Classical Department of Bryn Mawr.

57. *Braunschweiger Zeitung,* August 22, 1950.

58. January 15, 1955.

59. January 12, 1914, p. 10.

60. December 17, 1934, p. 9.

61. *Ibid.*

62. August 22, 1950. (Translated by P. Gallasch himself.)

63. See reviews *supra*, pp. 11-14.

64. Edwin Zeydel, "Knowledge of Hrotsvitha's Works prior to 1500." *Modern Language Notes, LIX* (1944), 382.

65. *Ibid.*

66. Munich, Staatsbibliothek, MS, Clm 14485.

67. Variable spelling of titles and proper names conforms with their source.

68. Cologne, Stadtarchiv, MS, W 101, fols. 1r-16v.

69. Goswin Frenken, cf. *Neues Archiv der Gesellschaft für ältere deutsche Geschichtskunde,* XLIV (1922), 101-114.

70. Munich, Staatsbibliothek, MS, 2552.

71. Klagenfurth, Studienbibliothek, MS, Perg.-Hs. 44.

72. H. Menhardt, *Zeitschrift für deutsches Altertum und deutsche Literatur,* LXII (1925), 233-236.

73. Wolfenbüttel: Verlegts Gottfried Freytag.

74. Hanoverae: B. Nicolai Foersteri et Filii.

75. H. Bodo. The work of this Benedictine Monk of the Monastery of Clus is preserved in the Archiv der Stadt Bad Gandersheim.

76. Basel, 1494.

77. Separat-Abdruck aus Bd. XV. der *Zeitschrift des Harzvereins,* Darmstadt, Janr. 1920.

78. *Ibid.,* Janr. 1926.

79. See *supra*, p. 191, n. 50.

80. Paris: Charpentier et Cie, Libraires-Éditeurs.

81. K. K. Hof- und Staatsdruckerei.

82. Berlin: Weidmann.

83. Leipzig.

84. Ed. Paul Zimmermann (Wolfenbüttel: Julius Zwissler).

85. Wolfenbüttel: Julius Zwissler.

86. Göttingen: W. Fr. Kaestner.

87. See *supra*, p. 191, n. 48.

88. See *supra*, p. 191, n. 54.

89. Zoltán Haraszti, "Hroswitha's Works," in *More Books, The Bulletin of the Boston Public Library,* XX, (1945), 87-119, 139-173.

90. Edwin Zeydel, *Modern Language Notes,* LXI (1946), 50-55.

91. Edwin Zeydel, "'Ego Clamor Validus'—Hrotsvitha," *ibid.,* pp. 281-283.

92. *Mitteilungen des Österreichischen Staatsarchivs,* III (1950), 362-403. (Hereafter cited as Goetting, "Zur Kritik.")
93. *Braunschweigisches Jahrbuch,* XXXI (1950), 5-52. (Hereafter cited as Goetting, "Die Anfänge.")
94. Sonderdruck aus der *Harz-Zeitschrift,* V/VI (1953/1954), 10-25. (Hereafter cited as Goetting, "Brunshausen.")
95. Konrad Algermissen, "Bischof Altfrid, der Mitbegründer von Gandersheim," *Unsere Diözese,* XXI (3./4., 1952), 53-76. (Hereafter cited as Algermissen, "Bischof.")
96. Konrad Algermissen, "Die Gestalt Mariens in der Dichtung Hrotsvithas von Gandersheim," *ibid.,* XXIII (3./4., 1954), 139-156. (Hereafter cited as Algermissen, "Die Gestalt.")
97. Christopher Dawson, *The Making of Europe* (New York: Macmillan, 1932), pp. 256-283.

Chapter II

1. F. Löher, "Hrotsvitha und ihre Zeit" (1858), *Zeitschrift des Harzvereins,* XV (1920), 468.
2. Kurt Reinhardt, *Germany, 2000 Years* (Milwaukee: Bruce, 1950), p. 35.
3. James J. Walsh, *High Points of Medieval Culture* (Milwaukee: Bruce, 1937), p. 38.
4. Reinhardt, pp. 56-57.
5. *Ibid.,* p. 56.
6. Christopher Dawson, *Religion and the Rise of Western Culture* (New York: Sheed & Ward, 1950), p. 54.
7. *Ibid.*
8. *Ibid.*
9. *Ibid.,* p. 55.
10. Robert William Southern, *The Making of the Middle Ages* (New Haven: Yale University Press, 1953), p. 12.
11. *Ibid.*
12. Reinhardt, p. 63.
13. *Ibid.*
14. *Ibid.,* p. 61.
15. *Ibid.,* p. 62.
16. *Ibid.*
17. *Ibid.,* p. 63.
18. Löher, p. 502.

19. *Ibid.*

20. Strecker, *Hrotsvithae Opera* (Leipzig: 1906), p. 221.

21. Southern, p. 161.

22. K. Algermissen, "Bischof Altfrid, der Mitbegründer von Gandersheim," *Unsere Diözese,* XXI, (1952), 53.

23. H. Goetting, "Die Anfänge des Reichsstifts Gandersheim," *Braunschweigisches Jahrbuch,* XXXI (1950), 9-10.

24. Algermissen, "Bischof," pp. 53-58.

25. Goetting, "Die Anfänge," p. 10.

26. *Ibid.,* p. 11. ". . . auf sicherer Tradition beruhen, also voll verwendbar sind."

27. *Ibid.,* p. 8.

28. *Ibid.,* p. 11. ". . . dass Hrotsvit zwar auf zuverlässigen Quellen fusst, dass aber ihr Werk mindestens an einer sehr entscheidenden Stelle der Gründungsgeschichte eine grosse Lücke enthält und im übrigen aus der Situation ihrer eigenen Zeit heraus mit deutlich spürbarer Tendenz geschrieben worden ist. Tendenziöse Darstellung war bisher nur der 'Gegenseite' vorgeworfen worden, nämlich den Hildesheimer Quellen zur Geschichte des Reichsstifts Gandersheim, . . . [Be this as it may,] so ist doch nicht daran zu zweifeln, dass die Tatsachen, welche uns die Denkschrift Thangmars und das spätere Chronicon Hildeshemense überliefert haben, . . . voll verwendbar sind."

29. *Ibid.,* p. 5 "Wer sich aus der Literatur über die Geschicke des nunmehr fast 1100-jährigen Reichsstifts Gandersheim, des ältesten Kulturzentrums des braunschweigischen Landes, unterrichten will, muss noch heute notgedrungen auf die Werke von zwei Historikern aus dem Anfang des 18. Jahrhunderts zurückgreifen, nämlich von J. G. Leuckfeld und J. Chr. Harenberg."

30. See *supra,* p. 16.

31. *Ibid.,* p. 6.

32. *Ibid.*

33. Goetting, "Die Anfänge," p. 7, n. 4. "Ebenda. Dieses Exemplar mit den Randbemerkungen Harenbergs befindet sich jetzt im Nds. StA. Wolfenbüttel, Dienstbücherei Q2278, 3. Expl."

34. *Ibid.,* pp. 6-7.

35. See *supra,* p. 17.

36. Goetting, "Die Anfänge," p. 7.

37. *Ibid.,* p. 10.

38. Goetting, "Das Fuldaer Missionkloster Brunshausen," *Harz-Zeitschrift,* V/VI (1953-1954), 10.

194

39. *Ibid.*

40. *Ibid.*, p. 11.

41. Goetting, "Die Anfänge," p. 24. "Das Kloster Brunshausen war demnach bereits vom Grossvater und Vater des späteren Sachsenherzogs Liudolf gegründet worden!"

42. Algermissen, "Bischof," p. 63. ". . . des Herzogs Liudolf, der selber um 840 Laienabt in Brunshausen war."

43. It was to this abbot, Adalhard, that Alcuin wrote of his concern for monks associating with *histriones* and *mimos*. See p. 189, n. 19.

44. Goetting, "Die Anfänge," pp. 26-27. "Von Westen her drang dann in den folgenden Jahrzehnten die von der karolingischen Königsippe gegründete und anfangs auch geleitete Reichsabtei Corvey vor, die das klösterliche Zentrum Sachsens wurde und der die sächsischen Adelsgeschlechter Güterschenkungen in noch weit grösserem Umfang zuwandten, als sie vordem Fulda zugefallen waren. Der nächste Schritt war dann die Errichtung eigener Familienklöster und stifter durch die grossen Grafensippen, die um die Mitte des 9. Jahrhunderts beginnt. Daraus erwuchs im Mittelpunkt des liudolfingischen Familienbesitzes die Gründung des Stifts Gandersheim." These statements coincide with Algermissen, *supra*, n. 42.

45. *Ibid.*, p. 27. "Nichts kennzeichnet mehr das Geltungsbewusstsein des liudolfingischen Geschlechts, als dass sein Oberhaupt, bevor noch das Gandersheimer Familienstift eigentlich ins Leben trat, mit königlicher Genehmigung eine Fahrt nach Rom zu Papst Sergius II. unternahm. Der Zweck dieser Romreise war, abgesehen von der Pilgerfahrt als solcher, die geplante Neugründung dem päpstlichen Schutz zu unterstellen, möglicherweise auch schon den Altersdispens für die als Äbtissin vorgesehene noch minderjährige Tochter Hathumod zu erwirken, vor allem aber Reliquien zu erwerben, deren Bedeutung für die damalige Zeit und das erst seit wenigen Jahrzehnten bekehrte Sachsen nicht hoch genug veranschlagt werden kann."

46. *Ibid.*, p. 28. "Der Zeitpunkt der Reise Liudolfs und Odas ist durch den Pontifikat das Papstes Sergius II. (Jan. 844 bis Jan. 847) bestimmt."

47. Algermissen, "Bischof," p. 62. "Wie wir aus anderen Quellen mit Sicherheit wissen, erfolgte in Brunshausen 852 die erste Gründung des Kanonissenstiftes durch Liudolf, 'bis ein günstigerer Ort gefunden wurde' (Hrotswith. vs. 107)."

48. Goetting, "Die Anfänge," p. 28.

49. Algermissen, "Bischof," p. 61.

50. Goetting, "Die Anfänge," pp. 30-31.

51. *Ibid.*, p. 44. "Kurz vor ihrem Tode nämlich beklagt Hathumod im vertrauten Gespräch mit ihrem Bruder Agius den 'status tenerrimus' ihres Stiftes und gibt ihrer grossen Sorge Ausdruck, dass es noch nicht im Königsschutz stehe ('sibi tamen hoc penitus displicere, quod [sc. locus] necdum regiae tuitioni commendatus denn ihr Bischof sei ihnen doch 'fidelis et familiaris(!)', auch esset'). Und als Agius erwidert, das liesse sich wohl beheben, werde man es mit Hilfe der Verwandten und Freunde am Hofe wohl durchsetzen können, meint Hathumod resigniert, das glaube sie schon, aber sie werde es nicht mehr erleben."

52. Algermissen, "Bischof," p. 58. "Es folgte Markward, der dann am 29. November jenes furchtbaren Jahres 874, in welchem Hunger und Pest ein volles Drittel der Bevölkerung Germaniens und Galliens vernichteten, am Sterbebette Hathumods stand."

53. Goetting, "Die Anfänge," p. 45.

54. *Ibid.*, p. 46. "Einzelne Übereinstimmungen mit der in der älteren Gandersheimer 'Gründungsurkunde' überlieferten echten Traditionsurkunde Liudolfs, die ich aus stilistischen Gründen dem Diktat des Agius zuweisen möchte, deuten auf die Möglichkeit hin, dass auch hier Agius von Corvey, der Bruder der Tradenten und der hervorragendste geistliche Vertreter der Stifterfamilie, an der Abfassung der königlichen Diplome für Gandersheim mitgewirkt und dabei Formularteile aus der Königsurkundenreihe seines Klosters verwendet hat."

55. K. Steinacker, *Die Bau- und Kunstdenkmäler* (Wolfenbüttel: 1910), p. 89. "At her death in 896, she was succeeded by Christine, the fourth daughter and the last abbess from the immediate Liudolfian family. Oda, the mother, who after Liudolf's death had withdrawn into the monastery to be with her daughters, died in 913, at the age of one-hundred-six years. The last son, Otto, had died in 912, and the death of Christine in 916 [Bodo's *Syntagma* gives Oda's years as one-hundred-seven and Christine's death as 919 (*bis ternis post obitu matris*)] marked the passing of the last of the immediate members of the Duke Liudolf family. Christine was succeeded as abbess by a religious named Hrotsvitha. This first Hrotsvitha, who ruled from 916 [*sic*] to 926, is often confused with the nun-poet-dramatist, Hrotsvitha, who cannot be associated with the monastery until sometime after 950. [According to Bodo's *Syntagma*, the first Hrotsvitha came from the monastery of Hano to take the position of fourth abbess of Gandersheim (*illam autem benedictione in abbatissam coenobio Hano venerabilem foeminam fuisse ex con-*

gregatione illa sancta electam litterae tradunt posteritatis notitiae)]."

According to Steinacker, Windelgard followed the abbess Hrotswitha in 926, and Gerberga II, a daughter of the Emperor Otto I and sister of Otto II, became the abbess of Gandersheim in 959 and governed the monastery until 1001. This period covered the proximate span of the lifetime of the poetess Hrotsvitha.

56. K. Strecker, *Hrotsvithae Opera* (Leipzig: 1906), p. 253, vss. 103-110.

> Quis fuit ecclesiae possessio denique parvae
> Trans ripas Gandae supra montana locatae,
> Unde locum celebrem vocitabant Gandeshemensem
> Illic, obsequio domini digne celebrando
> Dum locus investigari posset magis aptus,
> Communi multas vita iunxere puellas;
> Atque sui natam decreverunt Hathumodam
> His habitu similem fieri sociamque perennem.

57. Goetting, "Die Anfänge," p. 40.

58. Algermissen, "Bischof," p. 63. "Auch bot das anderthalb Kilometer südlich gelegene Gelände des späteren Gandersheim Schutz durch Wald und Sumpf; gleichzeitig bot es ausgezeichnete Verkehrsmöglichkeiten, weil sich hier zwei grosse Verkehrsstrassen kreuzten: die Westoststrasse vom Rhein zur Elbe, die alte Heerstrasse der fränkischen Truppen, und die Nordsüdverbindung Göttingen, Northeim, Lamspringe, Hildesheim."

59. *Ibid.*

60. *Ibid.* "Erst jetzt fand die Übersiedlung des Kanonissenstiftes von Brunshausen statt."

61. Goetting, "Die Anfänge," p. 30.

62. *Ibid.*, p. 40. "Altfried selbst habe dann nach vier Jahren den neuen Ort ausgesucht, ihm den Namen Gandersheim gegeben und dort mit Zustimmung des Herzogs den Bau begonnen."

63. *Ibid.*, pp. 40-41. "G. O. von Wersebe, Der Altfriddom zu Hildesheim und die Gründungskirchen von Essen und Gandersheim. Untersuchungen zur Bestimmung ihres Grundrisses und ihrer Planverwandtschaft mit Corvey und Werden. Phil. Diss. Göttingen 1937."

64. *Ibid.*, p. 41.

65. *Ibid.*, pp. 43-44.

66. *Ibid.*, p. 19.

67. Strecker, pp. 267-268, vss. 581-594.

68. Goetting, "Die Anfänge," p. 49. "Anders lässt such der völ-

lige Umschwung nicht erklären, der gegen die Mitte des 10. Jahrhunderts im Zuge der neuen Reichsklosterpolitik Ottos I. eintrat. Am. 2. Januar 948 liess nämlich der König durch Abt Hathumar von Fulda beim Papst Agapet II. in Rom ein Schutzprivileg für Gandersheim erwirken."

69. *Ibid.*

70. *Ibid.* "Der Papst betonte ausdrücklich, dass Gandersheim ('nostrum monasterium'), dessen Errichtung hier auf 'Otto comes de Saxonia' zurückgeführt wurde, ausschliesslich der Jurisdiktion des römischen Stuhles unterstehe und keine andere geistliche Gewalt ein Verfügungsrecht über das Stift haben solle. ('. . . ut sub iurisditione sancte nostre cui deo auctore deservimus, ecclesie constitutum nullius alterius ecclesie iurisditionibus submittatur. . . . Et ideo omnem cuiuslibet ecclesie sacerdotem in prefato monasterio ditionem quamlibet habere . . . preter sedem apostolicam prohibemus.') Jeder zuwiderhandelnde Bischof verfalle der göttlichen Bestrafung. Die Äbtissin solle dem eigenen Kapitel entnommen, sonst aber vom König eingesetzt werden!"

71. K. Algermissen, "Die Gestalt Mariens," *Unsere Diözese,* XXII (1954), 141.

72. *Ibid.*

73. Goetting, "Die Anfänge," pp. 50-51.

74. Algermissen, "Die Gestalt," p. 141. "Im Jahr 973 brannte das alte Kanonissenkloster samt der Stiftskirche nieder, und die tüchtige Äbstissin Gerberga liess ein neues Kloster mit Kirche errichten. Während an diesem Bau gearbeitet wurde und Hrotsvitha ihre Dichtungen schuf, trat um 985 die Tochter des schon verstorbenen Kaisers Otto II., Sophia, als Kanonisse ins Gandersheimer Kloster ein."

75. Algermissen, "Bischof," p. 75.

76. Algermissen, "Die Gestalt," pp. 141-142.

77. *Ibid.,* p. 142. "Hrotsvitha war bei diesem Ereignis schon nicht mehr am Leben. Allen übrigen Unruhen aber hat sie in Gandersheim mit erlebt. Welche Stellung sie in dem Streit einnahm, ist nicht überliefert. Ihre Freundschaft mit Gerberga und ihr hohes Alter lassen es als wahrscheinlich erscheinen, dass sie nicht auf Seite jener aufrührerischen Nonnen stand, die unter Führung der stolzen Sophia dem Bischof Bernward jene furchtbare Szene bereiteten, von der Thangmar im 17. Kapitel seiner 'Vita Bernwardi' berichtet."

78. Algermissen, "Bischof," p. 76.

79. *Ibid.*

80. *Ibid.* "Das war das Ende von Liudolfs und Altfrids einstiger ehrwürdiger Stiftung."

81. Strecker, p. 221. "Gerbergae, illustri abbatissae, cui pro sui eminentia probitatis haut minor obsequela venerationis, quam pro insigni regalis stemmate generositatis; . . . p. 223, fol. 132^v, vss. 1-2, 5; p. 224, vss. 1-2, 11-14; p. 222, fol. 132^r, vs. 1; p. 223, vss. 7-11.

Romani praefulgens gemmula regni, Oddonis,
. . .
Vilem ne spernas vilis textum monialis,
Quem praesentari, . . .
Ipse tui claris iussisti nuper ocellis;

. . .
Si tis praecepto non urgerer metuendo,
non foret ullomodo mihimet fiducia tanta,
Ut tibi praesentis scrutandum rusticitatis
Auderem satis exiguum praeferre libellum.

. . .
Pollens imperii regnator caesariani,
Oddo, . . .
Exiguum munus ne spernas carminis huius,
Iste sed oblatus laudum placeat tibi census
Quem postrema gregis solvit tibi Gandeshemensis.
Quem dulcis patrum collegit cura tuorum,
Continuumque tibi debet studium famulandi.

82. Löher, pp. 502-503. "Diese Gabe erkannten auch Gerberge und Erzbischof Wilhelm von Mainz in ihr. Mit dem letztgenannten in Otto des Grossen späterer Zeit hochbedeutenden Manne stand unsere Dichterin im nahen Verkehr, ebens mit vielen anderen berühmten Gelehrten. . . . Der junge König Otto war jedesmal der erste, der ihre neuen Gedichte lesen wollte. . . . Auf seinen Antrieb, dem Gerberge und Erzbischof Wilhelm auf das Lebhafteste zustimmten, begann Hrotsvitha ein historisches Gedicht von ihres grossen Zeitgenossen, des Kaisers Otto, Thaten."

83. C. Magnin, *Théâtre de Hrotsvitha* (Paris: 1845), pp. iv-vi. "L'aristocratie intellectuelle et cléricale. . . . A la place des cirques et des amphithéâtres, qui avaient autrefois réuni d'immenses populations dans une même idée comme dans une même enceinte, on vit s'élever les églises . . . qui recevaient aux jours solennels, et réunissaient, sans les confondre, les fidèles de tous les états, les barons et les clercs, les hommes d'armes et les artisans, les manants des cités et les serfs de la glèbe, et présentaient ainsi, malgré la separation profondes de toutes les classe, la chose dont le drame a besoin par-dessus toute autre, un grande auditoire prêt à s'unir dans une

pensée sympathique et à palpiter sous une émotion commune . . .
dans l'enceinte des monastères, ces asiles privilégiés, qui s'ouvraient
pourtant à toutes les conditions et, à de certains jours, conviaient
les séculiers à leurs fêtes. A l'abri de ces sanctuaires de la science,
de la piété et des beaux arts, le drame au moyen âge put se dé-
velopper plus hardi, plus poétique, plus affranchi de l'inflexi-
bilité des rites. . . . En effet, nous savons, à n'en pas douter, que
c'est dans une illustre abbaye saxonne que furent représentés les
drames de Hrotsvitha, probablement en présence de l'évêque
diocésain, et de son clergé, devant plusieurs nobles dames de la
maison ducale de Saxe et quelques haut dignitaires de la cour
impériale, sans compter, au fond de l'auditoire, la foule émer-
veillée des manants du voisinage et (qui sait même?) plus loin,
sur les marches du grand escalier, quelques serfs ou gens main-
mortables de la riche et puissante abbaye."

84. Löher, p. 489. "Der Kaiser mit seinen Rittern und Gelehrten, die Nonnen und die adligen Frauen der Umgegend sitzen
vor einer Bühne, welche höchst einfach . . . gebildet wird, in die
Thüren und Fenster drängen sich Dienstleute und Volk."

85. *Ibid.*, p. 496. "Nun, wenn eine Klosterfrau sie schreiben
konnte, so werden auch wohl ihre Mitschwestern sich nicht ent-
setzt haben, sie anzusehen."

Chapter III

1. C. Magnin, *Théâtre de Hrotsvitha* (Paris: 1845), p. xv. ". . .
sa magnifique église, ainsi que les bâtiments du monastère et leurs
dépendances, sont encore debout. Il serait bien désirable que la
gravure se hâtât de reproduire, pendant qu'il en est temps, tous
les détails de construction et de disposition tant intérieures
qu'extérieures de cette vénérable abbaye, à laquelle se rattachent
tant et de si précieux souvenirs."

2. See *supra*, p. 17.

3. H. Goetting, "Die Anfänge des Reichsstifts Gandersheim,"
Braunschweigisches Jahrbuch, XXXI (1950), 7-8.

4. K. Strecker, *Hrotsvithae Opera* (Leipzig: 1906), p. 262, vss.
391-395.

> Tunc tandem, cunctis ad cultum rite paratis
> Festi, Wicberhtus praesul domini benedictus
> Dedicat hoc templum domini sub honore decorum
> Omnibus ad laudem sanctis per saecla perennem,
> Quorum tunc festum digne fuerat celebrandum.

5. K. Steinacker, *Die Bau- und Kunstdenkmäler* (Wolfenbüttel: 1910), p. 115. "Bischof Wigbert weiht 881 (nach dem Chronikon Hild. 883) am Tage Allerheiligen, dem Jahrestage der lokalen Lichtererscheinung, und für alle Heiligen das vollendete Münster. Aber erst Bischof Sighart kann 926 auch den Bau des 'turris occidentalis' abschliessen; ..."

6. H. Bodo, *Syntagma ecclesiae Gandesianae* (1550), p. 502. "Illa Atelheidis secundo combustum monasterium dedicari fecit."

7. Steinacker, p. 129. "Ende des X Jahrh.: Chorrechteck, Umriss und Einteilung des westlichen Querhauses, die Ecken des Mittelschiffs, das äussere Gewände der Westtür. Daraus folgt, dass überhaupt der Körper des Gebäudes noch dem X Jahrh. seine wesentliche Ausdehnung verdankt."

8. *Ibid.*, p. 122. "Da nun in den Jahren 1063/94 eine neue Weihe überliefert ist, so dürfen wir mit dieser sehr wohl auf Grund der Kunstformen das Mittelschiff des Münsters in Beziehung bringen, das also demnach im letzten Viertel des XI. Jahrh. seine jetzige Gesamtform erhalten haben muss."

9. Goetting, "Die Anfänge," pp. 39-40.

10. Steinacker, p. 170. "Der Name Abtei begreift alle heute zur herzoglichen Domäne gehörigen, um das Münster gruppierten ehemaligen Wohn- und Wirtschaftsgebäude des Stiftes, insbesondere die Reste der ältesten, den Kreuzgang einst umschliessenden Klosterbauten, die Stätte der Dechanei und die Abteigebäude im engeren Sinne."

11. *Ibid.*, "... wonach die Äbstissin gegen den friedlich heranziehenden Bischof *turres et munitiora loca circa ecclesiam* mit Bewaffneten besetzen liess die *ita castellum muniunt*. (Leibnitz aaO. I, S455)."

12. *Ibid.*

13. *Ibid.*

14. André Michel, *Histoire de l'Art* (Paris: Libraire Armand, 1905), t.I, deuxième partie, pp. 481-482.

15. Steinacker, p. 172.

16. *Ibid.*

17. *Ibid.*

18. A. Nicoll, *Masks, Mimes, and Miracles* (New York: 1931), p. 153.

19. L. W. Jones and C. R. Morey, *The Miniatures and Manuscripts of Terence* (Princeton: 1931), pp. 214-215.

20. P. Chasles, *Le Moyen Age* (Paris: 1876), pp. 276-277.

21. Magnin, pp. v-vi, ". . . on sent un auteur qui écrit non pour être psalmodié du haut d'un jubé, mais pour être joué avec apparat dans la grande salle d'un noble Chapitre."

22. *Ibid.*, p. vi, "Un sujet obligé d'étude pour tout historien sérieux du théâtre."

23. David Dunford, "Canoness," *Catholic Encyclopedia*, III (1913), 255.

24. Anthony Allaria, "Canons and Canonesses Regular," *ibid.*, III (1913), 288.

25. J. Heineken, "Die Anfänge sächsischen Frauenklöster," (diss., Göttingen: 1909.).

26. Goetting, "Die Anfänge," p. 8. "Wenn man von der im gleichen Jahre (1909) erschienenen Göttinger Dissertation von Johanna Heineken, 'Die Anfänge der sächsischen Frauenklöster' absieht, die sich mit unzureichenden Mitteln und daher nur geringem Erfolg dieser Aufgabe unterzog, so ist weder vorher noch nachher die genannte Voraussetzung erfüllt worden. Das mag zunächst in dem Umstand begründet gewesen sein dass die Urkunden des Reichsstifts eben nur in den suspekten Drucken des 18 Jhs. vorlagen."

27. *Ibid.*, p. 28. ". . . dass von Anfang an eng mit dem Kloster Corvey verbunden, wahrscheinlich nur wenig jünger als dieses und das Vorbild der immer zahlreicher werdenden sächsischen Kanonissenstifter. . . ."

28. H. Goetting, "Zur Kritik der älteren Gründungsurkunde des Reichsstifts Gandersheim," *Mitteilungen Österreichischen Staatsarchivs*, III (1950), 368, 389, 396. "Supplik der Gandersheimer Kanonissen an Papst Paschalis II., einer originalen Littera clausa, . . . Brunshausener Vorläufer des erst 852 ins Leben getretenen Kanonissenstiftes . . . und war bei der Gründung des nahe bei Gandersheim gelegenen Kanonissenstifts Lamspringe . . ."

29. K. Algermissen, "Die Gestalt Mariens in der Dichtung Hrotsvithas von Gandersheim," *Unsere Diözese*, XXIII (1954), 141.

30. K. Algermissen, "Bischof Altfrid, der Mitbegründer von Gandersheim," *ibid.*, XXI (1952), 63. Erst jetzt fand die Übersiedlung des Kanonissenstiftes von Brunshausen statt. Der Konvent zählte damals 24 Klosterfrauen, . . . Bald wuchs das Stift immer mehr an. Es wurde zum reichsten des Bistums Hildesheim."

31. H. Goetting, "Das Fuldaer Missionskloster Brunshausen und seine Lage" *Harz-Zeitschrift*, V/VI (1953/1954), 9-10. "Von

dem etwa anderthalb Kilometer nördlich der Stadt Bad Gandersheim and der oberen Gande gelegenen heutigen Domänenvorwerk war vordem nicht viel mehr bekannt gewesen, als dass hier im Jahre 852 das spätere Reichsstift Gandersheim gegründet worden war. Hier waren, ehe der dann im Jahre 856 in Gandersheim selbst begonnene Bau des Münsters unde der Stiftsgebäude nach fünfundzwanzig Jahren seine Fertigstellung erlebte, die Kanonissen des Stifts provisorisch untergebracht gewesen. . . . Dass sich in späterer Zeit ein vom Stift Gandersheim abhängiges Nonnenkloster in Brunshausen nachweisen liess, wurde entweder damit erklärt, dass bei der 'Verlegung' des Stiftskapitels nach Gandersheim ein kleiner Konvent in Brunshausen zurückgeblieben, oder dass damals ebendort, 'eine neue Stiftung nach der Benediktinerregel gegründet' worden sei."

32. *Ibid.*, p. 10. "Und auch die Bemerkung des Agius von Corvey in der dichterischen, leider von bestimmten Angaben bewusst freigehaltenen Lebensbeschreibung seiner Schwester Hathumod, dass die zunächst in Brunshausen versammelten Kanonissen *extra in villula* untergebracht werden mussten, wird hier herangezogen werden dürfen."

33. Goetting, "Die Anfänge," p. 48. ". . . nachdem Äbstissen und Kanonissen von Brunshausen nach Gandersheim übergesiedelt waren. (Hrotsvit, *Primord.*, v. 396)."

34. See p. 202, n. 31.

35. Francis Aidan Gasquet, *Monastic Life in the Middle Ages* (London: G. Bell, 1922), p. 201.

36. Algermissen, "Die Gestalt," p. 140. "Ihr Leben war also wesentlich freier als das der Insassen der eigentlichen Nonnenklöster."

37. Gasquet, p. 201.

38. Algermissen, "Die Gestalt," p. 140. "Gandersheim war, . . . ein Kanonissenstift. Die eintretenden Jungfrauen, den Adelsgeschlechtern unserer Heimat entsprossen, wohnten und lebten, beteten und betrachteten in einem gemeinsamen Konvent, durften aber Gäste empfangen, sich eigene Dienerinnen halten und aus der religiösen Gemeinschaft wieder austreten."

39. R. Steinhoff, "Canonissin des Stifts Gandersheim, die älteste deutsche Dichterin" (1882), *Zeitschrift des Harzvereins,* XV (1926), 120.

40. Goetting, "Die Anfänge," p. 28. "Hathumod war im Jahre 840 geboren und wurde dem berühmten Stift Herford zur Erziehung übergeben, das von Anfang an eng mit dem Kloster

Corvey verbunden, wahrscheinlich nur wenig jünger als dieses und das Vorbild der immer zahlreicher werdenden sächsischen Kanonissenstifter war."

41. Strecker, p. 260, vss. 322-326.

> Sed sese Christo clam consecraverat ipsa
> Caelesti fera sponso velamine sacro,
> Omnino sponsum spernens animo moriturum.
> Nec tamen extimplo, pro seditione cavenda,
> Auro fugentes potuit deponere vestes,
> Induitur solito sed vestitu pretioso.

42. Heineken, p. 96. "Gerberg tritt zunächst nicht ganz in die Gemeinschat des Klosters ein, denn sie legt noch nicht die goldglänzenden Gewänder ab. Nur durch ihre Kleidung unterscheidet sich auch die Königin von einer Nonne. (Aeltere Vita c. 11 Scr. X579.) . . . Für eine besondere Form der kirchlichen Bindung, eine strengere oder leichtere, bedeutet die Tracht nichts."

43. Gasquet, p. 215.

44. Thomas Merton, *The Silent Life* (New York: Farrar, Straus & Cudahy, 1957), pp. 69-70.

45. Algermissen, "Die Gestalt," p. 139. "Denn in die vornehmen Kanonissenstifte Niedersachsens—und Gandersheim war eines der vornehmsten—wurden in den ersten Jahrhunderten der christlichen Geschichte Niedersachsens nur Töchter des eingesessenen Adels aufgenommen. . . . Hrotsvitha hat den Namen des Stiftes Gandersheim weltberühmt gemacht."

46. *Ibid.*, p. 141. "Sie errichtete neben der neuen Marienkirche ein zweites Kloster, ein Benediktinerinnenstift für 30 Nonnen. . . . Während an diesem Bau gearbeitet wurde und Hrotsvitha ihre Dichtungen schuf, trat um 985 die Tochter des schon verstorbenen Kaisers Otto II, Spohia, als Kanonisse ins Gandersheimer Kloster ein."

47. *Ibid.*, p. 142. "Sicher ist, dass Hrotsvithas dichterisches▪ Schaffen ganz in die Zeit der tüchtigen Äbtissen Gerberga II. fällt und in die gläzende Epoche der Ottonischen Renaissance. Als eine der grössten deutschen Frauen ragt die in jener Zeit empor."

48. F. Löher, "Hrotsvitha und ihre Zeit" (1858), *Zeitschrift des Harzvereins*, XV (1920), 502. ". . . wenn er sie, wie sie sagte, mit seinen hellen Augen anblickte."

49. Strecker, p. 222, fol. 131^v, 1. 11.

50. *Ibid.*, p. 115, fol 79^r, 1. 1-4.

51. Lina Eckenstein, *Women in Monasticism* (Cambridge: The University Press, 1896), pp. 148-152.

52. Strecker, p. 1, fol. 2^r, 11. 28-29; p. 2, l.1.

53. Strecker, p. 113, fol. 78^r, 11. 1-8.

54. Löher, pp. 467-470.

Chapter IV

1. C. Magnin, *Théâtre de Hrotsvitha* (Paris: 1845), pp. xx-xxii. "Hrotsvitha nous apprend elle même qu'elle vint au monde long-temps après la mort d'Othon l'Illustre, duc de Saxe, père de Henri l'Oiseleur, arrivée le 30 novembre 912. Ailleurs (préface de ses légendes en vers), elle se dit un peu plus âgée que la fille de Henri, duc de Bavière, Gerberge II, sacrée abbesse de Gandersheim l'an 959, et née, suivant toutes les apparences, vers l'an 940. Il résulte de ces deux indices combinés, que Hrotsvitha a dû naître entre les années 912 et 940, et beaucoup plus près de la seconde date que de la première, par conséquent, vers 930 ou 935. La date de sa mort est encore plus incertaine. Un seul point est hors de doute, c'est qu'elle poussa sa carrière fort au delà de l'an 968, puisque le fragment que nous reste du *Panégyrique des Othons* comprend les événements de cette année, et que postérieurement à ce poeme, Hrothsvitha en composa un autre sur la fondation du monastère de Gandersheim. Casimir Oudin dit qu'elle mourut l'an 1001; elle aurait eu soixante-sept ans, si nous ne nous sommes pas trompés dans nos précédents calculs. Oudin fonde son opinion sur ce que Hrotsvitha a célébré les trois premiers Othons. Il est vrai que le premier livre du poëme, le suel qui subsiste, finit à la mort d'Othon Ier; mais le titre même de l'ouvrage (*Panegyris Oddonum*), prouve que nous n'en possédons que la première partie. La seconde dédicace addressée à Othon, roi des Romains, qui devint bientôt Othon II, formait probablement le préambule du second livre, consacré aux actions de ce prince. Ajoutons qu'on lit dans une chronique des évêques d'Hildesheim, que Hrotsvitha a célébré les trois Othons. De ce dernier fait, s'il était bien établi, il résulterait que notre auteur aurait vécu au delà de l'an 1002, ce qui n'aurait, d'ailleurs, rien que de très-vraisemblable."

2. K. Algermissen, "Die Gestalt Mariens," *Unsere Diözese,* XXIII (1954), 139. "Als frühestes Jahr ihrer Geburt kann wohl 932, als frühestes Jahr ihres Todes 1003 angesehen werden. Sie ist also gut 70 Jahre alt geworden."

3. C. St. John, *The Plays of Roswitha* (London: 1923), p. x.

4. K. Strecker, *Hrotsvithae Opera* (Leipzig: 1906), p. 2, fol. 2^r, 11. 3-4.

5. Evangeline W. Blashfield, *Portraits and Backgrounds* (New York: Charles Scribner's Sons, 1917), p. 12.

6. Strecker, p. 1, fol. 2^r, 11. 28-29; p. 2, fol. 2^r, 11. 2-3.

7. *Ibid.*, p. 222, fol. 131^v, l. 21.

8. *Ibid.*, p. 224, fol. 133^r, vss. 11-14.

9. Blashfield, p. 25.

10. Magnin, p. xiii. "Suivant les uns, Hrotsvitha l'abbesse sortait de la seconde branche de la famille ducale de Saxe, et était fille du duc Othon l'Illustre, second fils de Ludolfe et père de l'empereur Henry l'Oiseleur."

11. Algermissen, "Die Gestalt," p. 139.

12. *Ibid.*, p. 141. "Die vierte Äbtissin, Hrotsvitha, vermutlich eine Tante unserer Dichterin, war 919 vom Konvent gewählt und vom Hildesheimer Bischof Walbert (903-919) eingesegnet."

13. When Hrotsvitha said of herself, "I, the strong [or loud] voice of Gandersheim," she provided a fertile source of comment for writers who have attributed many and varied meanings to her statement. Algermissen explains that her name signifies "strong storm . . . it actually is a compound of *Hroud* (sound) and *souid* (strong or clear), and according to the original, the spelling of her name should have been "Hroudsouid," ("Die Gestalt," 139). This is undoubtedly the simplest and most nearly correct interpretation for "Ego, clamor validus." Cf. p. 192, n. 91.

14. Algermissen, "Die Gestalt," p. 139.

15. Strecker, p. 114, fol. 79^r, 1. 32; p. 115, 11. 1-2, 16-19; fol. 79^v, 11. 20-23. "Vestra admiratione dignum duxistis et largitorem in me operantis gratiae. . . . Deum namque, cuius solummodo gratia sum id, quod sum, in me laudari cordetenus gaudeo; sed maior, quam sim, videri timeo, quia utrumque nefas esse non ambigo, et gratuitum dei donum negare, et non acceptum accepisse simulare. Unde non denego praestante gratia creatoris per dynamin me artes scire, quia sum animal capax disciplinae, sed per energian fateor omnino nescire."

16. *Ibid.*, p. 1, fol. 1^v, 11. 18-21; fol. 2^r, 11. 23, 28-29; p. 2, fol. 2^r, 1. 2. ". . . quanto in ipsa inceptione minus ulla proprii vigoris fulciebar sufficientia; quia nec matura adhuc aetate vigens nec scientia fui proficiens, . . . pro rusticitate, . . . sapientissimae atque benignissimae Rikkardis magistrae, . . . prona favente clementia regiae indolis Gerbergae."

17. *Ibid.*, p. 221, fol. 131^r, 11. 1-15; p. 222, fol. 131^v, 11. 5-14. Gerbergae, illustri abbatissae, cui pro sui eminentia probitatis haut minor obsequela venerationis, quam pro insigni regalis

stemmate generositatis, Hrotsvit Gandeshemensis, ultima ultimarum sub huiusmodi personae dominio militantium, quod famula herae. O mea domna, quae rutilanti spiritalis varietate sapientiae prae lucetis, non pigescat vestri almitiem perlustrare, quod vestra confectum si ignoratis ex iussione. Id quidem oneris mihi inposuistis, ut gesta caesaris augusti, quae nec auditu unquam affatim valui colligere, metrica percurrerem ratione. In huius sudore progressionis quantum meae inscitiae obstiturit difficultatis, ipsa conicere potestis, quia haec eadem nec prius scripta repperi, nec ab aliquo digestim sufficienterque dicta elicere quivi.... Nunc autem omne latus tanto magis caret defensione, quanto minus ulla fulcitur auctoritate; unde etiam verior me temeritatis argui tendiculasque multorum non devitare convicii, eo quod pomposis facetae urbanitatis exponenda eloquentiis praesumpserim dehonestare inculti vilitate sermonis. Si tamen sanae mentis examen accesserit, quae res recte pensare non nescit, quanto sexus fragilior scientiaque minor, tanto venia erit facilior; praesertim cum si meae praesumptionis, sed vestrum causa iussionis huius stamen opusculi coeperim ordiri."

18. L. Eckenstein, *Women in Monasticism* (Cambridge: 1896), pp. 160-161.

19. H. Goetting, "Die Anfänge des Reichsstifts Gandersheim," *Braunschweigisches Jahrbuch*, XXXI (1950), 10.

20. Strecker, p. 1, fol. 2^r, 11. 23-25; p. 2, fol. 2^r, 11. 6-12. "Unde clam cunctis et quasi furtim, nunc in componendis sola desudando, nunc male composita destruendo. ... Quamvis etiam metrica modulatio femineae fragilitati difficilis videatur et ardua, solo tamen semper miserentis supernae gratiae auxilio, non propriis viribus, confisa, huius carmina opusculi dactilicis modulis succinere apposui, ne crediti talentum ingenioli sub obscuro torpens pectoris (antro) rubigine exterminaretur neglegentiae."

21. Algermissen, "Die Gestalt," p. 139 "Die erste christliche Dichterin Niedersachsens und unserer Hildesheimer Diözese ist zugleich die erste deutsche Dichterin. Sie ist die erste dramatische Dichterin der ganzen christlichen Welt, deren Dramen den ersten Versuch einer christlichen Dramatik überhaupt bedeuten."

22. Robert H. Fife, *Roswitha of Gandersheim*, (New York: Columbia University Press, 1947), pp. 6-7.

23. Charles S. Baldwin, *Medieval Rhetoric and Poetic* (New York: Macmillan, 1928), p. 144.

24. P. Chasles, *Le Moyen Age* (Paris: 1876), p. 297.

25. Strecker, "Abraham," vi, 171, 27.

26. Chasles, pp. 305-306. ". . . le balancement et la molle ca-

dence de ces vers, ce sont en effet des vers modernes. On n'a, pour s'en convaincre, qu'à suivre pas à pas le latin de Hrotsvita et à calquer, vers pour vers, des lignes françaises d'un nombre égal de pieds et de rimes sous ses lignes latines: . . . Peut-on nommer cela de la prose? Evidemment la religieuse a écrit en vers sans le savoir."

27. *Ibid.,* pp. 307-308.

28. Magnin, pp. vi-vii. "Ce célèbre monastère a été pour l'Allemagne une sorte d'oasis intellectuelle, jetée au milieu des steppes de la barbarie."

29. Blashfield, p. 30.

30. Ernst Rudolf Köpke, *Die älteste deutsche Dichterin* (Berlin: E. S. Mittler und Sohn, 1869), p. 28.

31. A. Ebert, "Hrotsvith Opera," *Allgemeine Geschichte der Literatur des Abdendlandes,* III (1887), 285-290.

32. K. A. Barack, *Die Werke der Hrotsvitha* (Nurnberg: Bauer und Raspe, 1858), p. 54.

33. Strecker, p. 113, fol. 78^r, ll. 1-25; p. 114, fol. 78^v, ll. 11-18. "Plures inveniuntur catholici, cuius nos penitus expurgare nequimus facti, qui pro cultioris facundia sermonis gentilium vanitatem librorum utilitati praeferunt sacrarum scripturarum. Sunt etiam alii, sacris inhaerentes paginis, qui licet alia gentilium spernant, Terrentii tamen fingmenta frequentius lectitant et, dum dulcedine sermonis delectantur, nefandarum notitia rerum maculantur. Unde ego, Clamor Validus Gandeshemensis, non recusavi illum imitari dictando, dum alii colunt legendo, quo eodem dictationis genere, quo turpia lascivarum incesta feminarum recitabantur, laudabilis sacrarum castimonia virginum iuxta mei facultatem ingenioli celebraretur. Hoc tamen facit non raro verecundari gravique rubore perfundi, quod, huiusmodo specie dictationis cogente detestabilem inlicite amantium dementiam et male dulcia colloquia eorum, quae nec nostro auditui permittuntur accommodari, dictando mente tractavi et stili officio designavi. Sed (si) haec erubescendo neglegerem, nec proposito satisfacerem nec innocentium laudem adeo plene iuxta meum posse exponerem, quia, quanto blanditiae amantium promptiores ad illiciendum, tanto et superni adiutoris gloria sublimior et triumphantium victoria probatur gloriosior, praesertim cum feminea fragilitas vinceret et virilis robur confusioni subiaceret. . . . Si enim alicui placet mea devotio, gaudebo; si autem vel pro mei abiectione vel pro vitiosi sermonis rusticitate placet nulli, memet ipsam tamen iuvat, quod feci, quia, dum proprii vilitatem laboris, in aliis meae inscientiae opusculis heroico ligatam strophio, in

hoc dramatica vinctam serie colo, perniciosas gentilium delicias abstinendo devito." (Translation from Eckenstein, pp. 168-169.)

34. Eckenstein, pp. 169-170.

35. E. Zeydel, "Were Hrotsvitha's Dramas Performed?" *Speculum*, XX (1943), 447, n. 1.

36. *Ibid.*, "*Das deutsche Drama* in Verbindung mit Julius Bab, Albert Ludwig, Friedrich Michael, Max J. Wolff und Rudolf Wolkan herausgegeben von Robert F. Arnold. Munich, 1925."

37. *Ibid.*

38. Blashfield, pp. 20-23. "Hrotsvitha's comedies are, in spite of their archaic subject matter, comedies of manners. . . . It is no longer a comedy of movement and manners like that of Plautus, nor of situations and poetic declamation like the work of Terence. It seeks to become ethical like the drama of Greece."

39. Magnin, p. lii. "S'il est vrai, comme on l'a dit souvent, que la comédie soit l'expression de la société, la comparaison que nous sommes à portée de faire entre les deux pièces de Hrothsvitha, le colloque d'Érasme et le drame de Decker nous offrirait un moyen sûr et piquant d'apprécier la valeur morale des trois époques."

40. *Ibid.*, p. lv. "Ces six drames sont un dernier rayon de l'antiquité classique, une imitation prémédités et assez peu reconnaissable, j'en conviens; des comédies de Térence, sur lesquels le christianisme et la barbarie ont déposé leur double empreinte; mais c'est précisément par ce qu'ils ont de chrétien et même de barbare, c'est-à-dire, par ce que leur physionomie nous offre de moderne, que ces drames m'ont paru mériter d'être recueillis à part et traduits avec soin, pour prendre rang à la suite du théâtre ancien, et à la tête des collections théâtrales de toutes les nations de l'Europe."

41. Blashfield, pp. 20-21.

42. *Ibid.*, p. 21.

43. *Ibid.*

44. Magnin, p. xlvii. "Chose étrange! la langue de l'amour au Xe siècle est aussi raffinée, aussi quintessenciée, aussi précieuse qu' aux XVI et XVIIes siècles . . . dans le poète de la cour d'Élizabeth, le jeune amoureux se perd en *concetti* à la mode italienne, tandis que, dans Hrotsvitha, il s'epuise, suivant le goût de l'époque, en arguties scolastiques et en distinctions tirées de la doctrine des *universaux*."

45. Blashfield, p. 23.

46. Wilhelm Creizenach, *Geschichte des neueren Dramas* (Halle: Niemeyer, 1911), I, 19.

47. *Ibid.*
48. Blashfield, pp. 23-24.
49. *Ibid.*, p. 24.
50. *Ibid.*, pp. 25 and 33.
51. S. H. Butcher, *Aristotle's Theory of Poetry* (New York: 1951), p. 291. "In the *Eumenides,* months or years elapse between the opening of the play and the next scene. The *Trachiniae* of Sophocles and the *Supplices* of Euripides afford other and striking instances of the violation of the so-called rule. In the *Agamemnon,* even if a definite interval of days cannot be assumed between the fire-signals announcing the fall of Troy and the return of Agamemnon, at any rate, the conditions of time are disregarded and the march of events is imaginatively accelerated."
52. *Ibid.*, pp. 288-289.
53. Creizenach, p. 18.
54. Butcher, pp. 31-35.
55. *Ibid.*, pp. 187-188.
56. C. M. Gayley, *Plays of Our Forefathers* (New York: Duffield, 1907), p. 2.
57. Blashfield, p. 9.
58. *Ibid.*, p. 27.
59. Algermissen, "Die Gestalt," p. 142. "Dass eine Klosterfrau die römischen Dichter Horaz, Ovid, Vergil, Plautus and Terenz nicht nur las und verstand, dass sie auch daranging, jenen heidnischen Dichtern und ihren Werken ein christliches Dichtungswerk entgegenzustellen, musste aller Augen auf sich lenken."
60. E. Zeydel, "Were Hrotsvitha's Dramas Performed?" *Speculum,* XX (1943), 445.
61. *Geschichte der deutschen Literatur* (Berlin: Weidmann, 1899), pp. 57-59.
62. Zeydel, "Hrotsvitha's Dramas," p. 445.
63. Winterfeld-Reich, *Deutsche Dichter des lateinischen Mittelalters in deutschen Versen* (Munich: 1913), p. 449. "Man denke an Notker und Hrotsvit. Notkers beste Kraft liegt in seinem echt schwäbischen, an G. Keller gemahnenden Humor, mit dem er alles zu vergolden weiss: die Fabel vom kranken Löwen und das Lügenmärchen vom Wunschbock, das noch heute an des Bodensees Ufern lebendig ist, wie die Anekdoten vom Kaiser Karl, dessen überragende Grösse sich im Andenken der Nachwelt nicht schöner abbilden konnte, als es in Notkers Geiste geschehen ist,

alles umfassend, das Grösste wie das Kleinste. Der treue Lehrer seiner Schüler, an denen er hängt, auch wenn sie est ihm nimmer danken, dessen Briefe an Mörikes 'Musterkärtchen' erinnern, und der geniale Schöpfer der Sequenz, der die geistliche Lyrik auf Jahrhunderte in neue Bahnen wies, dessen Grösse es ist, dass er im Göttlichen stets das Reinmenschliche zu sehen weiss, dass er das göttliche Geheimnis dem Herzen nahe zu bringen versteht, er ist in seiner liebevoll sinnigen Art Schwabe durch und durch. Ganz anders die Nonne von Gandersheim. Herbe und verschlossen is sie, trotz Annette von Droste-Hülshoff, und verbirgt die tief innerliche Weichheit ihres Wesens, dass sie nur hier und da, wo sie von ihrem lieben Gandersheim redet oder liebevoll verweilt bei der Charakteristik ihrer heiligen Jungfrauen, die ihr Schwester, Kind und heiliges Vorbild zugleich sind, unerwartet und schier elementar durchbricht. Ist Notkers Kennzeichen die Lust am Fabulieren, die liebevoll das Bild aus tausend kleinen, feinen Einzelzügen zusammenstrichelt, die ihn in den Sequenzen befähigt, das ganze Lied auf ein Bild zu stellen, daraus aber auch alles hervorzuholen, was darin liegt, so liebt sie es, kurz und knapp, mit wenigen Worten ihr Bild zu umreissen, und führt in ihren Dramen, worin ein geistvoller Erklärer Nordseeluft zu spüren gemeint hat, mit sicherer Hand die Fäden der Handlung: man denkt unwillkürlich an Hebbel. Freilich muss man dabei nicht Massstäbe anlegen, die für ihre Zeit und deren so ganz eigen geartete Kunst nicht passen; doch darüber wird später zu reden sein."

64. St. John, p. xxvi.

65. *Ibid.*, p. xxvii.

66. *Ibid.*

67. Zeydel, "Hrotsvitha's Dramas," p. 450.

Chapter V

1. Edwin H. Zeydel, "The Reception of Hrotswitha by the German Humanists after 1493," *Journal of English and Germanic Philology*, XLIV (1945), 248-249.

2. S. H. Butcher, trans. *Aristotle's Theory of Poetry and Fine Art* (New York: 1951), p. 351.

3. *Ibid.*, pp. 360-361.

4. Cf. K. Strecker, *Hrotsvithae Opera* (Leipzig: 1906), p. 113, fols. 78ʳ and 78ᵛ, ll. 21-25. "Quia, quanto blanditiae amantium

promptiores ad illiciendum, tanto et superni adiutoris gloria sublimior et triumphantium victoria probatur gloriosior, praesertim cum feminea fragilitas vinceret et virilis robur confusioni subiaceret."

5. Strecker's 1906 Teubner edition is used for the Latin text and St. John's 1923 edition for the English translation in this chapter.

6. Production, *Mercy College Players*, Lydia Mendelssohn Theatre, University of Michigan, Ann Arbor, Michigan, January 15, 1955.

7. E. W. Blashfield, *Portraits and Backgrounds* (New York: 1917), p. 74.

8. For further examples, cf. Strecker, "Abraham," vi, vii, and viii in toto; "Pafnutius," iii, in toto.

9. See *supra*, n. 6.

10. Blashfield, p. 51.

11. R. H. Fife, *Hroswitha of Gandersheim* (New York: 1947), p. 13.

12. Butcher, p. 359.

13. *Ibid.*, p. 363. "Frequently, the whole action of a Greek drama would form merely the climax of a modern play."

14. Cornelia C. Coulter, "The 'Terentian' Comedies of a Tenth-Century Nun," *Classical Journal*, XXIV (1929), 529.

15. R. Steinhoff, "Canonissin des Stifts Gandersheim, die älteste deutsche Dichterin" (1882), *Zeitschrift des Harzvereins,* XV (1920), 119.

16. For further examples, cf. Strecker, "Gallicanus," I, ii, 120, 5 through 16; xii, 127, 14 through 28; "Dulcitius," xii, 145, 25 through xiii, 146, 2; "Calimachus," iii 150, 9 through 23; "Abraham," i, 163, 22 through 29; "Pafnutius," i, 179, 18 through 14; "Sapientia," i, 202, 8 through 15; iii, 207, 5 through 11; v, 209, 16 through 22.

17. Butcher, pp. 342-343. The Greeks used the term, *dianoia*, for "the intellectual reflexions of the speaker, the proof of his own statements, the disproof of those of his opponents, his general maxims concerning life and conduct, as elicited by the action and forming part of a train of reasoning." Butcher believes the use of this device was due to the influence of political debate and forensic oratory on the Greek theater. He explains that the characters did not use this device to discuss abstract truths, but rather to explain their own doing and to influence others. Nor does Hrotsvitha use the learned disputation or dialectics for the

212

exposition of an abstract truth but to confound an antagonist, as in "Sapientia," or to influence, as in "Pafnutius."

18. For further examples, cf. Strecker, "Gallicanus," I, v, 123, 1 through 16 (prayer); xii, in toto (narration); "Calimachus," iv, 151, 12 through 19 (prayer); ix, 159, 29 through 160, 5 (admonition); "Abraham," ii, 164, 24 through 30; vii, 174, 15 through 22 (admonition); "Pafnutius," i, in toto (dialectics) ; iv, 190, 34 through 191, 4 (admonition); x, in toto (narration); xiii, 200, 1 through 13 (prayer); "Sapientia," iii, 205, 1 through 207, 4 (disputation); ix, 218, 23 through 219, 21 (prayer).

19. Cf. Strecker, "Sapientia," iii, 205, 1 through 207, 4.

20. Butcher, p. 278.

21. For further examples, cf. Strecker, "Gallicanus," II, 5, 135, 3; "Pafnutius," x, 196, 1, 17; xii, 199, 11; xiii, 199, 26; "Abraham," iv, 169, 15; vii, 175, 29; "Sapientia," iii, 207, 13, 16; v, 208, 26; v, 215, 30; ix, 218, 10.

22. Cf. Strecker, "Sapientia," ix, 218, 10.

23. Kenneth Thorpe Rowe, *Write That Play* (New York: Funk & Wagnalls, 1939), p. 37.

24. For further examples, cf. Strecker, "Gallicanus," ii, 120, 18; xii, 127, 20; II, v, 6 through 29; "Dulcitius," xii, 145, 1; "Calimachus," ii, 149, 31; ix, 157, 3; "Abraham," ii, 165, 17; vi, 172, 13; 19 through 23; vii, 173, 25; vii, 174, 4, 15, 30; vii, 175, 5, 10; ix, 177, 16, 26; "Pafnutius," vii, 193, 27; vii, 194, 20, 25; xiii, 199, 28; iii, 203, in toto; iv, 207, 22; v, 211, 23.

25. Cf. 'irony' in the *Oxford Universal Dictionary*, p. 1045.

26. For further examples, cf. Strecker, "Dulcitius," xiv, 146, in toto; "Abraham," vi, 171, 15.

27. *Ibid.*, "Gallicanus," I, v, 123, 2; ix, 126, 15; xii, 129, 15; xiii, 131, 1, 21; xiii, 132, 3; II, vii, 136, 3; ix, 137, in toto; "Dulcitius," xi, 143, 19; xi, 144, 5; xiv, 147, 11; "Calimachus," iv, 151, 12; ix, 155, 11; ix, 157, 15; ix, 159, 5; "Abraham," ii, 164, 24; iii, 169, 13; ix, 178, 5,; "Pafnutius," i, 185, 29; iii, 188, 4; xiii, 200, 1; "Sapientia," iii, 206, 32; v, 211, 10; v, 214, 26; vii, 217, 10, 12; ix, 217, 33; ix, 218, 23.

28. Aristotle *Poetics* 13. 1453[a] 4. 12-13. "A well-constructed plot should, therefore, be single in its issue, rather than double as some maintain."

29. *Ibid.*, 7. 1450[b] 1, 2, and 3. 22-35.

30. *Ibid.*, ll. 1452[a] 1. 22-29.

31. Cf. Strecker, "Abraham," vii, 173-178.

32. *Ibid.*, "Gallicanus," I, ix, xii, xiii, 125-132.

33. For further examples, cf. Strecker, "Gallicanus," I, xii, 128, 35; xii, 129, 5; II, ix, 137, 10; "Dulcitius," viii, 142, 26; xi, 144, 10; xiii, 146, 10; xiv, 146, 27; "Calimachus," vii, 153, 8; viii, 153, 21; ix, 155, 20; ix, 157, 32; ix, 159, 12; ix, 160, 4; "Abraham," iii, 167, 4; "Pafnutius," x, 196, 17; xi, 197, 20; "Sapientia," v, 210, 10, 16, 22, 28; v, 211, 2; v, 212, 31; v, 213, 18; v, 213, 33; vi, 216, 18, 23; ix, 219, 22.

34. Aristotle *Poetics* 11. 1452ᵃ 2. 29-32.

35. Cf. Strecker, "Abraham," vii, 173.

36. *Ibid.*, "Pafnutius," iii, 187.

37. Aristotle *Poetics* 11. 1452ᵃ 3. 36-38.

38. *Ibid.*, 16. 1454ᵇ and 1455ᵃ 1-7.

39. Cf. Strecker, "Sapientia," iii, 204, 11.

40. *Ibid.*, "Calimachus," vii, 153, 9.

41. *Ibid.*, "Dulcitius," iv, v, vi, vii, 141-142.

42. *Ibid.*, "Abraham," vi, 172, 3.

43. *Ibid.*, "Calimachus," iii, 150, 24.

44. Aristotle *Poetics* 16. 1455ᵃ 8.

45. Cf. Strecker, "Gallicanus," I, x, 126.

46. Allardyce Nicoll, *The Development of the Theatre* (New York: Harcourt, Brace, 1937), p. 39.

47. Carl Robert, *Die Masken der neueren attischen Komödie* (Halle: Max Niemeyer, 1911), pp. 1-60.

48. L. W. Jones and C. R. Morey, p. 67. MS *Parisinus Latinus* 7899 (6.—P fol. 2ᵛ). This manuscript dates from a little after 820 A.D. and was allegedly copied from a fourth- or fifth-century Terence manuscript presumably lost.

49. For further examples, cf. Strecker, "Dulcitius," i, 138, 13 (your own rare beauty); vi, 142, 15 (her looks are wild, her hair unbound); "Calimachus," vii, 173, 8 (Take care! A monstrous serpent is coming toward us!); ix, 155, 5 (Hence, savage monster! Away from this man!); ix, 160, 1 (O, Fortunatus, brimful of Satan's bitter gall); "Abraham," i, 163, 7 (My only care is her radiant beauty); iii, 166, 1 (How did the devil seduce her? By the wiles of love. He dressed in a monk's habit and went to see her often); iii, 168, 28 (in the guise of a worldling, I will seek her out) ; "Pafnutius," i, 184, 29 (Her beauty is wonderful!); iv, 190, 1 (Come, all my evil lovers); "Sapientia," iii, 203, 23 (I am amazed at their beauty).

50. Cf. Strecker, "Pafnutius," iv, 170, 11.

51. *Ibid.*, "Dulcitius," vi, 142, 9.

52. *Ibid.*, vi, 142, 12.

53. *Ibid.*, "Pafnutius," x, 196, 6.

54. For further examples, *ibid.*, "Sapientia," viii, 217, 17; "Dulcitius," i, 148, 13; vi, 142, 15.

55. *Ibid.*, "Dulcitius," vi, 142, 6.

56. *Ibid.*, ii, 140, 6.

57. *Ibid.*, "Gallicanus," I, vii, 124, 24.

58. *Ibid.*, "Sapientia," v, 210, 2.

59. *Ibid.*, v, 212, 20.

60. *Ibid.*, v, 211, 28.

61. *Ibid.*, "Dulcitius," xiv, 147, 1.

62. *Ibid.*, xiii, 146, 17.

63. Coulter, p. 528.

64. For further examples, cf. Strecker, "Calimachus," ii, 149, 33; "Pafnutius," i, 179, 10; 180, 27; 184, 13, 23, 29.

65. *Ibid.*, "Gallicanus," I, iv, 122, 1; "Abraham," vi, 171, 18; "Pafnutius," iii, 188, 5; "Sapientia," iii, 204, 8, 30; v, 209, 12.

66. *Ibid.*, "Dulcitius," xiii, 146, 10; "Calimachus," viii, 153, 16; ix, 156, 7; "Abraham," iii, 167, 4, 22; vi, 172, 2; "Pafnutius," xi, 197, 20; "Sapientia," v, 213, 16.

67. C. Magnin, *Théâtre de Hrotsvitha* (Paris: 1845), p. 457, n. 43. "Les notes indicatives du jeu des acteurs, que les grammairiens grecs appelaient *didascalies,* se recontrent, comme on sait, fort rarement dans les ouvrages dramatiques anciens. Ces indications de mise en scène sont également fort peu nombreuses dans le théâtre de Hrotsvitha. Cependant, nous en signalerons dans *Gallicanus* deux, qui ont échappé à Celtes. Nous attachons, pour notre part, une grande importance à ces *didascalies,* parce qu'elles prouvent, de la manière la plus formelle, que ces drames n'ont pas été écrits seulement pour la lecture, comme le prétend M. Price, un des récents éditeurs de Warton (*History of English Poetry*)."

68. E. Zeydel, "Were Hrotsvitha's Dramas Performed?" *Speculum,* XX (1943), 452, n. 1.

69. Quintilian, *Inst.* ix. 2. 40.

70. *Ibid.*, viii. 3. 61, 62.

71. Zeydel, "Hrotsvitha's Dramas," p. 451.

72. P. Chasles, *Le Moyen Age* (Paris: 1876), p. 308.

73. Cf. Strecker, "Gallicanus," xii, 128, 6.

74. Coulter, p. 527.

75. Cf. Strecker, "Dulcitius," ii, iii, 140.

76. *Ibid.*, "Gallicanus," I, ix, 125.

77. *Ibid.*, "Pafnutius," i, 179.

78. *Ibid.*, "Gallicanus," I, vii, 124, 29; xii, 128, 29.

79. *Ibid.*, "Calimachus," v, 152, 9; "Sapientia," viii, 217, 29.

80. Nicoll, *Theatre*, pp. 51-52.

81. A. Nicoll, *Masks, Mimes, and Miracles* (New York: 1931), p. 135.

82. *Ibid.*, p. 152.

83. *Ibid.*, p. 165.

84. *Ibid.*, p. 138.

85. Winterfeld-Reich, *Deutsche Dichter des lateinischen Mittelalters in deutschen Versen* (Munich: 1913), p. 512. "Hatte Hrotsvit für ihre Märtyrerkomödien wirklich keine Vorbilder? Sie nennt nur Terenz; aber dass sie nichts anderes nennt, beweist wenig. Hier klafft einstweilen eine Lücke; aber ich kann sie zum Glück durch ein Beispiel ausfüllen, worauf Reich mich einmal nebenher hinwies."

86. *Ibid.*, pp. 512-513. "In seinem Mimus (I 82 ff. 566f.) hatte er ausführlich von den christologischen Mimen gesprochen, die den Glauben und die Zeremonien der Christen und ihr Martyrium der Spottlust der Heiden preisgaben. Das typische Beispiel ist der Mimus des Genesius. Der hatte, als Heide, alle christlichen Gebräuche erkundet, um sie mit seiner Bande realistisch darzustellen, zum Gaudium des Kaisers Diokletian. Der Inhalt des Mimus war dieser: Genesius brach in der ersten Szene auf offener Strasse zusammen und verlangte als Schwerkranker die Taufe. Wir müssen uns gegenwärtig halten, dass viele, wie auch Konstantin der Grosse die Taufe eben verschoben, bis sie das Ende nahe fühlten; einen solchen Halbchristen also gab Genesius wieder. Nächste Szene: Genesius liegt zu Bett; seine Freunde sind um ihn. Er fühle sich schwer und wolle leicht werden. Antwort der Umgebung: 'Wir sind doch keine Tischler, dich auf die Hobelbank zu legen und dir ein Stück abzuhobeln'—richtige grobkörnige Mimenwitze. Er macht ihnen klar, er wolle Christ werden. Lauter Beifall des Kaisers über diesen kostbaren Spass. Man ruft den Priester und Küster; sie kommen, fragen nach seinem Begehren, und es folgt (wohl gleich an Ort und Stelle) die Taufhandlung mit allem Zeremoniell. Aber schon erscheinen die Kriegsknechte, um ihn vor den Kaiser zu führen. Er bekennt sich als Christen—und nun sollte natürlich in Mimus Verurteilung und Hinrichtung folgen. Da tritt ein unerwarteter Zwischenfall ein. Den Mimen, der eben noch als Spötter das Christentum verhönnt hat, fasst plötzlich der Geist: er bekennt sich im Ernst zu dem, was er eben in seiner Rolle deklamiert hat, und fordert

in begeisterter Rede den Kaiser und das Publikum auf, sich zu bekehren. So wird aus dem Spiele blutiger Ernst; man ergreift ihn, er wird verurteilt und hingerichtet. So wird der Mime zum Heiligen; und dieser Fall soll sogar mehrere Male vorgekommen sein."

87. *Ibid.*, p. 519. "Hrotsvits Dramen aber mit ihrer Inhaltsangabe im Titel sind vollgültige Zeugen der Mimenpraxis ihrer Zeit: '(wir werden agieren) die wunderbare Historie von dem Herzog Gallican; dem hat Kaiser Konstantin seine Tochter versprochen' usw."

88. Nicoll, *Masks*, pp. 111-112. Delivered on the occasion of his famous artistic combat with Publilius Syrus in 46 B.C.

89. Winterfeld-Reich, *Deutsche Dichter*, p. 518. "Auch der Mimus wird, zumal in der Zeit, wo er das dramatische Element überhaupt einschränkte, den eigentlichen Prolog, den ein Schauspieler zu agieren hatte (die pronuntiatio fabulae), auf eine prosaische, die Zuhörer schlicht instruierende Inhaltsangabe reduziert haben, die etwa den ältesten Theaterzetteln entspricht, welche sich auch nicht auf den blossen Titel beschränken, sondern angeben, was in der Komödie 'vorgestellt' wird. Die langen Titel Hrotsvits aber sind ein Ersatz für die Periochen der terenzianischen Komödie und zwar in einer dem Mimus, wie sie ihn kannte, angepassten Form, in derselben kunstvollen Reimprosa wie das Drama selbst."

90. Cf. Strecker, "Gallicanus," p. 117.

91. Nicoll, *Masks*, p. 31.

92. Cf. Strecker, "Calimachus," vii, viii, 153; ix, 155.

93. Herman Reich, *Der Mimus (Berlin*: Weidmann, 1903), p. 134, quoting Beveridge, *Pandectes Canonum* I, S. 230. "Es sollten nur fernerhin im Mimus nicht die Tracht von Mönchen und Nonnen profaniert werden, und man solle nicht den christlichen Glauben und seine Institutionen verhöhnen."

94. Cf. Strecker, "Abraham," iii, 166.

95. Nicoll, *Masks*, p. 148.

96. Jones and Morey, Text (*Leidensis Lipsianus* 26), pp. 214-215.

97. Cf. Strecker, "Dulcitius," ii through vii, 140-142.

98. *Ibid.*, "Abraham," vi, 172, 5.

99. *Ibid.*, vii, 174, 19.

100. *Ibid.*, "Sapientia," iii, 203-207.

101. *Ibid.*, "Gallicanus," II, v, 133-135.

102. Winterfeld-Reich, *Deutsche Dichter*, p. 519. "Wohl aber

hat die Stauferzeit die Dramen Hrotsvits als Geist von ihrem Geist erkannt."

103. *Ibid.*, p. 521. "Ich meine, . . . Hrotsvit hat, als sie ihr erstes Drama begann, allerdings mimische Aufführungen gekannt und hat bei ihren vier ersten Dramen eine Aufführung ins Auge gefasst, wenn auch nur im stillen.

104. B. Hunningher, *The Origin of the Theater* (Amsterdam: 1955), p. 83.

105. Zeydel, "Hrotsvitha's Dramas," p. 445.

106. Magnin, pp. xxxix-lv and corresponding notes in appendix.

107. *Ibid.*, p. 459. The *amen* which customarily provided a formal closing in the religious plays of the middle ages corresponding to the *plaudite* of the pagan comedies.

108. *Ibid.*, p. xi.

109. *Ibid.*, p. 459.

110. *Ibid.*, p. 461.

111. *Ibid.*, p. xl. "C'est une farce religieuse . . . sans trop de disparate, à côté du martyre des trois héroïques soeurs."

112. *Codices apocryph. Nov. Test.*, t. II, p. 542.

113. t. I, pp. 271 and 547.

114. Magnin, p. 469.

115. *Ibid.*, p. 477, n. 81.

116. C. St. John, *The Plays of Roswitha* (London: 1923), pp. 131-158.

117. Cf. St. John for translation.

118. Dan. 3:20, 22-24, 49-50.

119. Cf. St. John, "Abraham," p. 88.

120. *Ibid.*, "Gallicanus," II, viii, 30.

121. *Ibid.*, ii, 25.

122. *Ibid.*, "Dulcitius," vii and viii, 41.

123. St. Luke. 15:7.

124. I Cor. 1:27.

125. Pss. 129:3.

126. *Ibid.*, 148, 4, 9-10, 14.

127. For further examples, cf. Strecker, "Gallicanus," I, v, 123, 23, xii, 129, 15; xiii, 132, 3; II, i, 132, 18; vii, 135, 24; vii, 136, 3; "Dulcitius," xi, 143, 19; xii, 145, 5; xiv, 147, 9; "Calimachus," ix, 155, 11, 20; ix, 157, 9, 21, 25; ix, 158, 18; ix, 159, 29; ix, 161, 6; "Abraham," i, 162, 14; ii, 164, 33; iii, 169, 5, 13; vii, 175, 31; "Pafnutius," viii, 195, 30; xiii, 200, 10; "Sapientia," iii, 203, 16;

iii, 207, 11; v, 208, 21; vi, 216, 23; vi, 217, 10, 12; ix, 218, 23; ix, 219, 22.

128. *Ibid.*, "Dulcitius," iii, 141, 1; "Abraham," iii, 167, 18; ix, 178, 5.

129. Nicoll, *Masks*, p. 177.

130. Cf. Strecker, "Gallicanus," I, xii, 127, in toto.

131. *Ibid.*, "Abraham," i, 162, in toto; iii, 165, in toto; ix, 177, in toto.

132. Hunningher, p. 87.

133. See *supra*, pp. 7-8.

134. For further examples, cf. Strecker, "Sapientia," iii, 204, 30 through 207, 4; v, 208, in parte.

135. Cf. Strecker, p. 113, fol. 78^r, 11. 13-18.

136. Chasles, p. 307.

137. *Ibid.*, "Elle a reçu, tel est le propre des esprits supérieurs, les impressions de son temps, et les a transmises en les épurant."

138. Cf. Strecker, pp. 113-114.

139. *Ibid.*, "Abraham," ii, 164, in toto; Magnin, p. 466, n. 46.

140. Nicoll, *Masks*, p. 81.

141. Chasles, p. 307. "Les nuances dans la peinture des senti-ments du coeur, l'union de la chasteté volontaire et de l'amour ardent, l'expression contenue des passions fortes, la métaphysique dans l'émotion, tous ces caractères essentiels de la civilisation moderne se trouvent, chez Hrosvita, . . . à l'état de premiers liné-aments et dans leur forme pour ainsi dire virginale."

142. *Ibid.*, pp. 306-307. "Lorsque l'ermite se révèle à Marie, et lui reproche ses deportements, le mètre, que nous venons de voir inégal et ondoyant comme le volupté, devient grave, régulier et alterné comme les sentencieuses leçons du dogme." Cf. also Strecker, "Abraham," vi, 171, 15 through vii, 176, 17.

143. Cf. Strecker, "Dulcitius" and "Sapientia."

144. *Ibid.*, "Gallicanus," "Dulcitius," "Calimachus," and "Sapientia."

145. John Gassner, *Masters of the Drama* (New York: Dover Publications, 1945), p. 27.

146. Nicoll, *Masks,* pp. 111-128.

147. Zeydel, "Hrotsvitha's Dramas," p. 451.

148. *Terence*, trans. John Sargeaunt (2 vols.; New York: G. P. Putnam's Sons, 1931). Concerning time, Terence wrote only one play, "Timorumenos," covering more than a few hours duration. (Afternoon, Act I, no lapse of time, Act II, daybreak next morn-ing, Act III, no lapse of time, Act IV, thirty minutes, Act V.)

Each of the other five plays has less than two hours passage of time between acts. In no instance does the locale change from the initial street scene or road.

149. St. John's translation.

150. W. J. Craig text.

151. For further examples of exits and entrances in dialogue, cf. Strecker, "Gallicanus," I, i, 118, 4; i, 119, 19; ii, 119, 24; ii, 121, 13; iii, 121, 22; v, 122, 18; v, 125, 6; vi, 124, 8; vii, 124, 13, 29; vii, 125, 4; viii, 125, 6; ix, 125, 13, 23; x, 126, 26; xi, 127, 13; xii, 127, 14; xii, 130, 14, 17; II, i, 132, 20; ii, 132, 21, 29; iii, 133, 3; v, 133, 15; v, 135, 10; vi, 135, 15; "Dulcitius," ii, 140, 6, 29; iii, 141, 3; iv, 141, 6; v, 141, 27; v, 142, 4; vi, 142, 6, 15; viii, 142, 30; xi, 143, 14; xi, 144, 14; xii, 144, 15; xii, 145, 23; xiii, 145, 25; xiii, 146, 23, 25; "Calimachus," i, 148, 15; ii, 150, 1; iv, 151, 21; vi, 152, 31; viii, 153, 26; ix, 160, 34; "Abraham," i, 163, 32; iii, 165, 16; iv, 169, 15; v, 170, 21; vi, 171, 15; vi, 172, 29; vii, 173, 1; vii, 176, 16; viii, 176, 30; ix, 177, 1; "Pafnutius," i, 185, 23; ii, 186, 31, 33; ii, 187, 5, 6; iii, 189, 33, 34; iv, 190, 1; v, 191, 5, 18; vi, 192, 2; vii, 192, 2; vii, 195, 15; viii, 195, 17; x, 196, 5; x, 197, 11; xi, 197, 23; xi, 198, 7; xii, 198, 10; "Sapientia," i, 202, 30; ii, 202, 32; ii, 203, 12; iii, 203, 18; iii, 207, 15; iv, 208, 12; v, 208, 19, 21; v, 211, 28; v, 212, 20; v, 213, 27, 31; v, 216, 1; vi, 216, 18; viii, 217, 29.

152. For further examples of body movement indicated in dialogue, cf. Strecker, "Gallicanus," I, i, 119, 11; ii, 121, 31; ix, 125, in toto; II, vii, 135, 27 and 136, 3; "Dulcitius," iii, iv, v, vi, vii, viii, 140 ff. in toto; xi, 144, 1; xii, 145, 14, 23; xiv, 146, in toto; "Calimachus," i, 148, in toto; iv, 151, in toto; vii, 153, in toto; ix, 154, 32; ix, 155, 5, 20; ix, 157, 32; ix, 159, 12; ix, 160, 6; "Abraham," v, 170 in toto; vi, 171, in toto; vii, 173, 3, 9, 13; "Pafnutius," ii, 186, in toto; iv, 190, in toto; vi, 191, in toto; xi, 198, 10; "Sapientia," v, 208, 19, 21; v, 209, 33; v, 210, 2, 3, 22, 24, 31, 32; v, 211, 2, 12, 15, 28, 30; v, 212, 20; v, 213, 6, 18, 24; v, 214, 24, 26; vii, 217, 1; viii, 217, 17, 19; ix, 217, in toto.

153. For further examples of posturings described in dialogue, cf. Strecker, "Gallicanus," I, ii, 119, 22; ii, 120, 2; iii, 121, 16; iv, 122, 27; v, 123, 20; vi, 124, 11; vii, 124, 13; ix, 125, in toto; xi, 127, 5; xiii, 130, 20; II, v, 134, 13; viii, 136, 11, 15; ix, 137, in toto; "Dulcitius," i, 139, 8, 11; iv, v, vi, vii, viii, ix, x, 141 ff. in toto; xii, 144, 16; xiii, xiv, 145 ff. in toto; "Calimachus," ii, 149, 17, 27, 31; ii, 150, 5; iv, v, vi, vii, viii, 151 ff. in toto; ix, 154, 10, 18; ix, 155, 18; ix, 157, 3, 13; ix, 158, 13; "Abraham," iii, iv, v, vi, 165 ff. in toto; "Pafnutius," i, 179, 8, 17; ii, 185, in toto; iii, 187, 20; iii, 188, 7, 9, 12; vii, 193, 22, 25; x, 196, 30; xi, 197, 14; "Sapientia," ii, iii, 202 ff. in toto; iv, 208, 16; v, 210, 15; v, 211, 15,

220

19; v, 212, 26, 31; v, 214, 12, 15; vi, 216, 9; vii, 217, 8, 14; ix, 218, 5, 23.

154. For further directions in dialogue indicating handling of properties, cf. Strecker, "Gallicanus," I, ix, 125,, 13; ix, 126, 12; II, vii, 135, 27; "Dulcitius," i, 140, 3; iii, 141, 2; iv, 141, in toto; v, 141, 29; xi, 144, 3; xiv, 147, 1; "Calimachus," vi, 152, 28; "Abraham," iv, 170, 17; vi, 172, 22 and 24; vi, 173, 1; vii, 175, 21; "Pafnutius," iv, 190, 7, 18; "Sapientia," v, 209, 9, 33; v, 210, 18, 24, 31; v, 212, 20; v, 214, 24.

Chapter VI

1. Eric Bentley, *The Play* (New York: Prentice-Hall, Inc., 1951), pp. 6-7.

2. *Ibid.*, p. 8.

3. *Ibid.*, p. 9

4. K. Reinhardt, *Germany 2000 Years* (Milwaukee: 1950), p. 62.

5. Bentley, p. 9.

6. Hanns Swarzenski, ed., *Early Medieval Illumination* (New York: Oxford University Press, 1951), pp. 16-18. "The sumptuous manuscripts of the Liuthard Group, executed for Otto III around the year 1000, represent the most perfect artistic embodiment of the time. Nowhere else is such convincing expression given to the hieratic and visionary imagination of the period with its mixture of mystical ecstasy and imperialistic dreams of expansion. . . ."

7. *Ibid.*, Plates X and XI.

8. *Ibid.*, p. 18.

9. Hans Jentzen, *Ottonische Kunst* (Munich: Bruckmann, 1947), p. 84.

10. *Ibid.*, p. 46.

11. Swarzenski, Plate IX.

12. Jentzen, p. 38.

13. *Ibid.*, p. 61.

14. L. W. Jones and C. R. Morey, *The Miniatures of the Manuscripts of Terence* (Princeton: 1931), Plates 334, 338, 373, 469, and 499.

15. C. Magnin, *Théâtre de Hrotsvitha* (Paris: 1845), pp. xl-xli. "Cet ouvrage, bien que composé, comme tous ceux du même écrivain, dans une pensée d'édification et de piété, remplit néanmoins la plus indispensable des conditions imposées à l'auteur

comique, celle d'exciter le rire et la gaieté. On peut même dire qu'à cet égard *Dulcitius* dépasse quelque peu les bornes du genre. Cette pièce est plus qu'une comédie, c'est une farce religieuse, une bouffonnerie dévote, une parade sacrée, qui se déploie, chose étonnante! sans trop de disparate à côté du martyre des trois héroïques soeurs, Agape, Chionie et Irène. Dans cette pièce, où les prestiges et le merveilleux dominent, les persécuteurs ne sont pas simplement représentés, selon l'usage, comme des bourreaux farouches et sanguinaires, mais comme des hommes ineptes, des niais en butte aux plus ridicules illusions et livrés aux mystifications d'une main cachée qui se joue d'eux."

16. *Ibid.*, p. 461. "It is because of the importance given to the comic role, I believe, that Hrotsvitha has given this comedy its title; not the revered names of the three heroines, but that of the hapless magistrate whose misadventures inject such alien gaiety into this tragi-comic piece." (Translation of note 27.)

17. E. Blashfield, *Portraits and Backgrounds* (New York: 1917), pp. 57-59.

18. Magnin, p. 462, n. 8.

19. *Ibid.*, p. 462, n. 31. "La présence des animaux dans les divertissements hiératiques n'était point une chose rare au moyen âge."

20. A. Nicoll, *Mimes, Masks, and Miracles* (New York: 1931), p. 123, n. 9.

21. *Ibid.*, p. 127.

22. *Ibid.*, p. 126.

23. *Ibid.*

24. K. Strecker, *Hrotsvithae Opera* (Leipzig: 1906), p. 143.

25. *Ibid.*, i, 138, 17.

26. *Ibid.*, xi, 143, 29.

27. *Ibid.*, iv, 141.

28. Nicoll, *Masks*, p. 105. "In the fourth century A.D. a poet describes the removing of weights, the descent of the great pageant-machine, the play of lights upon the stage, the fictional burning of the scenic towers."

29. Magnin, pp. 462-463, n. 31. "On pensera peut-être qu'il dut être assez difficile aux novices de Gandersheim de représenter le comte Sisinnius demandant à grands cris un cheval, comme Richard III dans Shakespeare, et poursuivant sur sa monture rétive l'innocente Irène. Mais il ne faut pas oublier que le cheval de Sisinnius ne fait que tourner, comme dans un manège, ce que simplifiait beaucoup les difficultés de cet exercice équestre.— D'ailleurs, la présence des animaux dans les divertissements hiéra-

tiques n'était point une chose rare au moyen âge. . . . On voit donc, sans que j'insiste ici davantage, que la mise en scène de *Dulcitius* ne dépassait pas les moyens d'exécution dont le drame hiératique était au Xe siècle en mesure de disposer."

30. See *supra*, p. 146.

31. See *supra*, pp. 147-148.

32. J. Gassner, *Masters of the Drama* (New York: 1945), p. 20.

33. Cf. Strecker, pp. 140-141.

34. *Ibid.*, p. 142.

35. C. St. John, *The Plays of Roswitha* (London: 1923), p. 151.

36. *Ibid.*, p. 152.

37. Cf. Strecker, p. 201.

38. *Ibid.*, p. 202.

39. Blashfield, p. 106.

40. *Ibid.*

41. Magnin, p. 408.

42. *Ibid.*

43. *Ibid.*, pp. 480-481. "Cette vieille mère . . . me semble rappeler un autre grand et noble type de maternité courageuse, la vénérable duchesse Oda, qui consacra cinq de ses filles à Dieu, en vit mourir quatre et, ne devançant la dernière que de peu d'années, descendit, en priant, dans la tombe. Hrotsvitha, dans son poëme sur la fondation du monastère de Gandersheim, a rappelé avec émotion la glorieuse vieillesse d'Oda et les tombeaux de la mère et des filles."

44. Cf. Strecker, "Sapienta," iii, 205, 11. "Karitas duas olympiades, iam volvit, Spes duo lustra, Fides tres olympiades.

45. St. John, p. 155.

46. Magnin, p. 441. ". . . souviens-toi de ta mère, qui t'a enfantée quand déja tes soeurs aînées avaient épuisé ses forces."

47. *Munich Codex*, see *supra*, p. 192, n. 66.

48. Strecker, "Sapientia," vii, 217. 15.

49. *Harper's Latin Dictionary*, pp. 629-630 and 1119-20.

50. L. Eckenstein, *Women in Monasticism* (Cambridge: 1896), p. 180.

51. Blashfield, p. 107.

52. Magnin, pp. 478-479, n. 86. "Hrotsvitha retombe ici dans une de ces digressions pédantesques où elle aime tant à se jeter en écolière émerveilée de son savoir de fraîche date. Ce ne sont pas cette fois des lambeaux de philosophie scolastique, comme dans *Callimaque*, ni une exposition technique de la science musicale, comme dans *Paphnuce*. Nous allons assister, bon gré, mal

gré, à une leçon sur la théorie des nombres. Il semble que Hrotsvitha ait eu à coeur de prouver sa compétence dans presque toutes les branches du *trivium* et du *quadrivium*. Elle a, d'ailleurs, laissé percer cette ambition dans la préface de ses comédies, sous une formule modestement orgueilleuse: 'Pour que ma négligence, a-t-elle dit, n'anéantisse pas en moi les dons de Dieu, toutes les fois que, par hazard, j'ai pu recueillir quelques fils ou légers débris du vieux manteau de la philosophie, j'ai eu grand soin de les insérer dans le tissu de mon ouvrage (*Épître à certains savants,* p. 13).' Il est impossible de tenir plus exactement ses résolutions. La savante religieuse ne laisse, en effet, échapper aucune occasion de se parer du bonnet doctoral, ou plutôt elle s'en affuble, comme ici, sans même avoir pour excuse la moindre apparence d'occasion."

53. St. John, p. xix.

54. Blashfield, p. 107.

55. Magnin, p. 477, n. 80. Magnin points out that the name, Diocletian, which appears in the title prologue is evidently a copyist's error since Hadrian's name is used throughout the interior of the play in the Munich manuscript. He imputes this potential for error to the original source (*Acta Sanctorum*), which does not state either the place of the martyrdom of the matron and her three daughters or the reigning monarch.

56. Nicoll, *Masks,* p. 69. The *bucco* is one of the stock characters of the mimes, the "babbling vehement type."

57. Gassner, p. 140. "The *Sapientia* is an allegory like *Everyman* with such abstract characters as Wisdom, Faith, Hope, and Charity."

58. Magnin, pp. 477-478, n. 81. "Les noms significatifs des principaux acteurs de ce drame m'avaient d'abord induit à croire que *Foi, Espérance et Charité, filles de Sapience,* étaient une pièce allégorique du genre de nos anciennes moralités, plutôt que la mise en action d'une légende. Je m'étais trompé. Un assez grand nombre d'auteurs grecs et latins ont mentionné l'histoire de cette mère intrépide et de ses trois jeunes filles. Les Bollandistes, à la date du 1er août (*Acta Sanctor.,* August. t. I, p. 16), donnent une notice des écrivains qui ont parlé de ces courageuses héroïnes, et regrettent que, hors leur martyre, on ignore ce qui les concerne. En effet, tous les agiographes, sauf le déclamateur Métaphraste, n'ont accordé qu'un très petit nombre de lignes à cettes histoire. Hrotsvitha a eu rarement moins de secours. Il faut encore remarquer qu'elle a un soin particulier de faire parler chaque personnage suivant le caractère que son nom suppose."

59. St. John, p. xix.

60. Cf. Strecker, "Sapientia," ii, 202-203.

61. *Ibid.*, v, 213, 29.

62. Cf. Strecker, "Sapientia," iii. 203-207.

63. See *supra*, p. 224, n. 56.

64. Cf. Strecker, "Sapientia," iii, 204, 30. "Placetne vobis, o filiae, ut hunc stultum aritmetica fatigem disputatione?"

65. Magnin, p. 479, n. 87. "Toute cette théorie des nombres se trouve dans Boëce, qui lui-même l'avait prise ailleurs. Il n'y a pas jusqu'à ces quatre nombres parfaits cités pour exemple, qui ne soient dans Boëce (*Arithm.*, lib. I, cap. 20).—Un jeune mathématicien de Franche-Comté, M. Grillet, me communique sur ce passage la note suivante. 'Les nombres parfaits dans l'ordre où l'on vient de les lire (6, 28, 496, 8128) sortent de la formule $2^n (2^{n+1}1)$ laquelle donne des nombres parfaits, toutes les fois que $(2^{n+1}1)$ est un nombre premier. On conçoit, d'ailleurs, que les arithméticiens du moyen âge se soient arrêtes à ces quatre nombres, car le plus petit que la formule fournit ensuite est 33,550336, pour $n=12$.'"

66. *Ibid.*, p. 480, n. 90.

67. Jantzen, p. 67. The rods were suggested by Plate 69, *Die Gefangennahme Christi* (ca. 1045).

68. See *supra*, p. 148.

69. Jones and Morey, Plate 499.

70. *Ibid.*, Plate 334.

71. *Ibid.*, Plate 469.

72. Nicoll, *Masks*, p. 111. "Josephus, the Jewish historian, reports a mime in which a robber-leader is captured and crucified; 'there was a great deal of artificial blood,' he adds, 'which flowed down the cross.' This last remark is corroborated by Suetonius; he too describes the scene of crucifixion, and declares that then 'the stage ran with blood.' On some occasions, however, fiction passed into reality. The part of the robber-leader was taken by some criminal already condemned to death, and the crucifixion at the end of the play made the stage run, not with artificial blood, but with the true blood of the tortured wretch. 'A Laureolus hanging on no false cross,' is Martial's terse and significant summary of the scene."

73. *Ibid.*, p. 113.

74. *Ibid.*, p. 143.

75. *Ibid.*, p. 120.

76. *Ibid.*, p. 123.

77. *Ibid.*, p. 115.

78. R. W. Southern, *The Making of the Middle Ages* (New Haven: 1953), p. 27.

79. Liudprand. See anecdotes in his *Antapodosis*, pp. 27-203.

80. Jon Whitcomb, "Kirk Douglas Makes a Violent Movie," *Cosmopolitan*, CXLVI, No. 6 (June, 1958), 16-19. "Douglas said that Norse history was an unplowed field as far as movies were concerned. 'The subject is so vast, and there's so much material, that it's hard to choose what to dwell on. The Vikings were very rough characters. They were unusual in that they had no fear of death. A warrior was eligible for Valhalla if he died with his sword in his hand.' I told him I had been so moved by his portrayal of Van Gogh in that picture that I had left the theatre to avoid the ear-cutting scene. This cowardly admission did not strike him as a compliment. 'Well, then,' he said shortly, 'we'll lose you a dozen times in *The Vikings*. I lose an eye to a falcon, on camera. Curtis gets a hand cut off at the wrist. In another scene he's tied up in a water-filled pit and attacked by giant crabs. The picture opens with a Viking raid on an English court. All the royal victims are murdered except the queen who is violated. In the tenth century, only the very brave lived to be old men.'"

81. Cf. Strecker.

82. See *supra*, p. 167.

83. Suetonius, *Julius* xxxix; *Caligula* xviii; *Claudius* xii, xxxiv; *Vespasian* xix.

84. Nicoll, *Masks*, p. 148.

85. Magnin, p. 464, n. 39. "Voilà un jeu de scène qui ne peut que donner une idée fort avantageuse de l'habileté du machiniste de Gandersheim." Here Magnin is alluding to a speech of Andronicus in "Calimachus," viii, 153, 24, who, upon seeing the apparition suddenly raised from sight, exclaims, "How suddenly he has been taken up to heaven!" Zeydel, in speaking of this compliment remarking the efficiency of the machinist, refers to it as the least convincing of Magnin's arguments for performance ("Hrotsvitha's Dramas," 452, n. 1).

86. Cf. Strecker, p. 208.

87. *Ibid.*, p. 217 between viii and ix.

88. *Ibid.*, xi, 144.

89. See *supra*, p. 91.

90. K. T. Rowe, *Write That Play* (New York: 1919), p. 388.

91. *Ibid.*, p. 403.

92. Magnin, p. liv. "Cette dernière scène, d'un effet religieux et grandiose, rappele un peu, si j'ose le dire, le dénoûment d'*Œdipe à Colone*."

BIBLIOGRAPHY

Manuscripts

Cologne. Stadtarchiv, MS W 101, fols. 1^r-16^v. Four plays, allegedly 12th-century copies. Discovered in 1922 by Goswin Frenken.

Klagenfurth. Studienbibliothek. MS Perg.-Hs. 4. Known as the Klagenfurth Fragments. Four sheets containing part of the legend "Maria" and part of the drama "Sapientia." Allegedly copied in the 11th century from the Emmeram-Munich Codex.

London. British Museum. *MS Cotton Tiberius A. III*, "Regularis Concordia," edited by W. S. Logeman in *Anglia*, xiii (1891), 426-428.

Munich. Staatsbibliothek. Codex 2552. "Gallicanus." Copied from the Emmeram-Munich Codex. Discovered by O. Holder-Egger in 1888.

Munich. Staatsbibliothek, Emmeram-Munich Codex. (Clm 14485.)

Edited and Translated Works

Aristotle. *Theory of Poetry and Fine Art*. A critical text and translation of *The Poetics* by S. H. Butcher. First American edition. New York: Dover Publications, Inc., 1951.

Biblia Sacra (Vulgatae Editionis; Vaticanis, Oeniponte; Sumptibus Librariae Academicae Wagnerianae, 1906). Translated by P. Michael Hetzewaver, O.C.

The Complete Works of Shakespeare. Edited by W. J. Craig. New York: Oxford University Press, 1919.

Duchesne, Louis Marie. *Christian Worship*. Translated by M. L. McClure. New York: Macmillan, 1931.

Fiedler, Conrad. *On Judging Works of Visual Art*. Translated by Henry Schaefer-Simmern and Fulmer Wood. Berkeley: University of California Press, 1949.

Hauser, Arnold. *The Social History of Art*. Translated in collaboration with the author by Stanley Godman. 2 vols. New York: Alfred A. Knopf, 1951.

Hrotsvithae Opera. Edited by Karl Strecker. Leipzig: B. G. Teubner, 1906.

Mantzius, Karl. *A History of Theatrical Art*. Translated by Louise von Cossel. 6 vols. New York: Peter Smith, 1937.

Monumenta Germaniae Historica inde ab anno Christi quingentesimo usque ad annum millesimum et quingentesimum, auspiciis Societatis aperiendis fontibus rerum Germanicarum medii aevi. Edidit Georgius Heinricus Pertz. Hanoverae, 1826. Epistolae Karolini Aevi. ii, t. iv.

Plays of Roswitha. Translated by H. J. W. Tillyard. London: The Faith Press, 1923.

Plays of Terence. Translated by John Sargeaunt. 3 vols. Cambridge: Harvard University Press, 1939.

Quintilian. *Institutio Oratoria*. Translated by H. E. Butler. 4 vols. Cambridge: Harvard University Press, 1943.

St. John, Christopher. *The Plays of Roswitha*. With an Introduction by Cardinal Gasquet and a Critical Preface by the Translator. London: Chatto & Windus, 1923.

Suetonius. *The Twelve Caesars*. Translated by J. C. Rolfe. 3 vols. Cambridge: Harvard University Press, 1944.

The Holy Bible. Translated by Msgr. Ronald Knox. 3 vols. New York: Sheed & Ward, Inc., 1950.

The Works of Liudprand of Cremona. Edited by G. G. Coulton and Eileen Power Routledge. London: Broadway House, 1930.

Winterfeld, Paul von. *Deutsche Dichter des lateinischen Mittelalters in deutschen Versen*. Edited by Hermann Reich. Munich: C. H. Beck, 1913.

228

Books

Artz, Frederick B. *The Mind of the Middle Ages.* New York: Alfred A. Knopf, 1953.

Aschbach, Joseph. *Roswitha und Conrad Celtes.* Vienna: K. K. Hof- und Staatsdruckerei, 1867.

Baldwin, Charles S. *Medieval Rhetoric and Poetic.* New York: Macmillan, 1928.

Barack, K. A. *Die Werke der Hrotsvitha.* Nurnberg: Bauer und Raspe, 1858.

Bentley, Eric. *The Play.* New York: Prentice-Hall, 1951.

Blashfield, Evangeline W. *Portraits and Backgrounds.* New York: Charles Scribner's Sons, 1917.

Bodonis, Fr. Henrici. *Syntagma.* De constructione caenobii Gandesiani, perfectione quoque & defectione eiusdem, 1531. Copy obtained from Archiv der Stadt Bad Gandersheim.

Bryce, James. *The Holy Roman Empire.* New York: Macmillan, 1907.

Cassidy, Frank P. *Molders of the Medieval Mind.* St. Louis, Missouri: B. Herder, 1944.

Chambers, Edwin K. *The Mediaeval Stage.* 2 vols. London: Oxford University Press, 1925.

Chasles, Philarète. *Le Moyen Age.* Paris: Charpentier et C^{io}, Libraires-Éditeurs, 1876.

Clapham, Alfred W. *Romanesque Architecture in Western Europe.* Oxford: Clarendon Press, 1936.

Clark, Barrett H. *European Theories of the Drama.* New York: Crown Publishers, 1947.

Conant, Kenneth John. *Benedictine Contributions to Church Architecture.* The Wimmer Lecture, 1947. Latrobe: Archabbey Press, 1949.

Creizenach, Wilhelm. *Geschichte des neueren Dramas.* Halle: Niemeyer, 1893.

Dawson, Christopher. *The Making of Europe.* New York: Macmillan, 1932.

———. *Religion and the Rise of Western Culture.* Gifford Lectures delivered at the University of Edinburgh 1948-1949. New York: Sheed & Ward, 1950.

Douhet, Jules comte de. *Dictionnaire des Mystères, Moralités, Rites Figurés et Ceremonies Singulières* in J. P. Migne, *Nouvelle Encyclopédie Théologique*, nouvelle ser. t. unique, XLIII. Paris, 1845.

Eckenstein, Lina, *Women in Monasticism*. Cambridge: The University Press, 1896.

Ellard, Gerald, S. J. *Master Alcuin, Liturgist*. Chicago: Loyola University Press, 1956.

Fergusson, Francis. *The Idea of a Theater*. Princeton: University Press, 1949.

Fife, Robert Herndon. *Hroswitha of Gandersheim*. Prepared for the Hroswitha Club. New York: Columbia University Press, 1947.

Frankl, Paul. *Die frühmittelalterliche und romanische Baukunst*. Wildpark-Potsdam: Athenaion, 1926.

Gallagher, John J. *Church and State in Germany under Otto the Great*. Washington, D.C.: Catholic University of America, 1938.

Gasquet, Francis Aidan. *Monastic Life in the Middle Ages*. London: G. Bell, 1922.

Gassner, John. *Masters of the Drama*. New York: Dover Publications, 1945.

Gayley, C. M. *Plays of our Forefathers*. New York: Duffield, 1907.

Gilson, Etienne. *The Spirit of Mediaeval Philosophy*. New York: Charles Scribner, 1936.

Gross, Peter. *Die Tropen und Figuren*. Leipzig: Heinrich Bredt, 1888.

Harenberg, Johann Christoph. *Historia Ecclesiae Gandershemensis Cathedralis ac Collegiatae Diplomatica*. Hanoverae: B. Nicolai Foersteri et Filii, 1734.

Haskins, Charles H. *The Rise of the Universities*. New York: Henry Holt, 1923.

Hunningher, Benjamin. *The Origin of the Theater*. Amsterdam: E. M. Querido, 1955.

Isidore of Seville, *Etymologiae seu origines*. LXXXII of J. P. Migne's *Patrologiae Latinae*. Paris: 1850.

Jantzen, Hans. *Ottonische Kunst*. Munich: Bruckmann, 1947.

Jones, Leslie W. and Morey, Charles R. *The Miniatures of the Manuscripts of Terence: Prior to the Thirteenth Century*. 2 vols. Text and Plates. Princeton: University Press, 1931.

Köpke, Ernst Rudolf. *Die älteste deutsche Dichterin*. Berlin: E. S. Mittler und Sohn, 1869.

———. *Hrotsvitha von Gandersheim. Zur Literatur Geschichte des zehnten Jahrhunderts*. Berlin: E. E. Mittler und Sohn, 1869.

Leuckfeld, Johann Georg. *Antiquitates Gandersheimenses*. Wolfenbüttel: Gottfried Freytag, 1709.

Magnin, Charles. *Théâtre de Hrotsvitha*. Paris: Duprat, 1845.

Mansi, J. D. *Sacrorum Conciliorum et Decretorum Nova et Amplissima Collectio*. Leipzig: Wetter, 1901.

Marique, Pierre J. *History of Christian Education*. 3 vols. New York: Fordham University Press, 1926.

Merton, Thomas. *The Silent Life*. New York: Farrar, Straus & Cudahy, 1957.

Michel, André. *Histoire de l'Art*. t. I, deuxieme partie. Paris: Librairie Armand, 1950.

Nicoll, Allardyce. *The Development of the Theatre*. New York: Harcourt, Brace, and Company, 1937.

———. *Masks, Mimes, and Miracles*. New York: Harcourt, Brace, and Company, 1931.

Reich, Hermann. *Der Mimus*. Berlin: Weidmann, 1903.

Reinhardt, Kurt, F. *Germany, 2000 Years*. Milwaukee: Bruce, 1950.

Robert, Carl. *Die Masken der neueren attischen Komödie*. Halle: Niemeyer, 1911.

———. *Der Neue Menander*. Berlin: Weidmann, 1908.

Rowe, Kenneth Thorpe. *Write That Play*. New York: Funk & Wagnalls, 1939.

Scherer, Wilhelm. *Geschichte der deutschen Literatur*. Berlin: Weidmann, 1899.

Southern, Robert William. *The Making of the Middle Ages*. New Haven: Yale University Press, 1953.

Steinacker, Karl. *Die Bau- und Kunstdenkmäler des Kreises Gandersheim.* Wolfenbüttel: Julius Zwissler, 1910.

Stratman, Carl J. *Bibliography of Medieval Drama.* Berkeley: University of California Press, 1954.

Swarzenski, Hanns, *Early Medieval Illumination.* New York: Oxford University Press, 1951.

Taylor, Henry Osborne. *The Classical Heritage of the Middle Ages.* New York: Macmillan, 1929.

———. *The Medieval Mind.* Cambridge: Harvard University Press, 1949.

Thompson, James Westfall. *The Middle Ages (300-1500).* New York: Alfred A. Knopf, 1931.

Tritheim, Johannes. *Liber de scriptoribus ecclesiasticis.* Basel, 1494.

Ulich, Robert. *2000 Years of Educational Wisdom.* Cambridge: Harvard University Press, 1954.

Vasiliev, Alexander A. *History of the Byzantine Empire.* Madison: University of Wisconsin Press, 1952.

Walsh, James J. *High Points of Medieval Culture.* Milwaukee: Bruce, 1937.

Winterfeld, Paul von. *Hrotsvithae Opera.* Berlin: Weidmann, 1902.

Young, Karl. *The Drama of the Medieval Church.* 2 vols. Oxford: Clarendon Press, 1933.

Articles and Periodicals

Algermissen, Konrad. "Bischof Altfrid, der Mitbegründer von Gandersheim," *Unsere Diözese,* XXI (1952), 53-58.

———. "Die Gestalt Mariens in der Dichtung Hrotsvithas von Gandersheim," *Unsere Diözese,* XXIII (1954), 139-156.

Allaria, Anthony. "Canons and Canonesses Regular," *Catholic Encyclopedia,* III (1913), 255.

Braunschweiger Zeitung. August 22, 1950.

The College News (Bryn Mawr, Pa.). May 7, 1952.

Coulter, Cornelia C. "The 'Terentian' Comedies of a Tenth-Century Nun," *Classical Journal,* XXIV (1929), 515-529.

Dunford, David. "Canoness," *Catholic Encyclopedia,* III (1913), 288.

Ebert, A. "Hrotsvith Opera," *Allgemeine Geschichte der Literatur des Abendlandes,* III (1887), 285-290.

Frenken, Goswin. *Neues Archiv der Gesellschaft für ältere deutsche Geschichtskunde,* XLIV (1922), 101-114.

Goetting, Hans. "Die Anfänge des Reichsstifts Gandersheim," *Braunschweigisches Jahrbuch* (1950), 1-52.

———. "Das Fuldaer Missionkloster Brunshausen und seine Lage," *Harz-Zeitschrift,* V/VI (1953/1954), 1-25.

———. "Zur Kritik der älterin Grundungskunde des Reichsstifts Gandersheim," *Mitteilungen des Österreichischen Staatsarchivs,* III (1950), 362-403.

Haraszti, Zoltán. "Hroswitha's Works," *More Books, The Bulletin of the Boston Public Library,* XX (1945), 87-119, 139-173.

Menhardt, H. *Zeitschrift für deutsches altertum und deutsche Literatur,* LXII (1925), 233-236.

The New York Post. December 17, 1934.

Steinacker, Karl. "Stift Gandersheim," *Jahrbuch des Geschichtsvereins für das Herzogtum Braunschweig.* VIII (1909), 1-46.

The Times (London). December 30, 1913 and January 12, 1914.

Whitcomb, Jon. "Kirk Douglas Makes a Violent Movie," *Cosmopolitan,* CXLVI, No. 6 (June, 1958), 16-19.

Zeydel, Edwin H. "The Authenticity of Hrotsvitha's Works," *Modern Language Notes,* LXI (1946), 50-55.

———. "A Chronological Hrotsvitha Bibliography through 1700 with Annotations," *Journal of English and Germanic Philology,* XLVI (1947), 290-294.

———. "'Ego Clamor Validus'—Hrotsvitha," *Modern Language Notes,* LXI (1946), 281-283.

———. "Knowledge of Hrotsvitha's Works Prior to 1500," *Modern Language Notes,* LIX (1944), 382-385.

———. "The Reception of Hrotsvitha by the German Humanists after 1493," *The Journal of English and Germanic Philology,* XLIV (1945), 239-249.

———. "Were Hrotsvitha's Dramas Performed During Her Lifetime?" *Speculum,* XX (1945), 443-456.

Other Sources

Heineken, Johanna. "Die Anfänge der sächsischen Frauenklöster," Göttingen: W. Fr. Kaestner, 1909.

Löher, Franz. "Hrotsvitha und ihre Zeit (1858), *Zeitschrift des Harzvereins*, Darmstadt: Brakebusch, 1920.

Steinhoff, R. "Canonissin des Stifts Gandersheim, die älteste deutsche Dichterin (1882), *Zeitschrift des Harzvereins*, Darmstadt: Brakebusch, 1926.